20 YEARS A FILMMAKER

by

Gabriel Rhenals

© 2022 Reveu LLC
All Rights Reserved
Cover design and art by Gabriel Rhenals
Portrait photos by Jon Funder

www.gabrielrhenals.com

ISBN: 9798355059736

To Mom and Dad
for their ever-present love and support

Contents

Acknowledgments | 12
Introduction (September 2022) | 14
Gabriel Rhenals' Filmography | 16
Part I: Formation (1986-2002)
1. Acquisition (December 2000)
   About my dad receiving a video camera for Christmas | 19
2. Ambition (January 1996)
   About my first original movie idea | 21
3. Attractions (April 1990)
   About my first theater-going experience | 24
4. Authorship (December 1992)
   About writing a book in 1st grade | 27
5. Birth (March 1986)
   About my birth and family | 29
6. Cropping (December 1999)
   About my purchase of widescreen VHS tapes | 30
7. Demo (February 2002)
   About my first time digitally editing video | 33
8. Digital (March 1996)
   About an experience creating digital art | 36
9. Disenchantment (February 2002)
   About my dismissal from New World | 38
10. Documentarian (January 2000)
    About my first allusion to a filmmaking career | 40
11. Drama (March 1999)
    About attending a drama class in middle school | 43
12. Exposure (July 1999)

About watching films on DVD with my older brother | 46
13. Fanfiction (June 1993)
    About writing a piece of 'Jurassic Park' fanfiction | 49
14. Identity (October 1990)
    About my parents identifying me as an artist | 52
15. Music (June 1998)
    About my love of classical and film music | 54
16. Outlining (March 2000)
    About my first exposure to outlining | 57
17. Photography (February 2002)
    About my interest in photography | 61
18. Physics (February 1996)
    About participating in a pinewood derby | 64
19. Pilot (December 2001)
    About my first location scout for a short film | 68
20. Prompt (October 1996)
    About writing my first long-form story | 70
21. Puzzles (May 1992)
    About creating puzzles for my classmates | 73
22. Reading (February 2002)
    About my reading habit after leaving New World | 75
23. Recognition (April 2000)
    About an art teacher's discovery of my first website | 78
24. Storytelling (October 2000)
    About the creation of 'Norstadt of Lanshire' | 81
25. Synthesis (January 1994)
    About my first time watching 'Star Wars' | 84
26. Terrorism (September 2001)
    About my experience on 9/11 | 87
27. Trinity (July 2001)
    About my movie-viewing habit one summer | 90

Part II: Short Films (2002-2017)

28. Advancement (August 2002)
    About being moved ahead in TV Production class | 95

29. Appraisal (October 2007)

   About a review of my short films by a UCF professor | 98

30. Aruba (October 2015)

   About my experience at an Aruban film festival | 101

31. Asocial (May 2006)

   About a strange old man's story about Steven Spielberg | 104

32. Atypical (October 2007)

   About a mock acting audition at UCF | 106

33. Audience (February 2016)

   About my opening night win at a Sanford film festival | 108

34. Brevity (July 2006)

   About figuring out the climax of 'Meat on a Grill' | 112

35. Capital (March 2007)

   About the making of 'March on the Pentagon' | 114

36. Casting (September 2002)

   About casting 'Mass Education' | 120

37. Cavalry (December 2002)

   About my dad's letter to Killian's principal | 123

38. Clemency (September 2008)

   About the making of 'The Nap' | 126

39. Co-Directing (October 2006)

   About the making of '12:03' | 129

40. Contest (June 2005)

   About the contest entry aspect of 'Does Free Speech Matter?' | 133

41. Counterculture (June 2004)

   About my political leanings at the end of high school | 135

42. Dedication (August 2014)

   About producing the money shots in 'Leo's Love Letter' | 138

43. Denied (July 2006)

   About a failed short film production | 141

44. Discovery (July 2005)

   About editing 'Does Free Speech Matter?' | 144

45. Earnesty (July 2006)

   About filming 'Meat on a Grill' at a supermarket | 147

CONTENTS

46. Economy (July 2005)
    About cutting down scenes on 'Does Free Speech Matter?' | 151
47. Encouragement (April 2006)
    About meeting producer Michael Hausman | 153
48. Engineering (May 2007)
    About watching a rough cut of 'Breakfast, Lunch and Dinner' | 156
49. English (May 2003)
    About Mr. Hill's class | 158
50. Exhibition (November 2003)
    About the first public screening of one of my short films | 161
51. Experimental (July 2007)
    About the making of 'Rough Cut' | 163
52. Expiration (June 2007)
    About my need for a new video camera | 166
53. Extremity (February 2012)
    About the writing of 'Semester of Madness' | 168
54. Facebook (August 2009)
    About my use of Facebook | 172
55. Feedback (June 2003)
    About my family's response to 'Mass Education' | 175
56. Feminine (July 2014)
    About my collaboration with Stephanie Maltez | 177
57. Festivals (February 2011)
    About my experience at a Tampa film festival | 180
58. Generativity (February 2017)
    About my experience substitute teaching | 185
59. Guidance (March 2004)
    About showing 'Mass Education' to my high school counselor | 188
60. Handcrafted (August 2016)
    About post-production on 'The Promotion' | 190
61. Hijacking (April 2005)
    About hijacking a group video project at FIU | 193
62. Idealism (September 2006)
    About my interaction with an Orlando film organization | 198

63. Indecisive (January 2007)
   About my indecision on an abandoned short film project | 201
64. Ingenuity (April 2007)
   About the making of 'Jesus Christ Goes to Mars' | 204
65. Initiative (January 2006)
   About the making of 'The Procrastinator' | 209
66. Inspiration (May 2008)
   About seeing 'Speed Racer' | 213
67. Kindred (March 2006)
   About my friend Cris Mertens | 216
68. Learning (May 2012)
   About my time at UM's student film festival | 219
69. Limitations (July 2015)
   About developing ideas constrained by limitations | 222
70. Madness (October 2007)
   About my first psychotic episode | 225
71. Mentorship (May 2016)
   About Mr. Hill's mentorship | 233
72. Moniker (April 2013)
   About determining my short film production company name | 236
73. NAMI (May 2017)
   About my experience at NAMI's film festival | 238
74. Occupy (December 2011)
   About the making of 'Occupy Miami!' | 241
75. Ostracization (April 2007)
   About dealing with a bully at UCF | 245
76. Outbound (July 2005)
   About deciding to attend UCF | 248
77. PBS (July 2017)
   About my involvement with 'film-maker' | 251
78. Philosophy (March 2004)
   About my time as a philosophy major at FIU | 255
79. Prequels (December 2005)
   About my love of the 'Star Wars' prequels | 258

80. Preserved (January 2007)
   About the making of '3,000 Too Many' | 262
81. Principles (September 2006)
   About an art class in film school at UCF | 266
82. Professors (May 2014)
   About some of my favorite professors at FIU | 269
83. Proud (November 2017)
   About my friend Kieron Williams | 274
84. Radical (October 2007)
   About my second trip to Washington, D.C. | 278
85. Recruitment (May 2003)
   About recruiting extras while making 'Mass Education' | 283
86. Refused (September 2003)
   About my failure to recruit actors for an unmade short film | 287
87. Rejection (July 2003)
   About my first film festival rejection letter | 290
88. Relapse (June 2009)
   About my second psychotic episode | 293
89. Rescue (May 2007)
   About the decision to finish 'March on the Pentagon' | 309
90. Resuscitation (October 2012)
   About the decision to finish 'Proteus' | 312
91. Retail (June 2004)
   About my first job at CVS | 316
92. Retooling (September 2012)
   About the evolution of my idea for 'Proteus' | 318
93. Return (August 2009)
   About my return to writing after hospitalization | 320
94. Revision (May 2004)
   About making changes to my short films | 323
95. Satellite (November 2016)
   About my personal website | 327
96. Scoring (November 2012)
   About my friend Ben Morris | 330

97. Search (February 2007)
   About the conception of 'Breakfast, Lunch and Dinner' | 334
98. Seniors (September 2005)
   About my first film set experience | 338
99. Shrine (December 2013)
   About my bedroom wall film posters | 342
100. Solitude (June 2002)
   About my time at the FIU library | 344
101. Speaking (April 2013)
   About Toastmasters | 347
102. Technology (September 2002)
   About my homemade Steadicam | 351
103. Trust (January 2006)
   About casting the lead in 'The Procrastinator' | 353
104. Twins (September 2005)
   About the Dastoli brothers | 357
105. Undeterred (May 2006)
   About my detainment while making 'May Day!' | 359
106. Uniform (August 2003)
   About my unconventional dressing habit | 362
107. Unprepared (November 2005)
   About a failed short film production at UCF | 365
108. Vagrancy (March 2008)
   About living away from my student apartment at UCF | 368
109. Variety (June 2012)
   About the making of 'Semester of Madness' | 371
110. Walking (September 2014)
   About my walking habit | 376
111. Zealous (March 2007)
   About an editing assignment at UCF | 379

Part III: Feature Films (2014-2022)

112. Adaptation (April 2020)
   About writing 'State v. Unknown' | 383
113. Collaboration (March 2018)

About working with a local band on 'For My Sister' | 386
114. Compromise (March 2014)
About writing 'The Cult of Truth' | 388
115. Disappointment (June 2019)
About the film festival rejections of 'For My Sister' | 392
116. Effective (September 2018)
About the making of 'For My Sister' | 396
117. Familiarity (October 2016)
About writing 'Omni' | 403
118. LLC (December 2018)
About starting Reveu LLC | 406
119. Mobile (August 2018)
About using a phone to film 'For My Sister' | 409
120. Premiere (June 2019)
About the premiere of 'For My Sister' | 414
121. Preview (May 2022)
About a sneak preview of 'State v. Unknown' | 420
122. Remote (July 2021)
About the making of 'State v. Unknown' | 426
123. Renewal (February 2018)
About writing 'For My Sister' | 432
124. Struggle (April 2019)
About writing 'Zenith' | 434
125. Validation (October 2019)
About the reviews of 'For My Sister' | 437
About the Author | 442

Acknowledgments

- Michael Hill, my mentor and former high school English teacher, for his moral support and generous advisement on almost any matter.
- Kieron Williams, an author and friend, for kindly lending a critical eye to my occasionally esoteric ideas about storytelling.
- Ben Morris, a composer and friend, for encouraging my productivity with his own prodigious output.
- Cris Mertens, a film editor and friend, for sharing banter with me about film, life and everything in between.
- Rubén Rosario, a local film critic and friend, for his constant online companionship and marathon conversations over a meal.
- Dr. Amy Jacobstein, my long-time doctor, for helping me maintain a healthy perspective on life and nip potential problems in the bud.
- R.J. De La Espriella, an aspiring author and friend, for endless conversations about film and writing.
- David Bush, an author and film director, for challenging me to keep up with his astonishing yield of film and literary works.
- Cryogenic, a fellow forum member at Naberrie Fields, for his constant inspiration and unmatched intellect.
- Mom (Patricia), my life-giver and biggest fan, for urging me to finally write my 1st book.
- Dad (Alonso), my closest ally and intellectual sparring partner, for putting up with my manic enthusiasm at every juncture of this book's writing process.
- My siblings Alonso, Juan and Daniel for their surprisingly solemn respect for this writing endeavor.
- The employees of my local Subway for tolerating my near-daily

habit of dining and reading in the corner of their restaurant.

- The makers of Scrivener for designing an amazing piece of software I regularly refer to as Photoshop for writing.
- Microsoft for being Promethean stewards of technology and making a top-quality, budget-conscious laptop (their Surface Laptop Go) which I used to write practically all of this book on.
- Kendall Branch Library, West Kendall Regional Library and Florida International University for facilitating my quiet, solitary retreat from a noisy, distracting world.

Introduction (September 2022)

Death cleaning is the process of organizing and generally decluttering areas of your home before you die in order to minimize the burden of your loved ones after you've passed. While my recent bedroom closet organizational effort didn't necessarily qualify as death cleaning, I regarded the task of cleaning up and optimizing the organization of the papery content in my closet just as seriously.

In order to locate a single document that I was interested in quoting for a chapter in this book, I would have to sift through an immense quantity of collected documents spanning approximately 25 years (since my time in middle school). The thousands of documents, mostly creative in nature, were distributed among 15 or so boxes in my bedroom closet.

In pouring through the sheer glut of content in search of that elusive, single document (ultimately found!), a striking realization occurred to me: I've had an unusually driving expressive habit from a very young age. It presented itself in visual art earlier than I can remember but an almost equally salient writing practice was evident from my early adolescence onward. Of course, filmmaking would present itself not too long after my early teens but my writing activity would continue, mostly in support of my motion picture-making obsession.

As I approached adulthood, I began to see all of these rampant creative energies in a highly political light. As I was increasingly exposed to different social ideologies through my individual reading pursuits, my affinity for ideas related to grassroots organization, anarchist theory and a DIY (Do It Yourself) mentality took strong and abiding hold of me.

Ensuingly, my early and modest filmmaking practice became more than about simply telling stories and entertaining an audience; at my diminuitive scale, it was active resistance against the corporate domination of the art form. And it's in this spirit of defiance that I would think and work as I started out as a filmmaker.

Later on, in 2015, it occurred to me that it might be time to share the wealth of experiences I had under my belt in the form of a book. After all, I had completed 15 short films and a first feature-length screenplay at the time - all achieved in close accord with the compelling political ideas that had beckoned me at the outset of my filmmaking pursuit. I had also successfully weathered two severe mental health crises that would no doubt lend greater human interest value to a potential book-writing effort. However, I wasn't quite ready to make such a weighty investment of time and effort.

Despite my mom and others pushing me to author an account of my unique menagerie of experiences, I finally decided to take the plunge into authorhood six years later in 2021. It felt like an appropriate time to do so having completed my 1st feature film *For My Sister*, freshly commenced work on my 2nd feature film *State v. Unknown* and in time for the 20th anniversary of the start of my very first short film production!

And, after approximately 11 months of writing, here we are!

A diverse and almost exhaustive repository of significant events from my creative and personal life, here I share a history, often of extraordinary calamity and fortune, of a micro-budget filmmaker with an immutable one-man band approach to his beloved art and science. Additionally, this book amounts to the most extensive writing project I've ever undertaken; far exceeding in man-hours even the most belabored of my five feature-length screenplays.

In terms of organization, the book's three parts (Formation, Short Films and Feature Films) are arranged chronologically but the chapters within each part are organized by theme and alphabetically so. This approach was inspired by a vade mecum style of writing which encourages non-linear interaction with the book it is applied to. So, this book can be read sequentially or dipped into at any particular chapter of interest without compromising the intended reading experience at all.

So, without much further ado, I hope you're entertained by the anecdotes, intrigued by the insights and inspired by the resolve.

You are now released to the plenty in waiting.

Please enjoy and thanks for reading!

Gabriel Rhenals' Filmography

Feature Films*

2. *State v. Unknown* (2022)
1. *For My Sister* (2019)

Feature Screenplays

5. *State v. Unknown* (2022)
4. *Zenith* (2020)
3. *For My Sister* (2018)
2. *Omni* (2018)
1. *The Cult of Truth* (2014)

Short Films*

16. *The Promotion* (2016)
15. *Leo's Love Letter* (2014)
14. *Proteus* (2013)
13. *Semester of Madness* (2012)
12. *Occupy Miami!* (2011)
11. *The Nap* (2008)
10. *Rough Cut* (2007)
9. *March on the Pentagon* (2007)
8. *Jesus Christ Goes to Mars* (2007)
7. *Breakfast, Lunch and Dinner* (2007)
6. *3,000 Too Many* (2007)
5. *Meat on a Grill* (2006)
4. *May Day! or: Two Americas* (2006)
3. *The Procrastinator* (2006)
2. *Does Free Speech Matter?* (2005)

1. *Mass Education* (2003)

*As writer, producer, director, cinematographer and editor

Part I: Formation (1986-2002)

1. Acquisition (December 2000)

It was the evening before Christmas Day and, as tradition would have it, my family was gathered in our living room to open the gifts we'd gotten one another. As usual, my mother had the honor of selecting each gift from below our tall, lit and amply decorated plastic spruce and reading from whom and to whom each gift was intended.

We'd reached the end of the yearly occasion but there remained one rather large present left under our tree.

"Who's that one for?" one of my older brothers inquired.

My mother had deliberately overlooked the large, boxed present until the end of the family ritual. With an innocent smile, she lifted the remaining present onto her lap and read the tag.

"Para Papa, de Mama," she shared.

My mom passed the present to my dad.

"Oh, thank you, Patry!" he exclaimed.

My parents kissed and my dad settled down with his sizable gift which he began opening carefully.

"What is it?" I asked, peering at the present with great interest.

My dad finished unwrapping the box and I immediately saw the graphic printed on the side.

"A camcorder!" my dad declared.

"We need it! No tenemos nada para filmar los eventos de la familia," my mother added.

"Excelente!" said my dad as he examined the specs listed on the box.

Some time later, I walked into my dad's office to find him at his desk casually reviewing the video camera's manual. The actual device was still safely stored in its box.

"Es digital!" my dad shared as he scanned the pages of the manual.

"Can I see it?" I asked.

My dad put down the manual and placed the box onto his desk. He reached in and gently freed the Sony DCR-TRV720 Digital Handycam from its confines, exposing it to air for the first time since its manufacture.

The device was more compact than I expected. Despite its rather diminutive size, it had a fairly large fold-out, LCD viewfinder which I knew appealed to my dad as he'd made mention of such a desired feature in the recent past.

"Es una maravilla!" he said with uncommon delight as he cradled the camcorder in his hands.

At that moment, I stared into the camera's cyclopean eye.

It stared back.

2. Ambition (January 1996)

The 5th Dimension's rhythm section springs forth! Its opening bars are aggressive and imposing! Brass and drums, full of jaunty bombast, are soon joined by supporting and no less spirited instrumentation.

A small, unified vocal ensemble breaks through the lively introduction like sunlight through the clouds. However, their song is a touch melancholic, somewhat haunting and almost hymnal:

Let the sunshine!
Let the sunshine in!
The sunshine in!

The ocean is furious! Churning in its ardor with massive, violent waves!

Let the sunshine!
Let the sunshine in!
The sunshine in!

The stories-high waves make landfall and tear into coastal metropoli. Buildings topple and droves of people scramble in panic!

Let the sunshine!
Let the sunshine in!
The sunshine in!

Further inland, dormant fault lines beneath the sprawling, developed surfaces of civilization are jogged from sleep. Their waking movement topple more buildings and stir up a greater frenzy!

In addition to the upset ground and sea, the sky also unleashes its fury! Tornadoes and hurricanes wreak further havoc upon already bedeviled cityscapes. Calamity and destruction reign across the globe!

Let the sunshine!
Let the sunshine in!
The sunshine in!

Amid utter bedlam, the world governments' intelligentsia soon discover the root cause of the berserk behavior of tide, soil and air: a black hole's increasing proximity to earth!

At the tender age of 10, this dramatic juxtaposition of music (5th Dimension's "Let the Sunshine In") and visuals represented my first, original cinematic imaginings. The premise or logic behind this spectacle of my mind's eye was preposterous, to be sure, but the laws and basic sense that typically govern epic cinematic storytelling mean nothing to the anarchic mind of a 5th grader.

I was undoubtedly influenced by the media landscape of the time, then characterized to some degree by a steady stream of generously-budgeted disaster films. The disaster films of the '90s harnessed the power of advanced visual effects techniques to tell stories that captured the existential anxiety of the millennium's end, typified by concerns like global warming and Y2K (remember that?!).

Films like *Independence Day*, *Waterworld*, *Deep Impact*, *Dante's Peak* and *Twister* were the main culprits in my recollection. Despite the fact that I didn't see a single one of those films in a movie theater (my parents were far from the movie-going sort), their essence reached me by friendly word-of-mouth and the peerless might of Hollywood promotion and advertising.

So motivated was I by my movie ideas that I decided to fill a three-prong notebook with notebook paper and label the cover "Chaos" with the intent of writing a movie around the apocalyptic vision described above! However, I left the notebook mostly untouched in the ensuing months. I knew there was a feature-length screenplay to be written but little did I know that it would take me 18 years to actually deliver on that promise.

3. Attractions (April 1990)

My mother secured me in my second-row baby seat as my two older brothers boarded the rear-facing jump seats in the back of our family's blue station wagon. With my mother by his side, my father pulled out of the driveway of my childhood home in Reading, Massachusetts.

We were on our way! But in all my few years of existence, I hadn't the faintest clue where we were headed.

Where the heck were we going?

A long commute followed. However, between a nourishing bottle of milk and the entertaining but strange verbalizations of my surrounding family members, I suppose I didn't mind this stretch of suspense too much.

Having made our way downtown, our vehicle slowed as we approached a large complex of brick buildings bathed in midday sunlight. Before long, we were enveloped by a great shadow as we entered the complex's adjacent parking garage.

My family had arrived at our destination - Museum of Science, Boston!

I recall a computer room; a massive atrium flanked by countless exhibits; a scale model of a Tyrannosaurus Rex; a massive ball-and-track apparatus; and so much more! It was sheer visual delight on an unrivaled scale!

Some time later during our visit, my family and I found ourselves in a long queue with other families and individual museum patrons in a narrow, dimly lit antechamber of some sort.

What were we waiting for?

What was the great mystery?

A museum employee opened the door at the far end of the space and motioned for those in line to begin advancing.

My family and I finally reached the long-awaited entry point. We passed through a long, dark hallway and into an equally dark room with a massive, domed wall opposite a cliff of seats. It was a theater! My mother guided me toward a row of seats but at so steep an angle were the rows of seats arranged that I surely thought I'd topple over to the stage area far below!

Soon enough, everyone gathered into their seats and any errant chatter was soon hushed by a booming demonstration of the room's impressive sound system.

After the sound demo, a narrator guided the audience through a series of New England vistas on the mammoth screen: a cityscape, a harbor, a sports stadium and...

The film suddenly took on a different character as the camera assumed the first-person POV of a car traveling down an inner-city highway. The music and speed of the camera started to go faster...

And faster...

    And faster...

        And faster!

Until the film, to my nascent eyes and ears, reached a dizzying and maddening intensity! My eyes widened in terror and alarm! I thought we were going to crash!

Thankfully, a hard cut to a serene river vista immediately followed the heart-stopping highway dash. A bit fazed but generally relieved, the harrowing introductory film came to a close and I enjoyed the ensuing and far less terrifying feature presentation without incident. A relatively sedate, educational film about some topic of scientific interest.

Per our membership, my family made fairly regular trips to Museum of Science, Boston when I was growing up and a stop at the Mugar Omni Theater was a staple of our visits. They were my earliest cinematic experiences and in large-format film to boot!

I think back on my reaction to the Omni theater intro film and compare it to the Lumière brothers' exhibition of one of the first motion pictures ever shown publicly, 1895's *The Arrival of a Train at La Ciotat Station*. It is believed that audiences at the time were so convinced of the reality of the projected image that they apparently reacted to the moving image of a train seeming to come directly at them by screaming and attempting to dodge it.

I could definitely relate.

4. Authorship (December 1992)

"The shape of a skull," I responded.

Ms. Taitz, my 1st grade teacher, proceeded to sandwich several sheets of regular paper between two sheets of construction paper and draw a skull-shaped outline on the topmost sheet. She then took a pair of adult scissors and carefully cut all the gathered paper along the lining of the oblong shape.

"And what's the title of your story?" she asked.

I took a moment to consider it.

"The Skull of the World," I responded in a dramatic tone.

Ms. Taitz then took a felt-tip marker and wrote out the title along with the byline on the front of the skull-shaped amalgam of cut-out paper. Then, she took out a ball-point pen and prepared to transcribe the story content I'd prepared in rough form onto the cut-out sheets of regular paper. She numbered each page as she went along.

"Page 1. The Skull Man was fighting the Duke," she dictated.

I nodded.

"Page 2. The monster was mad at the Skull Man and the Duke."

I nodded again.

"Page 3. The monsters were haunting the house."

I nodded. My story sounded so much better being read back to me, I thought.

"Page 4. They were going downstairs to kill the people."

My attention drifted to my other classmates a distance away but Ms. Taitz intervened, "Gaby!" I snapped back to attention.

"Page 5. The monster was mad. He attacked the Duke and the Skull Man."

I nodded.

Several pages later, Ms. Taitz completed her transcription of my story and asked one final question.

"Who would you like to dedicate your book to and why?"

I took a moment to decide. "My whole family... because they're nice to me."

Ms. Taitz wrote out my dedication in her elegant script and her immediate involvement in this book-making assignment was complete.

It was now incumbent upon me to furnish each of the 14 pages of *The Skull of the World* with an illustration of the transcribed text. I did so with great diligence and enthusiasm. When that was done, it was only a few days later before I received my book, stapled together with both its front and back cover fully laminated!

Ultimately, I completed about a handful of these little books in Ms. Taitz's 1st grade class. Already having somewhat of a reputation as a visual artist, I recall how impressed the class, including Ms. Taitz and her teaching assistant, were with my illustrations. Although the storytelling was rankly juvenile and nonsensical, these mock-publishing exercises were my first taste of authorship and would anticipate a significant high school English class storytelling assignment not too dissimilar from these early dabblings.

5. Birth (March 1986)

There was an issue with my respiratory functioning!

I had exited my mother's womb too quickly and the doctors were concerned. So, they ordered that I remain in observation for a period of ten days as a precautionary measure. My parents were, of course, deeply worried.

I was born Gabriel Enrique Rhenals on March 17th, 1986 in Boston, Massachusetts at Beth Israel Hospital around midday on a clear, late-winter day. My parents were both from Colombia and they had found themselves in New England on account of my dad attending Massachusetts Institute of Technology (MIT), subsequently finding employment in the area and, with my mom, deciding to start the family there. My family lived in Reading, a small town just north of Boston. I already had two brothers, Alonso and Juan.

My mom and dad made the long drive to the hospital each of the ten days I was in observation. They would stay at the hospital the entire day as they kept a watchful eye over me and awaited any important updates from the maternity doctors.

Thankfully, at the end of the those harrowing ten days, my doctors had seen satisfactory improvement in my condition and I was discharged from the hospital. My parents were greatly relieved as I could finally be brought to my loving, waiting home.

When I occasionally bring up this dramatic episode about my life's start to my parents, my mother always offers the reason I exited her womb too quickly.

"You couldn't wait to get started," she says.

6. Cropping (December 1999)

It was the holiday season and my parents finally replaced my family's old VHS player as they had promised. It had been with us for about 15 years and its replacement was long overdue. But I wasn't too excited about the prospect of a new VHS player alone. Rather, my interest lay more in the fact that my parents also promised to gift me a boxed set of the recently re-released *Indiana Jones* trilogy on VHS now that we had a piece of kink-free equipment to play it on!

So, my dad, younger brother Daniel and myself visited our local Best Buy to pick up my long-awaited boxed set.

When we arrived at the appropriate shelf of home video media, we found that the only version of the set in stock was that labeled with a blue sticker. "Widescreen Edition", it read.

"What's 'Widescreen Edition'?" Daniel asked.

Although I didn't know for sure, I responded, "It means there are black bars at the top and bottom of the screen... I think."

My younger brother groaned.

Not willing to leave Best Buy empty-handed, I insisted on purchasing what was available even if I was uncertain of what exactly "Widescreen Edition" meant.

My dad obliged, we plucked the item from the shelf and headed to the register.

We returned home with our bounty in tow but my enthusiasm had been slightly knicked over this unexpected "Widescreen Edition" business.

At home, I unwrapped the set, took out the cassette of the first film in the series and popped the tape into my family's new VHS player.

I held my breath as the film began.

Not only were there black bars at the top and bottom of the screen, they were thicker than I had anticipated. In fact, they comprised about 2/3rds of the entire screen!

What was going on?

The internet would soon provide me with the answers I needed.

From the 1950s to the early 2000s, television screens had a 1.33:1 (or 4:3) aspect ratio (ratio of width to height) and received broadcasted content shot for that aspect ratio. Theatrical films from the mid-'50s onward, on the other hand, were primarily shot and projected using more horizontal 1.85:1 or 2.35:1 aspect ratios. Therefore, when the home video market was established, film studios were faced with the problem of how to present wider-screen films on more square-like television screens.

Their solution? Pan and scan.

Pan and scan involved formatting widescreen film content for a television's 1.33:1 aspect ratio by cropping the film image. The process also involved the studios adding in-frame pans and cuts to particular shots (where key story information existed at far ends of the wider frame) to preserve narrative clarity in light of the cropped widescreen image, often beyond the supervision of the film's original director and editor.

Pan and scan was seen as a necessary compromise to satisfy a consumer base desiring use of the entire television screen for film content but many filmmakers regarded the practice as a disgrace to their art form. In cases of films with a 2.35:1 or wider aspect ratio, up to 55% of the widescreen image was discarded for the home video presentation!

Certain filmmakers with enough clout in the industry, however, were able to compel a studio to release their films on VHS in a letterbox format (meaning black bars at the top and bottom of the screen) in order to preserve their intended directorial vision but this was a rare practice.

Thankfully, with the arrival of DVD and televisions with a 1.78:1 (or 16:9) aspect ratio, films were now able to be presented as originally envisioned.

When I finally learned the truth, I became obsessed with letterbox and widescreen presentations. I watched my beloved *Indiana Jones* letterboxed VHSs over and over again, appreciating cinematography like never before; gaining an idea of what cinematography actually was in the first place. I even began framing some of my drawings in letterbox configurations. I felt as though I'd happened upon an oasis in a desert. I needed to see what I'd been missing for years because of this whole pan and scan scam. Pan and scam!

Although letterboxed editions of my favorite films up to then were extremely scarce, it would not be long before DVD would allow me to scratch this peculiar but demanding itch.

7. Demo (February 2002)

Following my dismissal from New World School of the Arts high school earlier in the month, I was in a bitter and depressed mood. I was acclimating well enough to the regular, non-arts-focused high school I was newly enrolled at but much about my future, and more especially my present, was uncertain. I felt rootless and adrift.

As the weekend approached, my parents suggested a visit to Coconut Grove Arts Festival. Despite a slackened interest in visual art, the principal cause of my having to leave New World, perhaps my parents believed I still possessed enough of an interest to attend the event. I honestly felt like I didn't have an interest in anything but I agreed to go, however reluctantly. Maybe a relaxed, seaside excursion would offset the pervasive gloominess of recent weeks.

So, that weekend we set off to Coconut Grove for the arts festival.

As we arrived at the coastal park setting of the event, the sun was at its zenith in a cloudless sky but that signature Miami heat was countered by a soothing breeze. At least the weather was pleasant.

My parents and I began walking the grounds.

We visited various booths and saw some impressive and some not-so-impressive examples of contemporary fine art. Prints of all sizes for sale.

But my dampened regard for visual art persisted. I did not see myself in these artists' shoes. Maybe I never did.

Then, I saw it.

"Oh, great..." I muttered.

My parents saw it too.

"Gaby, look! New World's here!" my mother announced.

The visual art department of my former high school was representing itself here at the festival. Some of my former art teachers and a few former classmates of mine occupied the booth.

I tried to walk away but my parents insisted on visiting the school's tented space.

As my parents engaged in friendly conversation with the teachers, whom they'd gotten to know as a result of my fateful performance deficit at the school, I smiled politely but kept to myself and avoided eye contact. I didn't even talk to the former classmates present. I was embarrassed and unsure of how to behave given such unfortunate circumstances.

But thankfully, my parents didn't stay too long and we were soon off to the next set of booths. I was relieved but, at the same time, somewhat saddened as I'd likely never see those once-so-familiar teachers and former classmates in-person ever again.

My parents and I continued through the festival grounds.

We soon approached a building with some indoor exhibits. As we entered, I was greeted by a representative from Miami Dade College, a local post-secondary institution. The kind young woman asked me if I'd be interested in participating in a demonstration of what appeared to be a video production setup in-use at the college.

I saw a small set with a bench and some props. Then, adjacent to this set was a set of computer workstations. Some other festival goers were busy at some of the consoles.

It looked like fun so I agreed to take part.

The college representative handed me a page of script. I would be acting out a scene from the 1994 film *Forrest Gump* and the resulting footage would then be transferred to one of the computers where I would use editing software to edit the scene together and export it to a VHS tape.

I performed the simple scene opposite another participant to the best of my very amateur acting abilities and was then ushered over to a computer where footage of the various camera angles of my scene was waiting to be edited together in a digital, non-linear editing system.

The process seemed like magic to me. Fast and efficient.

Although I'd never used video editing software before, I impressed the supervising representative with my seemingly instant grasp of the software's fundamentals. I put together something resembling a scene but, damnable novice that I was, I accidentally deleted the audio track before export and ended up transferring only the video of my scene to VHS tape.

In any case, this was my first experience with digital video editing! I was allowed to keep the VHS tape and soon my parents and I were on our way back to the parking lot. Our day at Coconut Grove Art Festival had come to an unexpected but oddly satisfying conclusion.

Months later I would acquire a FireWire card capable of capturing digital video to my own computer for editing and manipulation. Where there had been a pall of absence and gloom, there was now a sliver of promise and potential.

8. Digital (March 1996)

It was my turn to use one of the few Macintosh computers that lined a back wall of my 4th grade art class. I sat down and powered up the unit in front of me. It chimed that familiar Apple chime.

I waited as the GUI loaded and when it did, I accessed the familiar art-making software.

A white, rectangular digital canvas with an adjacent sidebar of a myriad of tools soon appeared before me.

The interface beckoned me and I dove right in!

I applied a base layer of rainbow tone to the entire canvas. Because why not?

Then, I used a clip art tool to add mountains and pyramids in the lower right-hand corner.

Between the mountains, in a kind of valley, I added a castle and surrounding village dwellings with the same clip art tool.

The mountains and village looked rather plain so I capped the tops of each with a single light bulb using the same stamp-like tool.

I then outlined a translucent figure, a giant of some sort, looming over the incandescent mountains and its valley's buildings. I gave this large creature large eyes and an oval, mouth-like orifice. Then, I used a thin brush to apply some fur to the unusual leviathan.

As for the sky above, I added multiple alien spaceships of various sizes.

I used the clip art tool again to sprinkle the scene with a menagerie of unusual characters: a weight-lifter with a sombrero, an Egyptian pharaoh, a pair of Oriental figures, a mermaid, a ballerina, a reptilian-like alien, a caterpillar, a surfer dude, a vulture, an elf, a deer and a few more aliens for good measure!

Lastly, a finishing touch: some rainbow-colored and magnifying orbs to top off this bizarre creation.

My time was up and content with what I'd made without breaking a sweat, I saved the file and logged off the computer.

Some months later, my family and I made a trip to our county's youth fair. After enjoying some thrilling rides and fine carnival dining, we visited the fair's exposition center.

After perusing a variety of exhibits, I was unexpectedly reunited with my Hieronymus Bosch-like concoction. It had been submitted by my art teacher to a local digital art competition and had in fact won 1st place!

I was amazed that something so whimsical and immoderate had garnered such attention and standing. I was flattered but all I remembered about making it was how quickly time seemed to pass while caught in the gleeful abandon of its creation - its digital creation.

This entire occasion - the art production and the ensuing recognition - represented my first significant artistic rendezvous with the burgeoning Digital Revolution.

And I liked it.

9. Disenchantment (February 2002)

On this somber occasion, my parents and I sat with my guidance counselor Mr. Seidenman in his office at New World School of the Arts. It was the formal, last step of my dismissal from the reputable art high school I'd attended for nearly two years. I believe the meeting was arranged to affirm the decision of the school administration and offer some degree of outreach to the parents of the student now in a transitional state.

Looking back, my forced departure seemed rather inevitable after months of both academic and artistic performance lapses; in addition to concerning behavioral issues.

I'd stopped doing my homework.

I'd failed to meet artwork quotas.

I'd started to act out inappropriately.

I'd feigned sickness and injury.

I'd often sit brooding and inactive for entire class periods.

To put it simply, I was a dysfunctional student. I'd fallen out of step and out of love with my visual arts education. I was also dealing with a failed attempt to establish a romantic relationship with a fellow art student.

Despite all of my teachers' and parents' concerted efforts to help me get back on track at New World, I knew I was too far gone. The weight of my world bore down on me like nothing I'd known up to that point.

So, there I sat as Mr. Seidenman kindly addressed all that needed to be.

My mother was lightly sobbing so I took her hand and consoled her.

"Mom, it's fine," I said.

She smiled through her tears and nodded.

After the meeting, Mr. Seidenman encouraged me to return to my in-progress art class in order to say goodbye to my friends and classmates. I took up the opportunity.

After briefly addressing the class in one of my earliest examples of impromptu oratory (I would join Toastmasters International 11 years later), I left the school building located at 25 NE 2nd Street in downtown Miami for the last time.

It had been a strange day.

On my way home, I pulled out a recently checked-out library book from my backpack.

The book? *A Cinema of Loneliness: Penn, Kubrick, Scorsese, Spielberg, Altman.*

10. Documentarian (January 2000)

I'd received a callback from the audition committee at New World School of the Arts. My family and art teachers were all absolutely thrilled! New World was considered one of the most respected arts high schools in the country and the opportunity to attend was regarded as a great honor and privilege.

About a month or so earlier, the first phase of my tryout had taken place and was primarily comprised of a time-limited abstract drawing assignment involving a prearranged still life in one of the studio rooms at New World's main building. Although the start of high school was at the other end of the year, my art teachers at Southwood Middle School wasted no time preparing their flock for auditions at New World and other arts-oriented high schools right from the start of our 8th grade year.

At any rate, I was particularly proud of the drawing I'd produced for the trial and I'd left that first appointment at New World fairly confident in what I'd demonstrated.

Now, in the first floor gallery of New World's main building, I waited to be escorted to a studio room upstairs where I'd sit across the three-member audition committee for a review of my audition piece, some artwork from my time at Southwood and my personal sketchbook. Of course, they'd also be interviewing me about my interests and aspirations.

An audition coordinator called out my name.

The time was nigh!

My parents wished me luck as I gathered my portfolio and sketchbook in my arms. I was then led by the coordinator to the visual arts floor above.

Following the coordinator down one of the building's checkered-floor hallways, we arrived at one of the studio rooms.

The coordinator opened the door.

The room was empty except for a set of three chairs before a table, a stool just ahead of the table and an easel holding my initial audition piece - the abstract drawing.

I was asked to lay out my work on the table and take a seat on the nearby stool. The coordinator said the audition committee would be along in a moment and then left.

I sat alone in the room. A bit nervous.

As I waited, I looked around at the surrounding walls, heavily covered in scuff marks and paint stains. A great deal of art-making went on in these rooms.

Soon after these observations, the door to the room opened and the senior visual art program triumvirate filed in and greeted me.

"Hi!" I responded.

The trio sat at the table and began commenting on my work to one another.

I was then asked about the abstract drawing I'd produced for the audition and I mustered a response that seemed to please them.

The committee then began commenting positively upon the techniques applied to the various Southwood pieces I'd brought in.

Following that, they descended upon my personal sketchbook, flipping through the almost-completely filled, hardbound artifact; perhaps the most compelling proof of my talent as a visual artist. They all seemed quite impressed.

Having reviewed my work samples, the committee then turned all of their attention to me.

During the rather brief interview which followed, one of the committee members asked me about my career aspirations.

"What would you like to do as a career?" they posed.

An unusual answer bubbled to the surface.

Months earlier, my parents had returned home from one of my younger brother's junior league baseball games with a surprise for me.

Having visited a library close to the athletics field (West Kendall Regional Library) after the game, my parents' surprise was a book they thought suited my obsessive interest in what else at the time? *Star Wars!*

The fourth film in the film series (*Star Wars: The Phantom Menace*) had released the year before and I was completely captivated by the franchise; by the formal aspects as much as by the storytelling. So, my parents sated my geeky predilection by bringing home a slim paperback, *George Lucas: Close-Up - The Making of His Movies*.

I dove in as soon as I could.

One of the most illuminating aspects of the book was the revelation - to me - that George Lucas had wanted to be an illustrator growing up. How familiar, I'd thought! And then how he'd attended film school and shifted his eye toward becoming a documentary filmmaker. Or a documentarian, as I chose to phrase it.

So, in identifying with an aspect of a renowned filmmaker responsible for so much childhood and early adolescent joy in my life, I adopted an alike career aspiration even if I didn't know the first thing about documentary filmmaking. It just made sense to me.

"A documentarian," I responded to the inquisitive committee member.

They were intrigued.

Another committee member chimed in with a reference to Hi8 video technology and I nodded along in understanding despite having only the vaguest familiarity with the term.

Finally, the committee members turned to one another with an unspoken, unanimous satisfaction.

This second and final stage of the audition was soon concluded and I was reunited with my parents on the first floor of the building.

"How'd it go?" my mom asked.

"Good," I responded.

I learned of my acceptance to New World two months later.

11. Drama (March 1999)

"You said you were interested in animation, right?" Ms. Gilpin, my 7th grade art teacher, asked.

"Yeah," I replied with a hint of suspicion.

"How'd you like to sit in on Ms. Lilly's class this afternoon?" she added.

I was a bit puzzled. Ms. Lilly was the Southwood Middle School theater teacher.

"You need to understand acting if you want to be a good animator," my art teacher clarified.

I agreed.

So later that day, I was given a hall pass and sent on my way from my art classroom to the school auditorium where Ms. Lilly would be waiting for me.

Toward the end of grade school, I'd had visions of my sketches in animated form. One of them involved, in loose and messy pencil strokes, a lean but muscular figure running, jumping and dodging their way through a dense jungle environment. This constantly replayed snippet of mental footage represented an ideal I could not yet fully articulate but which I understood in a deeply visceral way.

I wanted my characters to move!

Although I grew up on a steady diet of Saturday morning cartoons and Disney animated films, I was somewhat averse to learning about the animators and animation technique behind them because, even in my youth, I was turned off by their far too clean and streamlined appearance. I preferred a far rougher and more intense approach. For that reason, I found my own imagination considerably more appealing than any existing animated media as I entered adolescence.

Beyond mere movement, however, another artistic principle soon descended upon my impressionable, young artistic mind. On a lazy weekend afternoon, also toward the end of grade school, I happened upon a televised broadcast of Alan Parker's 1984 film *Birdy*.

I was particularly struck by the climax of the film in which one character (played by Nicolas Cage) desperately attempts to coax another, suffering from a traumatic tour of duty in Vietnam, out of a state of catatonia in a sanitarium. After so many failed efforts, a response from the cruelly afflicted character is at last elicited when the desperate friend breaks down in frustration after bringing in and emptying out a case filled with countless baseballs the pair had hit over their neighbors' fences when they were younger.

The film left an indelible mark on my budding psyche and actually fueled a short-lived desire to become an actor myself. But that desire later cooled and settled into an interest in creating characters that could perform as powerfully as I'd seen on the screen.

I wanted my characters to act!

Arriving at the auditorium, I entered and found it empty save for Ms. Lilly and another teacher. They welcomed and invited me to sit down next to them.

"We're going to be reviewing some of the monologues that our students will be auditioning for high school with," Ms. Lilly informed.

I nodded and sat quietly with great reserve.

The first student was beckoned.

Student #1 delivered his monologue and then retreated to the backstage area.

The teachers convened. "That needed more spontaneity," Ms. Lilly insisted. The other teacher nodded.

The teachers reset and called out the second student.

Student #2 delivered her monologue and then retreated to the backstage area.

The teachers convened. "Not enough movement," Ms. Lilly suggested. "Yeah, she's too planted," the other teacher affirmed.

The teachers reset and called out the third student.

Student #3 delivered his monologue and then retreated to the backstage area.

The teachers convened. "Wrong material for him," Ms. Lilly noted. "His first choice was better," the assistant responded.

The teachers reset and called out the fourth student.

Student #4 delivered her monologue and then retreated to the backstage area.

The teachers convened. Ms. Lilly looked pensive. The other teacher waited. "Her line should be 'stone creature' instead of 'gargoyle,'" Ms. Lilly insisted. The other teacher nodded.

The teachers reset but then Ms. Lilly called time. Those were all the monologues they'd be reviewing that afternoon.

The teachers then turned to me and asked if I'd learned something from the precedings.

I had.

In fact, so enchanted was I by the experience that I expressed an interest in switching out of the visual arts program and joining the theater program for my final year at Southwood. The teachers responded with great encouragement and upon my leaving, wished me luck on all my endeavors.

Some time later, I did in fact audition for the Southwood theater program but I was not accepted. I learned that there's a marked difference between capturing performance as a potential animator and embodying the craft effectively as an actor. I would be staying squarely in my visual arts lane for a bit more time to come.

12. Exposure (July 1999)

Owing to his employment at a local Best Buy, my older brother Juan was regularly surrounded by the latest in home electronic equipment and media at his workplace. And taking full advantage of employee discounts and the store's open-box inventory, he was able to swiftly and cheaply acquire some choice items for himself.

As a result, his bedroom soon contained the following:

- A 32" CRT television (large for its time)
- A complete, 5.1 surround sound system
- A set of wireless headphones for lone-viewing occasions
- A state-of-the-art DVD player
- And lastly, a bed positioned directly across from the television for maximum comfort

With this literal home theater setup contained entirely in his room, film viewings were an occasion I greatly looked forward to after school or on the weekends.

On top of this tricked-out living space, my brother also had a relationship with someone who worked at a local Blockbuster and was able to procure a large collection of DVDs, both new releases and older ones. Consequently, I was exposed to a wide range of films during the few years my brother and I had good enough relations to enjoy them together.

On one particular occasion, I was invited by Juan to watch a film I was only vaguely aware of but that I knew wasn't a mega-budgeted, star-studded, CGI-laden Hollywood film; the type of film I'd grown accustomed to and that major studios spent untold millions advertising the hell out of. Rather, the film in question had gained its reputation in my eyes almost solely on account of its award potential and critically-ordained artistic merit. For the first time in my moviegoing life, a film appealed to me based off a peculiar, new metric - prestige.

So with great enthusiasm, I settled into a relaxed position on the TV-facing bed as Juan powered up his mighty entertainment system, drew the shades, hit the lights and settled in himself.

It was showtime!

The film was Wes Anderson's 1998 indie hit *Rushmore*.

In the mid '90s, due to the immense critical and commercial success of independent films, like 1989's *sex, lies and videotape* and 1994's *Pulp Fiction*, the preeminent Hollywood studios were newly determined to harness the wind of a developing independent film craze around the country. Accordingly, the major North American film studios formed subsidiary companies to produce and market low-budget films with more specialized, niche-based appeal.

And the maneuver worked! The late '90s and early '00s saw an explosion of new, visionary filmmaking talent rising to great notoriety and acclaim; some closely allied with those subsidiaries and others less so.

The concurrent Digital Revolution also greased the wheels of this new trend in the industry. The advent of DVD and its remarkable superiority as a home media format over VHS and LaserDisc opened up a major new revenue stream for the latest independent releases as well as older, catalog titles. By virtue of the supplemental features typically added to a film's DVD release, pulling back the curtain on the filmmaking process, the format presented the culture of moviemaking, independent and otherwise, to legions of budding cinema enthusiasts and potential filmmakers.

It was a time like none other!

During this latest film viewing in Juan's souped up bedroom, we had been captivated by the seriocomic exploits of the eccentric Max Fischer in *Rushmore*. But I was more than simply intrigued by the film's story. I was exposed to a new kind of filmmaking that bore a strong, personal and highly askew stamp. This one had hit different.

In the year or two to follow, Juan and I would be awestruck by Neo's transcendent, climactic transformation in *The Matrix*; shocked by the brutality of the Allies' D-Day landing in *Saving Private Ryan*; exhilarated by Andy Dufresne's incredible feat of deception in *The Shawshank Redemption*; charmed by the sympathetic depiction of the evil Alex DeLarge in *A Clockwork Orange*; thrilled by Maximus' death-defying acts of heroism in *Gladiator*; enraptured by the tragic ascendancy of Michael Corleone in *The Godfather* and *The Godfather: Part II*; mesmerized by the beauty and wonder of the forest in *Princess Mononoke*; and riveted by the supernatural revelations surrounding David Dunn in *Unbreakable*...

Indeed, Juan and I explored films of many different genres and filmmakers during the few years we remained open to watching films together in his room. And the experience, more than a mere time-killing diversion, helped open my eyes to the venerable tradition and sheer power of cinema!

13. Fanfiction (June 1993)

I was transfixed by the television as a distinctly appealing movie advertisement played.

"...From the DNA in that blood, science was able to recreate those giants. And for the first time, man and dinosaur shared the earth. It happened at a place called... *Jurassic Park!*"

My eyes were wide and I gulped hard.

"This summer, director Steven Spielberg will take you there!" the advert's narrator promised as the iconic logo appeared and the tease concluded.

I bolted from the downstairs family room of my childhood home and reached my parents upstairs in the kitchen.

"Jurassic Park!" my 7-year-old self announced ecstatically.

My parents were puzzled.

"Can I see it when it comes out?!" I begged.

My parents looked at each other, unsure. My family rarely made trips to the movie theater.

"We'll see," they said.

In the ensuing months, I encountered a steady cavalcade of other TV spots, TV news segments, toy ads, print ads and, most influentially, talk among friends about what else? *Jurassic Park*! The hype surrounding the film was unbelievable! It was everywhere!

As the film's release rolled around in June of 1993, I asked my dad if I could finally go see the film that had practically engulfed my entire childhood mediascape.

"No," he said plainly.

I stared in derision.

"I have a friend who saw it and he said it's too violent for young children," my dad reasoned.

My jaw dropped. I soon learned that no quantity or quality of argument could make my dad and, by extension - my mom, budge. Their word was law and I did not possess the permitting social connections to circumvent their parental decree.

Toys, a museum exhibit, puzzles, activity books, incessant talk among friends, a junior novelization, newspaper features, TV specials and more - all bearing the mark of a certain fictional park of the future - existed as if to torture me.

I was resigned.

But I was also obsessed.

So enraptured was I by the promise of what lay in store by the relentlessly teased film, I began writing a work of fan fiction based on what I knew of *Jurassic Park* despite not having seen the actual movie. The premise of my story involved a malfunction of the park's security system resulting in prehistoric mayhem (surprise!). I collaborated with a fellow classmate and friend of mine at the time, Brian Koenig, who may or may not have seen the film. He shared a credit in the work's byline.

I finished a basic manuscript and not too long after, my dad caught wind of what I was up to. The grudge against my parents over my cinematic deprivation was surprisingly short-lived and I accepted my dad's proposal of having my writing typed up on our home computer and printed out using a newly acquired laser printer.

My dad assisted me with all of the technical particulars. And when I saw the printed result of my writing emerge from the printer, I proudly remarked, "It looks professional!" I'd never seen anything I'd written in such a form.

On each printed page, the text was relegated to the bottom of the page with space above for illustrations. I recall producing a few drawings for the piece but I never fully completed it.

My dad later reported that he'd shown my fan fiction to a friend of his in publishing and he'd been quite impressed. Even at a young age, I appreciated the attention my creative writing had received.

Ultimately I would have to wait well over a year after its theatrical release before I finally saw *Jurassic Park* (on the occasion of its VHS release in the fall of 1994). However, the images and feelings that consumed me in anticipation of the film fueled my imagination and creativity like few things did in my childhood. That said, I've probably seen *Jurassic Park* over 30 times, including once in theaters when the film was re-released in 3D in 2013.

14. Identity (October 1990)

The final, summarizing chorus of the song arrived...

This old man, he plays one.
This old man, he plays two.
This old man, he plays three.
This old man, he plays four.
This old man, he plays five.
Knick-knack, paddy-whack!

A group of four and five-year-olds, some seated cross-legged and others more casually reclined on the carpeted floor before the teacher, Ms. Moynihan, concluded their sing-along of yet another Raffi Cavoukian favorite.

Ms. Moynihan stopped the tape player and gently applauded the class for their spirited participation in yet another of one of the class's fairly regular sing-along activities.

One of the pupils requested another song.

"No, that's enough for today," Ms. Moynihan responded. She continued, "Today's Friday and what do we do on Friday, everyone?" Ms. Moynihan prompted.

"Free time!" most of the youngsters exclaimed enthusiastically.

"That's right! So let's get on our feet and go to our station of choice, okay?" Ms. Moynihan encouraged.

Getting to my feet, I raced to the painting station at one corner of the large, multi-purpose room.

Restless and impatient, I grabbed and donned one of the over-sized shirts covered in dried paint stains. I then arranged a large sheet of paper on one of the junior-sized easels and retrieved my crucial implements - a brush and some paint.

I stood in front of the easel and began to paint.

My sense of time slipped swiftly away.

Even as a child no older than four, I had already demonstrated a precocious knack for visual art. Much later on in life, my dad would describe how I would express myself through line drawings before I was sufficiently verbal. To express anger and frustration, I'd produce sharp, jagged lines on paper. If I was feeling calm and sanguine, my lines would be gently drawn and smoothly curved.

About half-an-hour later, Ms. Moynihan stopped by my station.

She saw me putting the finishing touches on a painting of a large, one-eyed creature with numerous spindly tendrils emanating from its head. The beastly entity filled the entire canvas and was rendered in a warm color scheme of mostly oranges and yellows. Some red.

I was quite proud of what I'd painted and Ms. Moynihan seemed quite impressed.

Later that day, when my mom arrived to pick me up from my preschool class at Baptist Day School, Ms. Moynihan showed her the painting I'd made earlier in the afternoon.

"Your son is quite talented," Ms. Moynihan commented as she smiled at me.

My mom, the caregiver to whom I was most attached, responded with some pride.

"He's an artist."

15. Music (June 1998)

Alarm clocks had sounded.
Breakfast cereals had been eaten.
Buses had delivered their passengers.
Notebooks had been pulled out of backpacks.
Teachers had lectured at length to their students.
Dirty drawings had been stealthily passed around.
Video game secrets had been traded between classes.
Books had been read during sustained silent reading time.
Moments from episodes of *The Simpsons* had been re-enacted.
Hands had been raised with questions about homework or an exam.
Laughter had erupted over flubs in the principal's school-wide address.
And ceiling tiles had been counted in boredom enough for the year...
For now, school was finally out for the summer!

At the very conclusion of what was my first year at Southwood Middle School, I'd received a birthday party invitation from a friend I'd made over the course of the school year. Invitees were beckoned to the local cineplex to see the latest Jim Carrey film *The Truman Show* and afterward we'd all be picked up and driven to my friend's house for the remainder of the occasion's festivities.

I assumed *The Truman Show* would be a riotous comedy in line with the headlining actor's earlier films. At least that's how the film had been advertised on TV. In any case, I looked forward to a theater screening, a fairly rare occurrence in my youth up to then.

The day of the party finally arrived.

All of the partygoers assembled just outside the theater. After a headcount, we strolled into the cavernous theater lobby and onto our auditorium. We soon found our seats and settled in for the show.

* * *

My parents often played classical music for their offspring in our early years of development. In addition to providing a rich, cultured home environment, my parents wanted to expose their children to music that had stood the test of time. As such, my father collected various classical music compilations on CD and routinely played them on a state-of-the-art stereo system in the living room of my childhood home in Massachusetts. So, from a very early age I developed an appreciation for a fair amount of popular classical music. Three pieces which stand out as particular favorites were Rimsky-Korsakov's "Flight of the Bumblebee (from the opera, *The Tale of Tsar Saltan*)", Khatchaturian's "Sabre Dance (from *Gayane Suite No. 3*)" and the whole of Tchaikovsky's *The Nutcracker*.

Famed film composer, John Williams, was another significant musical influence in my household growing up. My parents knew him best as the principal conductor of the Boston Pops Orchestra (on account of living just north of the city) but as a child I knew of him as the composer of a certain cinematic space opera. In 1997, I purchased a two-disc set of the soundtrack of *Star Wars: A New Hope* on account of the 1997 re-release of the film and would listen to the score religiously. My dad recalls how on one occasion, we sat down to watch the 1977 film and I would anticipate and point out each significant musical cue as it occurred. That music was in my blood!

As the end credits rolled on *The Truman Show* and the lights came up in the theater auditorium, I was stunned. This was no mere run-of-the-mill Jim Carrey vehicle. This was cinema on a level I'd never experienced!

Although it would be years before I could properly contextualize the film experience as a sublime contemporization of Platonic ideas about the nature of reality, it was enough that the film was as powerful and profound as it was to my unsuspecting 12-year-old mind.

As bold and affecting as the film's high-concept story was, another aspect stood out to me just as much - its music! The film predominantly featured an original score by Burkhard Dallwitz but it also included some remarkable needle-drops in the form of a few Philip Glass (a composer I'd grow to love some time later) selections and, most personally significant of all, some classical music!

The use of Mozart's "Turkish March" from his Piano Sonata No. 11, in particular, made an indelible impact on me and I immediately sought out a recording of the piece upon my return home from the ho-hum remainder of the birthday party. Freshly re-introduced to me, this relatively simple piano piece deftly conveyed harmony and stateliness with a slight air of sadness. It evoked images from my childhood and seemed to unlock powerful new images and feelings. I would never be the same again.

In the years to follow, I began a habit of listening to the local classical music station regularly on the radio (rest in peace, WTMI 93.1 FM); amassing a large collection of music, mainly classical and film music, in a digital format; and remaining acutely sensitive to the type of music featured in the films I would see. It was precisely the result of said experience and many others like it that fueled these new habits which would persist in some form or another up to the present and beyond.

16. Outlining (March 2000)

You didn't want to cross Ms. Siegel. Her height was imposing, her manner was strict and her expectations were alpine. She was perhaps the least fun, least hip and least sparing of teachers at Southwood Middle School. She taught English.

I walked into her classroom for yet another 6th period class of hyper vigilance and self-monitoring. The last thing any student of hers wanted to do was draw her ire. Even if a pencil so much as accidentally rolled off your desk and hit the floor, she would turn the rest of the class's attention to it and make a point about how the incident reflected your inadequacy and insincerity as a student (which actually happened to me on one occasion).

Ms. Siegel had been my English teacher in 7th grade, the previous year as well. Luckily, I'd survived. But as an 8th grader, her class now involved a far more singular and demanding curriculum. We were expected to write a seven-paragraph essay almost every week. She'd provide the prompt and we'd provide the essay.

I settled into my assigned seat.

My class's outlines were due at the end of the period.

Outlines...

Always with the outlines.

For every essay we wrote in Ms. Siegel's class, an accompanying outline was also due.

Every single time.

It never ended with the outlines.

Of course, the first step of outlining was defining a thesis statement. It was a single sentence that presented the main idea which the entire essay was attempting to substantiate. It would be included in the introductory paragraph along with some background information and then restated in the concluding paragraph.

Then? A list using three Roman numerals. One for each section of our essay:

I. Introduction
II. Body
III. Conclusion

For the second section, "Body," three alphabet characters for three body paragraphs of increasing importance:

II. Body
    A. First argument (least important)
    B. Second argument
    C. Third argument (most important)

Lastly, another subset but of numerical values for three supporting details per paragraph.

II. Body
    A. First argument
        1. Supporting detail #1
        2. Supporting detail #2
        3. Supporting detail #3

The same for all body paragraphs.

The "A, B, C" and "1, 2, 3" items served as placeholders for actual arguments and supporting details that were specific to each essay.

This was the basic structure of the outline Ms. Siegel expected from her class.

I took out some pages worth of internet research I'd conducted at home for the current essay and set myself to task, working out yet another outline.

As I weighed the various options I had in arranging my gathered information, the classroom door swung open and a tall Black man boisterously entered the room.

"This teacher!" he announced.

He was overcome with emotion as Ms. Siegel rose from her desk in utter surprise.

"Listen to her!" he spoke adamantly.

Ms. Siegel walked over to the man.

"Listen to what she says!" he continued.

The two embraced and the man revealed himself as a former student of Ms. Siegel. Perhaps from a decade or so ago judging by his age.

Ms. Siegel blushed as the man continued to address the class, insisting on the absolute and resounding value of her tutelage.

"She changed my life!" he exclaimed.

On a few occasions, I'd witnessed adult former students enter a teacher's class to say hello and catch up a bit but I'd never seen an example like this of such strong, almost immoderate emotion. What was he saying? Ms. Siegel was a cruel, old witch who drank her student's tears.

The man soon left but not before leaving me with a memory I associate with profound empathy.

Why profound empathy?

Out of the habit of producing outlines for every essay in Ms. Siegel's 8th grade English class, I internalized a necessity for preparing one for every significant writing effort from that year onward. I can't speak for my fellow classmates but to me, Ms. Siegel beat the practice of outlining so persistently and relentlessly into my conception of writing that I couldn't imagine not doing so from that point forward.

Outlining allows a writer to clearly build, oversee and re-arrange the super-structure of a written composition. Before I learned how to outline, effective writing for me was mostly affixed to the precarity of chance. To this day, however, I outline practically everything I write. A habit that has served me most well precisely because of my 8th grade English teacher's seemingly excessive tendency.

That former student who dramatically interrupted my 6th period

English class that day to honor Ms. Siegel with his ecstatic, prescriptive words?

It might as well as have been me.

17. Photography (February 2002)

"To make a film... you may not have to know very about anything else, but you must know about photography."
-Stanley Kubrick

My dismissal from New World School of the Arts signaled an end to my interest in and practice of the fine arts. Frankly, I was never sincerely committed to achieving great competency in still lifes, figure drawing, painting, sculpture and other related activities at New World. My sketchbooks of the period, replete with fantastic imaginings and later film-inspired illustrations, confirmed this fundamental and early-on disconnect from the fine arts curriculum. By the time I left New World, film and filmmaking had reserved my creative mental space almost entirely.

Newly enrolled at Miami Killian Senior High for the remainder of my high school education, filmmaking was the prevailing focus but music and photography also entered the picture as supplemental interests. Music, primarily classical and film music scores, had been an obsession of mine since late childhood. Photography I was less familiar with but considered it a gateway to filmmaking on account of the many shared characteristics with cinematography.

While my musical ambitions would flounder after a few months despite a period of rather intense application of effort at my family's electronic keyboard with the aid of a newly purchased instructional manual, photography seemed far less demanding and more in tune with my acuity for visual art.

Acting on my photographic inclinations, I borrowed my dad's Minolta SLR camera and regularly brought it to school with me.

This tool which I'd only known through my dad's limited use in capturing certain family moments or events, represented an exciting, new road to travel with filmmaking as the eventual destination.

In my attempt to gain competency in photography, I readily dove into reading about this fascinating art form with a basic guide my dad owned and a variety of books from my local library. I also grew familiar with several online resources and gained a great deal of insight from frequent access to those as well.

As I grew more familiar with my borrowed SLR's manual controls and acquired a wide-angle lens, my subject matter tended toward the unusual. After school hours, I wandered around Killian capturing unoccupied spaces with a one-point perspective orientation. Owing to some of the imagery from the films of Stanley Kubrick, I had become enamored with the conversion of receding lines in an architectural space toward a center-most vanishing point. The clean geometry and unnerving barrenness of such imagery greatly appealed to me. I also took photos of more mundane subject matter at home.

After my sophomore year came to a close at Killian, I expressed interest in enrolling in a summer photography class at a local college. After several months of grappling with the mechanics of photography completely on my own, I thought a basic primer in the form of a class would be most opportune.

Lasting only two weeks or so, I found the class rather elementary but I admired the attention its instructor gave to my occasional questions and comments. The first few sessions of the class were pure theory and the latter portion of the class involved some photography outside of the classroom on the campus grounds.

Unfortunately and quite miserably, my dad's SLR, which he'd purchased in the 1980s, stopped working days before my class was set to partake in the more practical part of the summer course. As a result, I could not participate in the field work and my experience in the class ended rather anti-climatically.

Instead of replacing my dad's broken-down camera with a replacement SLR of some sort, I opted to borrow a digital still camera he owned with a built-in viewfinder screen. This far smaller and more technologically advanced device allowed for more inconspicuous photography and its mostly automatic functions hastened the entire image-making process. I carried this camera around with me at Killian as well and used it to capture far more conventional subject matter in my junior year. However, in that same year, my photographic activity would be eclipsed by the production of my first short film.

Despite its discontinuation, the experience of wielding a still photography camera, whether analog or digital, was a valuable introduction to a medium of expression I'd never fully embraced before. It provided me with a basic understanding of lenses, angles, lighting and composition that would prove instrumental as I began my journey into short filmmaking. Additionally, an understanding of the technical rudiments of photography (e.g., aperture, depth of field, shutter speed and focus control) would also transfer over rather seamlessly to my technical facility in filmmaking despite the difference of a video format.

And for what it's worth, I am infinitely grateful my dad raised little objection to my surreptitious seizing of his cameras during my time in high school. Thanks, Dad!

18. Physics (February 1996)

The day of the local pinewood derby was finally here!

It was a longer car ride than I was used to as my parents and I drove to some place south of Miami-Dade, our county of residence, on a warm near-spring day.

When we arrived, my dad parked on the outskirts of a vast field where some of the mothers of the other Cub Scouts were gathered. My parents made polite small-talk as I scoped out the stretch of land before us. It was a sprawling, barren field with a gathering some several hundred feet away.

Soon enough, my dad joined me as I trekked toward the distant assembly with my pinewood racer. Upon arrival, I encountered many kids and adults I didn't know but also some familiar Cub Scouts from my pack and their fathers whom my dad and I greeted.

There was much activity related to registration and proper contest protocol. One of the adults received my racer and assigned it a number.

At the center of this busy gathering was a large wooden track. It was long, curved and made up of separate lanes. For every race, the racers would be situated at the top and caught in place by a holding mechanism. When the hold of the racers was released, they would barrel down the track driven by gravity alone. The racers would speed down a long slope to the red-marked area at the base, flanked by a USA flag and a checkered one.

Not too far from the track was a table with all of the contestants' racers. There was a great variety and virtually all of them were much more visually impressive than mine. I actually felt a bit dispirited. My entry sat alongside the showy fleet with its gold finish and a crudely, free-hand drawn white star gracing its top. Simple but plain.

Laid out near the racers were some ribbons to be awarded to the scouts with winning racers. They had clearly been laid out with care.

Near that table on the ground was a platform labeled, "Winner's Circle". I assumed that the winner would stand atop the slightly elevated mount for a deserving photo opportunity.

Surrounding all of these interesting sights were many father-and-son pairs. It seemed like this pinewood derby was a long-held tradition and an important bonding experience for many involved. It certainly was for me.

My dad and I returned to the area on the outskirts where a makeshift rest area with chairs and snacks had been set up by the Cub Scout mothers. I excitedly relayed news of the imminent start of the derby to my mom. I was thrilled; this being my first pinewood derby!

Not long after, the races began and I soon returned to the summit of activity on that sun-baked field to witness the unique spectacle.

After a few races, it was my racer's time to demonstrate its metal.

My heartbeat was revved up and my eye sight was fixed on my racer as it was put into position by one of the designated derby officials.

As my racer and its first round competitor were set into place at the top of the track, I traded glances with my dad. He seemed just as psyched as I was.

"Ready..." the announcer announced.

"Set..." he continued, almost teasingly.

"Go!" he finally yelled.

Weeks earlier, my dad and I had convened in our shed to put together the block of pine, four metal nails (or axles) and four plastic wheels included in the pinewood racer kit that had been provided at an earlier Cub Scout meeting.

I had expressed some interest in entering the competition but I was far from convinced that I had any chance of winning. I'd never competed in anything like a pinewood derby except in video games. My dad, on the other hand, saw a fighting chance and ventured an idea involving a simple modification of the wood block's center of gravity.

As we huddled in the swelteringly hot shed behind our home, my dad explained how embedding a simple weight beneath the wooden body toward the front would give our racer a substantial advantage; in addition to some aerodynamic carving and rounding of its shape. Ever the man of science, my dad seemed absolutely confident and convinced. So, we set to work applying my dad's ideas in swift and eager fashion.

When our assembly of pinewood, nails and wheels was complete, we spray-painted the body of our racer in gold and I applied the finishing touch - a crudely, free-hand drawn white star gracing its top. Simple but plain.

My racer plunged down the track with remarkable speed!

First place by a substantial margin!

I sported the widest grin and glanced at my dad who was also quite pleased.

A designated official scooped up my winning racer and reset the track for another race. A new competitor was placed next to my racer for another bout.

Those familiar words ringed out from the announcer once again.

"Ready..."

"Set..."

"Go!"

Once more, my racer blazed down the track to again win first place and with a significant lead!

I was ecstatic!

My little racer went on to win a few more races when it was finally deemed the winner of the day's event.

I was awarded a bright blue, first-place ribbon before being asked to stand atop the "Winner's Circle" platform for a photo.

I was one proud Cub Scout.

At the end of the day, my dad's formative training as a scientist yielded an astounding victory! He knew that the understanding and application of even the most rudimentary laws of physics would be enough to upset the competition or at least prove our effort formidable. An invaluable lesson!

Although I'd been somewhat intimidated by the flashy external appearance of the other scouts' pinewood racers, my own humble entry turned out to have the upper hand in the only department that actually mattered. A similar underdog victory amid intimidating opponents would take place two decades later but in a wholly different context - the film festival circuit.

19. Pilot (December 2001)

At New World School of the Arts, the prestigious arts high school I was attending, my interest in visual art began to wane. It wouldn't be long before my withering commitment to classwork and homework assignments registered to my teachers and guidance counselor. Now, a fervent interest in film and filmmaking was taking root.

For several months, character and scene ideas for a first short film began to crystallize in my mind. I'd started to keep a composition notebook handy to catalog all of the worthy results of a growing and very solitary meditative habit. I increasingly dissociated from friends and spent more time alone with film books borrowed from the library and ever-trusty paper and pen.

And my newfound habits were yielding results!

I was on the cusp of completing a first draft of a short film script titled "Concerning Arthur Roderick". At 10 pages in length, it told a high school-set love story between two misfit students. No dialogue involved; just visuals and music.

Before the first draft was complete, however, I endeavored to borrow my father's digital camcorder in order to perform a preliminary location scout; admittedly, more of an excuse to venture out into the bustling world with a camera than an absolutely practical necessity at that point in time.

The evening before I would head downtown to the familiar grounds of New World and thereabouts to perform my location scout, I thought I'd commemorate the occasion with a brief statement read on-camera.

Lacking a tripod at the time, I placed the camcorder on my computer tower and positioned myself accordingly.

My statement read as follows:

"*Hello and welcome to what I call the prologue to my first day ever of filmmaking! I'm very happy that everything's been going really well on the filmmaking or, rather, digital filmmaking front for me. There's a long road ahead and it's good to know that I'm prepared. I like good films and I plan to make good films.*

"The other day I was gazing vastly into a screen and now I'm about to gaze vastly into my DV camera. I'm making a short film! I promise compelling storytelling and visuals that will leave you completely satisfied. I believe this introduction represents the beginning of something great."

I was clearly primed.

The following day, I readied my camcorder with fresh tape and arranged to have my parents drive me downtown and drop me off for an hour or two as I explored potential locations for eventual production.

Owing to winter break, the various locations I visited were almost completely devoid of people and I was able to perform my amateur location scout with no interference or suspicion. As I explored a variety of interesting architectural spaces, my eyes were glued to the camcorder's LCD viewfinder. For the first time in my life, I felt like an actual filmmaker!

I would finish my first draft of "Concerning Arthur Roderick" some weeks later. And when it was finished, I prepared a casting call notice and actually had it approved by New World staff for posting on a bulletin board in the school's building.

Sadly, with my coming dismissal from New World, what would have been my first short film never entered production.

But a major fuse had been lit.

20. Prompt (October 1996)

I sat quietly in my 5th grade class before the morning bell had sounded, continuing work on yet another sketch of an original character intended for a prospective comic book project. The name of my intimidating, muscle-bound and masked character was Rampage.

Heavily inspired by the art of Todd McFarlane, I had developed the look of the character over the course of several weeks and the name had been chosen from a page I'd filled with possible monikers. This particular endeavor drew the fascination of those around me, including my adult educators, and I was very proud of my work.

At any rate, the morning bell soon rang and I continued tickling my practically finished sketch until the last possible moment before Ms. Murray would notice my off-task activity and, fascinated or not, politely ask me to put my sketchbook away.

After my class's routine pledge of allegiance recital and watching the school-produced morning announcements, Ms. Murray asked all of her students to take out their composition notebooks. She then proceeded to write out the following words on the classroom white board:

As I opened the door, I heard a sound. I looked inside and...

She then explained that what she'd written on the board would be our journal writing prompt for the day. We were instructed to spend a quiet half-hour or so using the prompt as a jumping-off point for whatever our boundless imaginations so decided to conjure in written form.

As I sat in the uncomfortable gap of time between instruction and activity, I weighed several possibilities of where I could take my writing. The clock ticked away as I fretted over the empty pages of my composition notebook. But then, the obvious dawned on me: I should tell the story of Rampage!

Bingo!

I immediately began filling the first page of my composition notebook!

Half-an-hour later, the teacher called time but I was still busy putting pencil to paper. I was on a hot streak as ideas cascaded from my mind and out through the tip of my writing utensil. Guns, cars, fighter jets, secret bases, dungeons, muscles, gore, piranhas, barracudas? My story had it all! I committed my ideas to paper with the same youthful delight and exuberance I'd wield in playing with my action figures at home. I couldn't stop!

On every subsequent journal writing opportunity I was given in class, I'd use it to add to my story. And my feverish scrawling didn't stop at the classroom. I continued to write at home as a form of gladly self-assigned homework. The carte blanche nature of the assignment had uncovered a vast reservoir of creative potential I never knew existed within me until then.

In the days that followed that initial assignment, I filled up nearly half of my composition notebook and racked up a total of 10 chapters for my story, titled *Rampage*. With chapter titles like "The Secret Crystal Necklace", "The Escape From the Building of Death", "The Expedition" and "The Isle of Death", it was the lengthiest and most ambitious writing project I'd ever undertaken up to that point.

Some time later, Ms. Murray asked the class if anyone would care to share their latest journal entry. Although I was recovering from a slight cold, I spiritedly volunteered to read my multi-part journal entry to the class from end to end. So, I walked up to the front of the classroom with my notebook in hand and began reading aloud.

Although my voice was somewhat raspy and in pain from that passing bout of illness, I soldiered on regaling the class with my story of the adventures of Rampage. But after about five or ten minutes of reading my journal aloud, Ms. Murray cut into my presentation, "Sorry to interrupt, Gabriel, but how much more is left?"

I indicated the number of remaining pages. Quite a few.

"Okay, that's enough. Thank you for sharing, Gabriel!" she announced.

I returned to my seat.

Despite the cut-short exhibition of my story, I was satisfied with what I'd been able to present. While I'd ultimately never realize a Rampage comic book, this particular journal writing assignment allowed me to flex my plotting, pacing, detailing and other general fiction writing abilities without any guidance for the very first time.

It was an invaluable experience!

21. Puzzles (May 1992)

Creativity was a major part of my childhood. Of course I watched a generous amount of television and spent a great deal of time playing video games but if I wasn't occupied by those activities, I was usually making things or making things up.

As a child, I produced countless pencil, marker and crayon drawings. I also went on sprawling adventures around my home and its outdoor areas with my action figures and other toys. And throughout grade school, I found myself providing illustrations for as many assignments as I could. Suffice to say, my creative abilities had ample opportunity to grow and develop in my youth. But this seemingly inexhaustible creative tear would early on be coupled with a peculiar sentiment.

One day during my kindergarten years, it simply occurred to me that I could cut a large drawing into smaller pieces to, in effect, create a makeshift jigsaw puzzle. What an incredibly discovery, I thought!

I soon relayed this revelation to my mom and she encouraged me to create a few of these homemade puzzles to share with my kindergarten class.

I hopped to it and quickly churned out a few. I kept each in a neatly labeled plastic bag. My class was going to love this!

The following day, I presented my original puzzles to Ms. Budney and she approved them for storage and use in the classroom. I was elated!

Even at such a young age, I felt the appeal of creating experiences for others. It had occasionally revealed itself in my mimicking a stuffy, *Masterpiece Theatre*-like opening for an invisible audience before an afternoon of playing with my action figures. Or in my determining what movie or TV show property the play of invited-over friends would imitate as we climbed my front yard apple tree or explored the woods behind my home. I also remember an occasion where I gathered the members of my family in our family room to perform some type of extremely abbreviated magic/variety show.

I enjoyed creating experiences for other people!

As I watched over my classmates grappling with the challenge of putting together one of my puzzles, I felt proud and humbled that something I'd created was being honored with the interest, time and effort of others.

Even at such a young age, I understood and relished this.

22. Reading (February 2002)

The wound of having had to leave New World School of the Arts was fresh and gaping. Although I'd invited my exit from New World by my failures as a visual art student, it hurt that I was now irrevocably severed from the friendships and familiarity that had developed at the prestigious art high school over the nearly two years I'd attended. I was also affected by the now-compromised direction of my future. If not visual art, then what?

On a morning like many others to follow, I entered the more local (New World was located downtown), run-of-the-mill Miami Killian Senior High School for the first time as a student there. However, I felt like some wildly out-of-place being, wholly apart and different. I'd been dropped into the fray of a new school environment right in the middle of a bustling school year well in-progress. So began the continuation of my sophomore year.

As I would pass groups of socializing students on my way to my first period class at Killian, I might as well have heard a rowdy exchange of alien language. From elementary school on, I was accustomed to being in a calm and quiet atmosphere amid many gifted young people, artistic or otherwise, and gently encouraging adults. This was far removed from anything like those halcyon times. The setting was loud and abrasive and I'm sure the security guards, of which there were many, certainly had their work cut out for them. In all, these surroundings were a stinging reminder of my seeming fall from grace.

At any rate, I would grow accustomed to arriving at my first period class's classroom well before any of the other students. Sitting in the hall just outside, I'd greet the arriving teacher who'd proceed to unlock the door and allow me to join her in the otherwise empty room for a good 15 or 20 minutes before the other students filed in at the first bell's ringing.

Entering into the room, I'd retreat to my seat at the far end of the space and sit quietly. Initially, I did nothing but look around my immediate circumstances without any significant preoccupations. Time to think. But that would change soon enough.

The rest of the day would carry on like the orderly corralling of inmates in a penitentiary. Misbehavior among students and discipline or threats of discipline from instructors was rampant. But despite this degraded schoolscape, I maintained my best behavior at all times; always raising my hand and refraining from irrelevant, recreational chatter. In fact, I would go on to develop a better rapport with certain teachers than almost any of my fellow classmates over the course of the next two-and-a-half years of my time at Killian.

But I wasn't so adrift as it would seem when it came to my personal interests and a sense of future vocational pursuits. Although I was pushed out of a major art school, my creative spark was far from extinguished. Around this time, I was beginning to show a greater interest in photography and writing on account of their importance to an increasingly alluring interest in filmmaking.

At some point during my first few days at my wonderful new high school, I felt compelled to visit its library and immediately peruse its collection of books about film and filmmaking. Little did I know that I was starting on a path that would run for miles.

For the rest of the second half of my sophomore year at Killian, I nearly always had a book in my hand during any disposable pocket of time. And during my lunch period, I would avoid the outdoor courtyard areas where virtually every student routinely collected and escape to the regularly empty library to read and bask in my utterly serene domain of solitude. The books I read were mostly on filmmaking, screenwriting and photography but my scope of interest soon grew to include politics, history and media studies.

I must have touched nearly every filmmaking book in the library at Killian! And the more I read, the more in love I grew. The films of Alfred Hitchcock and Sergei Eisenstein were major focal points. Many of the books I read were littered with breakdowns and analyses of their films as well as those of other storied filmmakers. I quickly acclimated to a new world of filmic concepts, terms and theories. It was this ancient practice of deriving knowledge and understanding from mere characters on a page that principally guided my entrance into the world of filmmaking.

And my book supply didn't just stop at Killian! I tasked my older brother Juan with borrowing books from Green Library at Florida International University (the university he was attending) and, as a result, I had access to certain film theory texts which were far more involved and intense than the reading material I extracted from my high school's library. I was in heaven!

Amid all this prodigious reading activity, something even more significant began to take place. The ideas that would eventually inform my first completed short film began to coalesce in my mind and even find their expression in offhand notes and sketches. I began thinking in terms of the shots, scenes and sequences... of my own creation.

23. Recognition (April 2000)

I should've been more on-task during my class's session in the computer lab but I couldn't help admire my digital handiwork. It was 5th period at Southwood Middle School which meant art class. My fellow art students and I were expected to perform some online research for an assigned research paper. However, as soon as our art teacher Ms. Gilpin was out of sight, I'd defiantly access a certain tab on my computer's taskbar and pull up something unrelated to the requisite academic research. One of my friends sat next to me in the lab and I showed him too.

So, what was this object of my wayward fixation?

Some weeks ago on a fairly uneventful Sunday morning, I woke up early and caught an episode of a television show *Computer Chronicles* which had been introduced to me by my dad and which we were both fans of. The show, off the air since 2002, was a showcase for the latest in computer technology and services. On the particular episode which aired that morning, the hosts were presenting an online service called Homestead which offered free website building and hosting (it still exists!). I was intrigued.

Feeling properly inspired later that day, I set out to design and publish my first website using Homestead. The web-based application was easy enough to use and I was able to select a basic site template and make swift progress. Over the next few hours, I would stake my ground on the world wide web and dub my first foray into web authorship *The Garnobian Outpost*!

What did Garnobian mean? It's a long story but it was essentially based on a made-up root word "garnob," which I'd invented out of whole cloth one day. I had earlier titled my hard-bound sketchbook at the time

The Garnobian Chronicles.

I loaded up my new personal website with scanned drawings from my sketchbook, downloadable MP3s I'd acquired through legally questionable means, a live chat area, links to my favorite websites, a view counter, a front-page section for news and updates about the website and my creative work. Its construction came so naturally to me and I was very proud of the end result!

I couldn't see Ms. Gilpin anywhere.

"Where'd she go?" I inquired to my neighboring friend as I sat with my personal website in clear view on my computer's monitor. But assured that Ms. Gilpin was nowhere nearby, I continued proudly scanning over my internet craftsmanship.

"What are you looking at?" A voice boomed from behind me.

My pulse quickened and I involuntarily pulled up another tab on the screen that suggested dutifulness in appearance only.

"Nothing!" I shot back innocently.

But it was too late, Ms. Gilpin was hot on the trail.

"Was that your artwork on that website?" she asked.

She'd seen it.

"Yeah. It's my personal website," I confessed.

"Let's see," she encouraged.

Surprised by her cool about it, I pulled up the tab in question on my computer's taskbar. I pulled up the front page of my website with its title in full sight.

"Garnobian?" she queried.

I gave her the long, rambling story about the origin of the word and took out my hard-bound sketchbook so she could put two and two together.

"Gabriel, I am really impressed!" she replied.

I sat unnerved by this surprising turn of events but I ended up giving my art teacher a guided tour of the rest of my site.

Soon enough, my class's time in the computer lab came to a close but not before I'd invited a special kind of regard from Ms. Gilpin. She was far kinder to me for the remaining few months of that 8th grade year than ever before.

The Garnobian Outpost actually became quite popular among a small group of my fellow art students when they soon learned about it. The website acted as a sort of social lubricant, allowing me to engage with the other young people in my art class in ways I would've never had an occasion to otherwise.

My humble slice of the internet would stay up for many month past the end of my time at Southwood and go through several major redesigns and shifting of content before I ultimately took it down as high school stresses encroached upon my life. Still, it was a memorable, worthwhile experience and an important prelude to my second and far more substantial web design effort in 2016 with *GabrielRhenals.com*.

24. Storytelling (October 2000)

I'd volunteered to present a short story I'd written as part of a major 9th grade English class project at New World School of the Arts but despite my willingness to share it with the room of fellow high school freshmen, I had difficulty quelling my nerves.

In any case, I approached the front of the class with my rough draft in hand. The English teacher Ms. Craig sat behind me at her desk, as intent on hearing what I had to offer as any of her students. When I stood squarely before my class of 30 or so, I cleared my throat and began my presentation. I was trembling but eager to share.

The title of my story was *Norstadt of Lanshire* and some of the story elements were clearly inspired by the work of J.R.R. Tolkien and the 1996 film *Dragonheart*. I also borrowed a name or two from the *Star Wars* films.

My story took place in an ancient past in a part of the earth called Lanshire where a residing human kingdom was caught in a devastating and escalating conflict with a tribe of dragons. Roth, the largest and most lethal of the dragons, was their leader. But luckily among the human population in Lanshire, there existed a class of dragon slayers; the most renowned being Norstadt the Dragon Slayer, our daring protagonist!

My story basically follows Norstadt as he plans and executes a risky plan with his good friend Quaid to kill Roth and end the conflict between men and dragons. The desperate ploy involves a loan of men from the human kingdom and Roth's peculiar anatomical vulnerability. However, when Norstadt and Quaid's plan falls apart, Norstadt is left to face Roth one-on-one in an action-packed climax!

In the end, Norstadt proves the victor and Lanshire returns to a state of peace and prosperity.

When I reached the end of my read-through, you could hear a pin drop in the classroom before the class erupted with vigorous applause. Ms.

Craig, in a parent-teacher conference some months later, would attest to my parents how impressed the students had been over this instance of oral storytelling.

After my nerve-wracking but encouraging presentation, I set myself to refine the text of my story and had a final draft approved for the next step of the project - binding. Although I didn't have access to a professional document binding service, I thought up a clever solution involving a separately purchased spiral-bound sketchbook.

What I did was figure out how many pages I'd need for text and illustrations. Then, I ripped out all but that number of pages from the sketchbook. After that, I affixed the printed out pages of text to every other page leaving the blank pages for accompanying illustrations. Now, it was time to do what I did best at the time - draw!

With a looming deadline on the horizon, I had thankfully prepared preliminary thumbnail sketches for nearly every illustration required by the project. But despite the quick and steady progress I made illustrating my story, I couldn't help but feel a bit dissatisfied by the results of my graphite pencil sketches.

They just didn't move.

My mind's eye was filled with sequences of grand kineticism but the drawings I produced, while more than sufficient for the assignment, left me wanting.

Nevertheless, I put aside those unimportant concerns and ultimately completed the assignment on-time and to the delight of the friends I shared it with. And a few weeks later, Ms. Craig had some good news for me.

What was it?

Ms. Craig informed me that *Norstadt of Lanshire* would be showcased at Miami Book Fair that year. New World was located across from the Miami Dade College campus downtown where the book fair was regularly hosted.

When the book fair rolled around, I ventured to the fair grounds with a few of my friends during our lunch break to find my book and see it on display.

I headed to a particular room on a particular floor of a particular MDC campus building and there it was! *Norstadt of Lanshire* was prominently featured along with several other examples of noteworthy student work.

Additionally, a New World administrator had left me a kind note thanking me for sharing my work with the book fair. They wrote, "Your writing, creativity and artwork are all outstanding in a unique way that highlights your talents. Your book *Norstadt of Lanshire* is delightful and I'm sure it was enjoyed by many at the Book Fair."

All told, not too shabby a reception for what was basically my first major original writing and illustration effort!

25. Synthesis (January 1994)

It was pizza night in the Rhenals' household.

My family and I all sat at our kitchen table enjoying the occasion's usual order of pepperoni and cheese pies from a local vendor. My two older brothers, Alonso and Juan, joked amongst themselves as my parents discussed matters related to work, family and finances. At the same time, my mom was busy cutting up a slice of pizza and feeding the more child-friendly pieces to my toddler-aged, younger brother Daniel.

All of a sudden, Juan disturbed the relatively quiet atmosphere by posing a question to me in a rather frank manner. "Hey Gab, have you ever seen *Star Wars*?" he tested.

I looked on dubiously and responded, "Is that the one with the robots?"

"Yeah," he said.

I had some faint recollection of having been exposed to at least one of the films in the series when I was younger than 7 (my age at this time) but it belonged to a cloudy and mostly inaccessible part of my brain's memory store.

Juan looked around with a devious look in his eyes while everyone else resumed their dining and casual enjoyment of the evening.

"Let's watch *Star Wars* tonight!" Juan spiritedly suggested.

My parents looked at each other as Juan eagerly nodded in their direction.

"Sí, pero después de la comida," my mom assured.

After we'd all had our fill of pizza, we moved our party to the family room and settled in for a proper movie viewing. While we didn't own an official home video copy of *Star Wars: A New Hope*, we did have a VHS recording of the film from a past televised broadcast even though it was missing the first ten minutes or so of the film.

Juan retrieved the tape, swiftly inserted it into our VCR and lay down next to me on the carpet right in front of the television as the VCR wound to life.

"No se pongan tan cerca de la televisión," my mother warned from the couch as our viewing began.

Star Wars: A New Hope of course tells the story of a farmboy named Luke Skywalker on a remote, desert planet. When his step-parents are killed by the evil Empire, Luke joins his sage mentor, along with two robots, a smuggler and his furry co-pilot, on a mission to save a princess, join the Rebel Alliance and bring peace to the galaxy....

My family and I enjoyed the humor of the two bickering robots, the charm of the strange alien cantina patrons, the suspense of a harrowing trash compactor sequence, the swashbuckling antics aboard a massive space station and the thrill of our heroes fending off enemy starfighters after a daring escape.

But something remarkable happened during the film's climactic space battle. Something I'd never experienced before.

As the Rebel fleet dwindles in number, the aerial fight soon comes down to Luke in his starfighter against a frightening, black-clad warrior-pilot in hot pursuit. Barreling down a lengthy trench on the massive space station's surface toward a vulnerable exhaust port, Luke's attempt to land a fatal blow against the planet-destroying space station is the Rebel's only chance for survival. The stakes couldn't be higher...

And then it happens:

While Luke summons his targeting computer in preparation for a critical torpedo firing, a sudden calm descends over the proceedings. The music takes on a lush, mystical quality and the assuring, disembodied voice of Luke's mentor, who died earlier in the film, is heard giving counsel. Then, a moment later, a point-of-view shot from Luke's perspective as he zooms through the trench appears. The seemingly endless stretch of gray trench consumes the entire frame. The shot, lasting only 30 frames (or just over a second), coupled with the stirring musical cue powerfully encapsulates the dynamic combination of enchanting romanticism and vast technological bleakness at play in the film.

While the ensuing climax of the film was richly satisfying, I recall the distinctly visceral sensation of that preceding moment like it was yesterday despite an intervening period of nearly 30 years! It was my first taste of the sublime possibilities of cinema even if I was far, far from being able to articulate or understand it completely.

It's also safe to say that I was in love with *Star Wars* from that point forward.

26. Terrorism (September 2001)

I was downtown attending New World School of the Arts that morning. During the first class of the day, rumors began to swirl of a suspected freak accident in New York City but no one seemed to know for certain what had happened. In any case, all of the students at my high school were soon being diverted from our 1st period classes to our respective homeroom classes.

When I arrived at my homeroom class, the television cart had been rolled out to the front of the room and everyone, including our teacher Dr. Kirn, had their eyes glued to the screen. Turned to a national news broadcast, a news helicopter relayed images of the World Trade Center towers emitting smoke from two gaping holes among them. Ground-level images were also presented of men and women being guided away from the towers by emergency personnel, some seriously injured and covered in soot from head to toe. The news anchors affirmed the likelihood of the events being part of an elaborate terrorist attack against the U.S.

As a feeling of grave mystery and shock pervaded the usually calm and orderly morning ambiance, I excused myself to go to the restroom.

I walked down a length of hallway alone. However, I wasn't alone upon entering the restroom. A figure stood before me in front of the sink counter, dressed as I was dressed and as still as I was still. I fixed my gaze squarely at his eyes and he did just the same to mine. We both took a moment to breathe deeply, consider the profundity of what was occurring and quell the creeping fear and anxiety.

Some time later, all students were directed to the class period which followed homeroom. While traversing the school's hallways to our new destination, one could feel an unusual spirit of amnesty and peace between teachers and students and among the students themselves.

Settled into a new classroom on this unusual day, students were allowed to make phone calls to arrange for an early pick-up as the downtown transit we all relied on to get home had been suspended. I called my parents and they told me they'd head out to get me as soon as possible.

As my fellow classmates and I waited on notice from administrators about the arrival of our rides back home, a prayer circle was proposed and met with unanimous approval. All of my classmates began arranging their desks in a circular fashion. I was asked to participate but I must have cited my atheism. Either way, I stayed apart from the group as they took turns expressing their candid fears and hopes.

Some time later, I was notified that my parents had arrived to pick me up. I met them just outside the main school building and we drove back home making plenty of conversation about the upended nature of our day.

When I arrived home, the television was on and turned to a local news broadcast. I watched in horror as some of the more dramatic and terrifying visuals were replayed by the news media. Later on, U.S. government officials began making statements about the various attacks, attempting to bring a measure of calm and surety to an unnerved population.

In the days to follow, my dad would offer a differing perspective on the attacks than the one touted by the government and the lock-step news media. He was highly critical of U.S. foreign policy and, in particular, cited a double standard involved in the government's response to an act of domestic terrorism in Oklahoma City several years earlier. No stranger to politics as an active local political figure himself, he met any patriotic, hawkish sentiment in his household with serious rebuke.

As a result of my dad's influence, my awareness of greater systemic forces beyond the myopic, day-to-day feed of events took root. An understanding of more complex historical, political and social realities was encouraged by my home environment. In turn, I began to speak up in school with a bit more force and frankness about my developing views on topics previously deemed the province of old men. An important, personal maturation was underway.

The currents of social criticism spawned in light of the 9-11 terror attacks would continue throughout my time in high school and beyond. In the years to follow, they would also inform the themes of a certain, highly belabored form of personal expression - my short films.

27. Trinity (July 2001)

Upon returning home from my summer school geometry class, I consumed a small snack in the kitchen and then checked to see if my older brother Juan was at home. He wasn't. So I went to my bedroom, grabbed a particular DVD from one of my shelves and proceeded to Juan's vacant abode. His bedroom was a major attraction for me because it housed a huge television, a DVD player, a surround sound system and ample room to lay back and enjoy any variety of audio-visual media. A literal home theater setup!

The film I'd selected from my small but gradually growing DVD collection was the 1968 sci-fi epic *2001: A Space Odyssey*. I gently removed the disc from its snapper case and loaded it into my brother's DVD player.

The film began.

2001: A Space Odyssey is a sprawling adventure story that traces the evolution of humankind from its humble origins in a prehistoric past to a relative peak of advancement in a speculative space-faring future. The central narrative involves the mission of *Discovery One*, a Jupiter-bound spaceship carrying a human crew, of whom all but two (Bowman and Poole) are in artificially-induced hibernation, and a sentient computer (the HAL 9000) in charge of the ship known as Hal. The purpose of *Discovery One*'s mission is known only to Hal but is ultimately revealed to involve the investigation of possible alien life. During the mission, Hal malfunctions and turns on his human counterparts, killing everyone but Bowman. After Hal's murder spree, Bowman deactivates Hal, departs the doomed vessel in a space-pod and soon finds himself on a journey that will take him to the farthest reaches of space and beyond.

Some years before, my dad had rented the film by mail using a new movie rental service called Netflix. He was finally following through with a recommendation to see the film made by a colleague of his at MIT - thirty years later! So, my dad invited me to watch the film with him but about midway through he lost patience with its deliberate pace and threw in the towel. I, on the other hand, finished watching the film on my own even if I didn't think too much of it either.

However, in the year 2001, appropriately enough, I began to appreciate how strikingly austere and transporting the experience of watching that film had been compared to most films I was exposed to at the time. The boldness of its narrative scope, crisp visuals and eclectic choices of music all made *2001: A Space Odyssey* stand out in ways that thrilled me as a developing cinephile and soon-to-be filmmaker.

The next day...

I got home, ate a snack, confirmed that Juan wasn't home, grabbed another DVD from my room and headed to my brother's room once again.

The film I'd chosen this time was the 1962 war epic *Lawrence of Arabia*. I eagerly slipped the first of two discs (the film is nearly four hours long) into Juan's DVD player.

The film began.

Lawrence of Arabia tells the real-life story of a British officer T.E. Lawrence who travels to the Middle East during the First World War to assist British forces against the Turkish army in the region. In the desert, Lawrence finds himself sympathetic to the cause of uniting the Arabs in the war effort and successfully leads several tribes to victory against a shared enemy, the Turks. Despite skepticism from British high-command, Lawrence continues leading the Arab Revolt but his progress is soon undone by tribal in-fighting and his own unwinding psyche. As Lawrence's fame and legend grows, his own hubris and over-sized ambition prove to be his downfall.

Growing up, I was familiar with the iconic musical theme from *Lawrence of Arabia* despite knowing virtually nothing about the film itself. But not too long before this particular summer, I felt an irresistible urge to finally cross the threshold and uncover what that stirring melody was all about. So, with the help of my brother Juan, I was able to acquire a copy of the film and watch it. I fell in love instantly!

Despite the grand and operatic scale of the film's musical score and desert sequences, *Lawrence of Arabia* appealed to me just as significantly as a psychological exploration of the character of T.E. Lawrence. I was awed by how the film's war epic trappings were all fundamentally in service to a penetrating study of such a tragic and enigmatic figure. It's also to the film's credit that I couldn't stop humming parts of the musical score for weeks on end.

The next day...

Home, snack, check, DVD, room.

The film was the 1977 sci-fi drama *Close Encounters of the Third Kind*. I quickly deposited the disc into the player.

The film began.

Like *2001: A Space Odyssey*, *Close Encounters of the Third Kind* also deals with the theme of extra-terrestrial intelligence. In the film, we follow Roy Neary, a blue-collar worker with a family, as he undergoes a strange transformation as a result of contact with a mysterious, and presumably alien, flying object. As Roy's behavior becomes more obsessive and alarming, his wife and children soon abandon him. Later, Roy befriends a woman whose child was abducted and they both travel to a particular location telepathically communicated to them as a result of their alien encounters. But despite the government's best attempt to keep their operation at that same location secret, Roy and the woman soon arrive at the site of an impending inter-species encounter which will soon sweep Roy away to the distant stars.

I had been eagerly anticipating the release of *Close Encounters of the Third Kind* on DVD since it was first announced. I didn't know too much about the film but the design of the alien mothership featured prominently on posters and other promotional material had captured my imagination for some time. It was brilliant, colorful and mysterious! I regarded it as the epitome of alien spacecraft designs without even having seen its film of origin. However, I would rectify that situation in short order when I raced out of school on an afternoon that previous May to purchase the newly released two-disc set of the film.

I was particularly intrigued by the distinctively dark turn of having Roy's relationship to his wife and children dissolve over his seemingly deteriorating mental state. Beyond the human drama involved, however, I admired the presentation of the alien vessels seen throughout the film which are lent a luminous glow by the special photography effects involved and a particularly magical quality by the lyrical orchestration that accompanies their appearances. But it's the climax of this film that takes said interplay of light and music to stirring emotional heights only a great film can achieve!

It would be seen that I watched either one of these three films almost every single weekday and weekend afternoon for the duration of that summer. After this experience, my love of film would only continue to grow.

In the first half of the ensuing 10th grade school year at New World School of the Arts, I would begin losing interest in my formal visual arts education; pay more attention to new film releases; read more about films, filmmakers and filmmaking; watch short films on the internet; spend more time talking to my friends about film; curate lunch period DVD viewings in the school computer lab; and start envisioning film projects of my own.

The seed had been planted.

Part II: Short Films (2002-2017)

28. Advancement (August 2002)

On the first day of my junior year at Miami Killian Senior High, I arrived for the first time to one of the two elective classes I'd selected the previous school year: Intro to TV Production. Arriving before any of my fellow classmates, I greeted the instructor Mr. McClendon and took my seat in the amphitheater-like classroom.

Upon getting seated, I saw before me a wall of large, tinted glass windows behind the lowest level of the room where the teacher's desk was located. As I peered into the dark space beyond those windows, I could make out a large news desk before a pair of professional-grade video cameras atop wheeled stands. There were also large light fixtures hanging from a series of ceiling rails. This was the studio where the morning news were recorded for broadcast school-wide every homeroom period.

My eyes drank it all in.

However, I soon learned that this alluring studio space would only be used for training purposes later on in the school year. I'd have to be patient for the time being. In any case, this introductory course was as close as I could get to Filmmaking 101 at Killian so I made sure to relish every moment.

As class began, I paid rapt attention to every detail of instruction. I had questions about nearly every topic introduced: cameras, lighting, sound, etc. I cared and I wanted to convey to the instructor that I cared.

A day or two later, Mr. McClendon introduced the class to a professional video camera and allowed his students to pass around the large, usually tripod or shoulder-mounted device. It got around to me pretty quickly and I began to examine every square inch of the machine. During my close and thorough inspection, I immediately shot off a round of questions about some of the features I was looking at and Mr. McClendon was more than happy to field them.

A short time later, Mr. McClendon asked me to see him after class.

As the other students were clearing out of the room, I made my way over to Mr. McClendon's desk.

"I want to put you in TV Production I," he said.

I was shocked. TV Production I was the more advanced class which produced the morning news.

"Really?" I asked.

"I think that'd be a better fit for you," he reasoned.

I was speechless.

And so, after an adjustment to my schedule was made so I could attend TV Production I in the mornings, I looked forward to making the most of this fortunate re-assignment.

On my first day in the new class, I was overwhelmed! I observed the seasoned TV Production students, mostly seniors, totally on top of their game prepping and executing the school's televised morning news. The previously empty and dark studio space was now lit up, fully functioning and bustling with activity.

As the students busied themselves with producing the news segment, I quietly and unobtrusively walked around the studio in absolute awe at the spectacle of collaboration between almost everyone and the practice of what was essentially a form of filmmaking.

I was in the right place.

In the months that followed, I was continually regarded as a TV production newbie and thus wasn't allowed to get too involved in helping to produce the morning news segments. However, owing to my experience working on my first short film during that school year, I quickly developed a reputation as an amateur filmmaker. So, I would spend a good deal of time in-class working on my short film and occasionally offering consultation on some of my fellow classmates' scriptwriting, editing and other more film-related activities.

One of the perks of being in the class that I regret not taking too much advantage of was having access to the school's television network. It was liberally controlled but the only content of mine that was ever broadcast school-wide was a brief music video (featuring the music of Berlioz and Rimsky-Korsakov) which I'd shot and edited; highlighting one of the school's volleyball matches. I should've done more of that.

In any case, I greatly valued the opportunity to jump ahead in my TV production class that school year and it all helped fortify the growing sense I had of myself as a filmmaker.

29. Appraisal (October 2007)

During my time in University of Central Florida's film program, Professor Randy Finch was an associate professor and a former film producer. Good-humored and always willing to impart insight and wisdom about the film industry, he was a man I immediately looked up to.

My first encounter with him was at the first Fall 2005 meeting of UCF's film club. It was one of the first events I attended at UCF just after my arrival and situating. At the meeting, Randy presented a coming-of-age film he'd produced in the late '90s titled *Outside Providence*, written by the Farrelly brothers (*Dumb and Dumber*, *There's Something About Mary*, *Kingpin*). It was an evening to remember as Randy shared his first-hand experience producing an indie film with major talent.

Between that experience and his regular co-conducting of the film program's weekly colloquium with the film school chair, I knew he was a serious member of the faculty and deeply committed to the quality of his students' education.

At the start of my second year in UCF's film program, I hadn't yet made an effort to interact with him one-on-one. So, I made an effort to politely stop him in the hallway one morning and relay my interest in sitting down and doing so. He was delighted at the prospect. I told him that I wanted to show him my short film work and he accepted my invitation.

I soon joined him in his office.

There, he allowed me to transfer my short films from my USB thumb drive (I regularly wore one around my neck in those days) to his iMac. I did so and he told me to return to his office later in the afternoon after he'd had time to review my work. No problem!

That afternoon upon return to Randy's office, the elder professor handed me a print-out with his thoughts on my shared short film work. I was overwhelmed. This would count as the first professional assessment of my filmmaking I'd ever received up to that point. That and how comprehensive it was meant a great deal to me and I surely conveyed as much right away.

Before I had a chance to properly read over what Randy had written, he singled out one of my short films as having great festival potential.

I followed him out of his office and down a hallway as he tracked down and queried another faculty member about festivals that could potentially be interested in programming a short film with the "crunchy granola" vibe mine gave off. I immediately took note of the new information but at the time I was not in the habit of submitting my films to festivals so I regrettably did not follow-through with his recommendation.

In any case, Randy and I soon returned to his office where he expressed some additional encouraging thoughts about my work, including a remark that "I'd figured some things out" that many students hadn't. Randy also invited me to keep up with him as I progressed through the program. Leaving his office, I felt cared for and supported as a student, filmmaker and as a person.

Now, what did Randy think of my work?

On *Does Free Speech Matter?* (2005), he saw a "well-intentioned piece" where the "raw materials necessary for filmmaking are evident (for example in the spare and effective use of the [child actor] and the calm use of camera and editing)" but thought the short film "relies on narration (too heavily in [his] opinion)."

On *The Procrastinator* (2006), he found a "nice bit of visual-storytelling that shows a flare for comic short making and editing" and thought "[my] silent hero follows in the stone-faced tradition of other silent sad clowns."

On *Meat on a Grill* (2006), Randy was particularly charmed by what he regarded as a "sharp and effective little film" which showed "further evidence of [my] skills as an editor and shot-maker." This is the short film he'd seen as having "festival potential," citing "very strong student filmmaking" and regarding it as "a crowd-pleaser served-up with filmmaking chops and refreshing humor."

On *3,000 Too Many* (2007), Randy admitted that there was "nothing profound in the filmmaking" but I'd done an "intelligent job of recording and editing together a short narrative that effectively tells what happened." However, he took issue with its "introductory titles that smack of naive propaganda" and suggested that "the film that follows [the introductory titles] speaks eloquently without voiceover or other commentary."

On *Breakfast, Lunch and Dinner* (2007), he charged that his "failure to get the message from this essentially dialogue-free movie makes it [his] latest favorite of the bunch" but "even here there is a forward motion and sureness to the editing that [he admires]."

On *March on the Pentagon* (2007), Randy found that "the title cards (which are freighted with opinion) undermine the strength of the images." He added that "a lack of footage concerning the most dramatic event alluded to in the titles (i.e., the 'ruthless' arrest of students) and the anticlimactic ending to the demonstration make the film seem weaker than it might otherwise."

Randy was honest and frank where he needed to be and I'd greatly appreciated his review of my work.

Unfortunately, that delightful meeting with Randy would be one of the last substantial interactions I had with any faculty member in the film program before a serious bout of mental illness forced me to return home a few weeks later.

30. Aruba (October 2015)

An abbreviated recounting of my experience at the 5th Annual Aruba International Film Festival... in reverse chronological order (all times approximate):

Saturday, October 10th

2:30pm - Both arriving safe and sound in Miami, Daniel and I say farewell to each other and part ways.

11:00am - Daniel and I board the plane but I sit apart to appreciate the vantage point of my window seat.

9:45am - Daniel and I enjoy some film-related conversation in the terminal as we wait to board our plane.

9:30am - By chance, I encounter a former FIU classmate of mine Daniel Tarasiuk at the baggage check-in area of the airport.

9:00am - After checking out of my hotel, I catch a ride to the airport via the shuttle.

Friday, October 9th

9:15pm - Considered a natural compass as all their branches point south-west, I purchase a small desk ornament of Aruba's national tree.

9:00pm - Encountering a distributor on the way back to my hotel room, our contact information is exchanged.

8:45pm - Plenty of warm embraces and promises to keep in touch from friends new and old at an evening party; my final event of the festival.

7:45pm - After viewing their film, I offer some feedback to Chris and Zach.

6:15pm - After hearing so much about Chris and Zach's film *Salam Neighbor*, I settle into a screening of the film.

6:30pm - Attempting to split my time between two films playing at the same time, I watch some of Alain's animated film *Battledream Chronicle*.

4:30pm - My first feature film viewing is Alexis' documentary *Vanishing Sail*.

4:15pm - Producer Cassian Elwes participates in a Q&A and I briefly meet him afterward to hand him a business card.

2:30pm - At a second showing of the dramatic block of short films featuring my own, the audience's response is encouraging in this instance as well.

10:30am - New filmmaker friends of mine Alexis, Alain and Angel all take part in a panel about Caribbean cinema.

Thursday, October 8th

12:15am - After kindly attending my screening, my cousin Joanna and her family invite me to dinner. My only non-film-related indulgence.

9:30pm - My short film *Leo's Love Letter* plays in a dramatic short films block and a Q&A follows. Cousins and a family friend in attendance.

7:45pm - Having met Angel the previous day, I attend a screening of his feature film *La Granja*.

6:45pm - Surprised by a radiant sunset viewed from the pier, I snap a few photos of it with my phone and promptly return to socializing.

5:00pm - Rejoining some familiar faces at a social event on a pier, I engage in a conversation with one of the festival's attending distributors.

4:15pm - After attending a panel with the director of the festival's opening night film Zachary Sluser, I briefly speak with him.

1:00pm - Interested in the topic to be addressed, I attend a gender equality panel featuring Ms. Madsen.

12:30pm - At a luncheon (or in my case, bruncheon), I meet some media personnel and a particularly enterprising woman Dilma Arends German.

Wednesday, October 7th

7:30pm - Interested in visiting a local food truck, Aaron drives filmmaker Angel Manuel Soto and myself to indulge in a burger. I resist.

6:30pm - Noticing a young woman sitting alone and looking lonesome, I avert my gaze and engage with an event photographer about film instead.

6:00pm - At the festival's opening night party I meet a writer for Empire magazine, actress Virginia Madsen and filmmakers Chris Temple and Zach Ingrasci.

5:30pm - To obtain my festival badge and other credentials, I meet with festival directors Aaron Hose and Rebecca Roos at the festival's base camp.

5:15pm - Filmmakers Alexis Andrews, Alain Bidard and I are transported from the airport to our hotel by shuttle.

4:30pm - After arriving safe and sound in Aruba, I am eventually greeted by Dexter Lacle, driver of the festival's courtesy shuttle service.

1:00pm - My Miami-Aruba flight departs. I intend to promote my 15th short film *Leo's Love Letter*, watch films and meet filmmakers. No fluff.

31. Asocial (May 2006)

During my first year at University of Central Florida, I lived at a university-affiliated, off-campus housing complex called Pegasus Pointe. It was an ideal setting for any student with plenty of amenities highly conducive to work, study and relaxation.

However, as I didn't have a car during my time at UCF, I relied on the complimentary shuttle service between Pegasus Pointe and campus; the distance between them about one mile. The shuttle service was always reliable and used by many UCF students.

One night late into the Spring 2006 semester, I caught a ride as I had on so many other similar occasions over the past year. Taking a seat toward the front of the transport, I sat next to slightly disheveled man who looked to be in his 50s or 60s. I doubt he was a student but it wasn't too unusual for interlopers to hitch a ride on the shuttle service once in a while.

I soon found myself in conversation with the man.

"My daughter's named Kathryn Morris," he told me. Continuing, "She was an actress in Spielberg's film *Minority Report*."

The man was holding a photograph of the actress who he purported to be the father of. A small photo with worn edges.

Accessing IMDb some time later, I would confirm that Kathryn Morris was in fact in Steven Spielberg's 2002 sci-fi thriller *Minority Report*. She was also in Spielberg's antecedent film, the 2001 sci-fi drama *A.I. Artificial Intelligence*.

I had a hard time taking this strange man at his word but I listened on. He proceeded to mention a facet of the personal life of the famed Hollywood director.

"While he's making movies, he has no social life at all. He doesn't go to parties or anything," the man claimed.

Admittedly, a part of me was rather intrigued. If what this man was saying was indeed true, it confirmed what I understood as a personality trait of many world-class artists and seemingly validated my own lifelong, asocial disposition.

Years later I'd later learn from an early-'80s interview with Spielberg that he regarded his life as "monastic" and almost singularly devoted to the art of moviemaking.

The curious gentleman offered little else and the shuttle soon approached my stop on its route. I bid farewell to the older passenger and hopped off the bus.

What an unusual encounter, I thought.

I never saw that man again.

Days later I'd relay that experience to a fellow UCF student and Pegasus Pointe resident. He knew exactly who I was talking about and referred to the man as "that crazy guy" in a dismissive manner.

Maybe that old man was deranged.

That made sense too.

32. Atypical (October 2007)

At the start of my second year in University of Central Florida's limited-access Film BFA program, I absolutely relished my new slate of fall semester classes. They included courses in film theory, sound design and cinematography. But chief among them was Directing II which was taught by the avuncular Professor Wolfe and focused on the theory and practice of working with actors.

In addition to the requirement of producing a performance-centric short film as part of the course, the entire class was also expected to cast and direct a separate short film as a group from a script chosen by the professor. The latter assignment would help prepare us for the challenges of auditioning actors and working with them on-set on our personal short film projects.

With classes in full swing, it was an invigorating environment of great potential edification for the diligent and committed. However, something was not quite right in the state of Denmark.

After several weeks into the new semester, I found myself less inhibited socially and somewhat defiant of social norms. I initiated conversations with fellow classmates more readily and often peppered my talk with bold, somewhat transgressive notions about power and sexuality. I also found myself participating far more spiritedly in class and sharing what I believed were incredibly profound personal insights about filmmaking and creativity.

I may have put off some of my classmates with my behavior but I doubt anyone suspected what was actually happening. I was slowly becoming psychotic.

Although far more concerning (and devastating) behavior would eventually rear its head, I would be sane enough to participate in an upcoming Directing II class activity without any issue. The class would be rehearsing a pivotal scene with a local actress for the group short film project.

On the day of that activity, my fellow classmates, our professor and the local actress named Peggy met in the film department's sound stage to conduct the activity. The activity called for a pair of students to each have a chance to direct Peggy, who'd be acting opposite a volunteer, before a camera and tripod set up for the occasion.

A few pairs of my classmates had their turn working with Peggy before it was my turn at bat. I had been paired with a friend of mine named Denyonta.

Called to direct Peggy with my partner, I readily approached the setup at the head of the class and enthusiastically greeted the Orlando-based actress. She was charmed.

Despite this being practice or mock directorial duty, I was so caught up in the thrill of directing Peggy that I hardly let my partner Denyonta get a word in. I was absolutely respectful but allowed my emotions to play a much larger part than the more calm, level-headed pairs before me. In one particularly memorable moment, I suggested Peggy play a particular line like Dirty Harry and my relishing of the result was outwardly observed.

After a few minutes, the scene was over and Professor Wolfe offered some words of positive feedback. Peggy chimed in and expressed that she'd felt "as though [I wanted her] to succeed." I was flattered and soon took my seat. Several of my classmates complimented me on my performance.

Later on in that same class session, the professor prompted me for my opinion about how to handle a particular hypothetical situation with an actor. I offered my thoughts and he was glad to hear it. I'd clearly made a strong impression on him and the class with my uncommon gusto and extroversion. Little did they know...

Several weeks later, I would be Baker Acted (in Florida that means involuntarily committed to a behavioral clinic).

33. Audience (February 2016)

One late evening, I received word that my 15th short film *Leo's Love Letter* would be an official selection at the 6th Annual Love Your Shorts Film Festival in Sanford, Florida. I was thrilled! But I was even more thrilled about the fact that my short film would screen at the opening night of the festival with a slate of other short films. The match between the festival's calendric and thematic proximity to Valentine's Day and my film's decidedly sentimental focus was pure kismet.

I would be traveling to Sanford with my parents for a one-night stay in the central Florida town to attend the festival's opening night festivities and my short film's screening.

All aboard my parents' comfortable sedan, we departed Miami in good spirits but I kept something to myself: a highly ruminative mind.

Why was I ruminating?

While I was ecstatic about my short film's imminent exhibition at a well-regarded film festival, the excitement about my latest short film idea was wavering. I had completed a first draft of its script but despite my intent to produce it, my enthusiasm wasn't at peak. I was merely content with what I'd written. Not a good sign.

In any case, I enjoyed the time I spent with Mom and Dad as we traveled northward, reminiscent of the many trips we'd make to Orlando together during my time at University of Central Florida. We shared plenty of conversation and shared anticipation about the prospective film festival event.

After arriving to our hotel in Sanford and grabbing a quick bite, my parents and I arrived at the theater venue for the opening night showcase. It was a cozy, recently renovated theater on a street with other buildings that evoked the small, remote towns of the Midwest. In rhyme with the small-town appearance, the general social climate was one of cohesion and ease of approachability. A refreshing modesty and neighborliness hung in the air; far different from alike Miami events.

Outside the venue, I was greeted warmly by Nelson and Christina Beverly, the founders and directors of the festival. They were supported by a tightly knit band of staffers. Both the Beverlys and their staff were most hospitable, making every guest feel welcome and appreciated.

After everyone was ushered into the theater for the festival's opening night program, I was impressed by the turnout (no doubt mostly local townsfolk). With over 100 people in attendance, I eagerly awaited the reception to my work by so great an audience.

The program included some rather heavy-weight competition with some boasting rather impressively elaborate production value. I was quite intimidated! By comparison, my short film was a fairly austere, reigned-in and minimalist affair. But that may have proved to be an advantage. In any case, the audience seemed to enjoy my film. They laughed in all the right places.

After all of the evening's short films were screened, audience members were instructed to vote for their favorite using their phones. Not more than ten or so minutes later, voting was concluded and a result arrived at...

Leo's Love Letter won the Opening Night award by audience vote!

With the announcement came my receiving of the festival's highly coveted "Monroe" trophy; an impressive film camera-shaped metal sculpture given to all festival winners.

Then guided onto the stage before the audience entire and handed a microphone, I was expected to give an award acceptance speech. Confident and uncompromised by any nerves due to my several years of being a proud Toastmaster, I started my brief speech that night by dubbing my short film "the little short film that could." I went on to thank Emmanuel Franco, Stephanie Maltez and Ben Morris (none present). I also thanked the audience for their gracious support of our film. A generous helping of their applause followed.

The after-party immediately following the film-viewing portion of the evening's festivities took place next door at a posh studio space. Live jazz music and dim blue lighting enveloped all attending guests.

Although more than ready to call it a night so early, I made some effort to engage socially with an old friend and several important new faces:

- Aaron Hose, a fellow filmmaker who I'd first met at a Tampa film festival five years prior and who'd invited me to Aruba film festival (he was programming director there) to screen *Leo's Love Letter* the previous year, was glad for my win. Always kind and supportive, he charmed me that night when he referred to me as "such a sweet guy" in conversation with my parents.
- Quincy Perkins, another fellow filmmaker who I'd met at a Miami short film showcase he was participating in, was so impressed by *Leo's Love Letter* that he invited me to submit it to the Key West film festival that he was director of. I expressed my fondness for the work of his I'd seen in Miami.
- Dr. Lisa Mills was a UCF film professor who I'd never met but was aware of her reputation. Learning about her involvement in a panel taking place as part of the festival, I better appreciated her deep commitment to her job an an instructor. Also, we bonded over our mutual high-regard for Chris Walker, a former close friend of mine and an accomplished documentary filmmaker who used to be one of Professor Mill's students.
- Cameron Meier is a central Florida film critic whose pedantic nature I found quite endearing. We had a brief but delightful exchange about our preference for seating in auditoriums for film screenings.
- T.L. Westgate was a local filmmaker whose prodigious short film output I'd later learn about and be quite impressed with.
- Lukas Hassel, actor and filmmaker, was a most amicable new face. He was the only other opening night filmmaker present at the festival and I enjoyed our brief interaction.

Despite all the celebration and positive tidings, I soon retired from the festivities with my parents after saying farewell to all of the wonderful people I'd met, both new and familiar. My parents and I returned to our hotel for a night's rest as we'd be setting out for Miami the next morning.

As I tried to quiet my mind enough for slumber, I couldn't quell a certain unsettled feeling. I was filled with a freshened desire, on account of my night's win, to honor such recognition with a better follow-up short film than the one already set for production. Although this wasn't my first filmmaking award as *Leo's Love Letter* had netted Best Screenplay at a monthly short film showcase hosted by an organization called FilmGate Miami, it meant more to me by virtue of the fact that the win had been bestowed by an audience of regular audience members. My uncertainty about the course of my short film plans were my final thoughts before I fell asleep.

In the days following my experience in Sanford, I would abandon that earlier idea and from its ashes would rise an almost completely different short film idea. It would be my 16th and final short film, titled *The Promotion*. I would proceed with its script writing and production with utmost confidence and enthusiasm!

34. Brevity (July 2006)

In 2014, I delivered a speech about the making of my 5th short film *Meat on a Grill* in 2006 while at a layover at my oldest brother Alonso's home in Tampa. The occasion was a weekly meeting of Florida International University's Toastmasters club where I was a member. Here is an excerpt from my speech:

There was a scene involved where the main character is cooking some meat on the grill. And I wanted to add some spectacle, some fireworks - literally - to this scene. And I wanted to cut it up and make it more of a jolt and make it more of a snap. And keep it really simple. It was originally a much more elaborate scene.

And so what I did was- well, two words came to my mind almost immediately: lighter fluid. If any of you have ever used lighter fluid with flames you know that you're in for quite a treat, for quite a show because you spray just a little of that sucker on an open and lit grill, flames fly up five feet into the air. It's exhilarating!

So what the scene required was that [Alonso] stand in front of the grill looking into the flame with a sinister visage on his face and just off-camera be squirting the lighter fluid onto the grill. And these flames were just inches from his face, licking the air just in front of him.

While I was satisfied with the content and delivery of my speech, I wasn't being exactly forthright about the origin of my desire to make the scene "more of a jolt and make it more of a snap." That approach had only entered my mind after an early failed attempt at the scene and some thoughtful reconsideration.

I'd been rather apprehensive about the meat-grilling climax from the start of production because I knew it had to be somewhat impressive.

After all, the film would be titled *Meat on a Grill*. The titular subject had to be presented especially well.

That first failed attempt at the scene involved some rather basic staging of my brother barbecuing a variety of meat. A diverse array of over-the-shoulder shots and close-ups were recorded. But something was missing. The construction of the scene I was considering in my head resembled a fairly basic montage with jump cuts and great angles but it all lacked an intensity and fire (no pun intended) I knew it needed. This short film deserved something truly special for its dramatic pinnacle but I didn't know what right away.

Since time at my brother's home was limited as I had to return to Miami before I started up school again at University of Central Florida in the fall, I had to come up with a solution quickly.

So, I thought and thought and thought and thought...

Then, at some point I recalled a video I'd seen online of some empty-headed frat boys playing with lighter fluid and an open flame. Not one second later, I asked my brother Alonso about the possibility of using lighter fluid to achieve certain (and potentially dangerous) pyrotechnic effects. He looked at me warily but he ultimately agreed to drive me to the supermarket to pick up a bottle of the highly inflammable liquid. This might just work, I thought.

As evening approached for the shooting of this crucial scene, I had determined to make the scene exactly as I'd described in my speech. It would definitely feel like a jolt or snap.

Additionally, my speech's description of the effects of lighter fluid was also dead-on. It did the trick exactly!

While the risk to my brother's safety was quite great and I remained on-edge throughout most of the setups, we were ultimately able to acquire all of the required shots within the hour. After we'd concluded filming I came away supremely confident in my ability to spin the spectacular footage I'd captured into a stand-out climax.

Brevity was once again the key... and a bit of insanity helped out too.

35. Capital (March 2007)

There is no end in sight to the UNITED STATES OF AMERICA's catastrophic occupation of Iraq. The U.S.-installed government, indifferent to sectarian tensions among the population, has bitterly divided its people against themselves but strongly united them against U.S. forces. There is no safety in the ravaged country.

Expectedly, the new Democrat-controlled U.S. Congress has sided with President Bush, recently approving a major war funding bill that expands military presence in Iraq and also grants the president the ability to launch another preemptive, and potentially nuclear, strike against its neighboring nation of Iran.

On the fourth anniversary of the start of the Iraq War, the Students for a Democratic Society (sds) join thousands of demonstrators at the nation's capital to demand an immediate withdrawal of U.S. troops from Iraq and protest the sinister combination of the government's overgrown military establishment with the relentless profiteering of the country's private defense industry....

In my second year at University Central Florida, I decided to join a group of my fellow sds'ers on a weekend trip to our nation's capital Washington, D.C. I'd been involved with sds, a student political organization at UCF, for about a year and regularly attended their meetings and events.

The last time I visited D.C. was on a tourist trip with my family when I was no more than three or four years old. But now, my purpose for travel wasn't sightseeing or recreation. No, the intent of my compatriots and I was to march against the Iraq War and the dreaded war machine that made it possible - and profitable. We would be joining thousands of other demonstrators at the very seat of U.S. power on the fourth anniversary of the infamous, preemptive invasion of the Middle Eastern country. I suppose it's worth mentioning that the march would take place on March 17th, my birthday.

I arrived at a parking lot on the UCF campus, met with the assembled group of sds'ers and was soon assigned to a carpooling SUV. My fellow passengers included the driver of the SUV, an Iraq War veteran, two students and a young activist with a tall mohawk who I don't believe was attending UCF at the time. We soon boarded the vehicle and set off north.

Over the course of the day-long car ride to our destination, I maintained a somewhat asocial disposition and kept to myself. But I listened as much was talked about; from the trivial to the serious. The veteran, a young man in his 30s, was the more involved conversationalist among us and regaled us all with stories from boot camp training to his tour of duty in the embattled country of Iraq. He also spooked us with rumors about impending government repression of activists and dissidents.

I must add that throughout the drive we listened to some rather appropriate music. We heard many selections from the punk-rock band Anti-Flag and other decidedly non-mainstream artists. New and alluring sounds to me.

At a rest stop just over the Virginia state line, we felt a dramatic drop in temperature and saw patches of snow. I had dressed suitably for the expected climate change but I hadn't felt such a northern chill or seen snow since my time in Massachusetts as a child. It almost seemed like I was traveling back in time as much as I was traveling up north.

As our party approached the capital well into the night, the roadway seemed to undulate in a wave-like manner. The cityscape grew closer. Then, I saw it in the distance: the Washington Monument. The red light atop the mighty obelisk instantly reminded me of the scorching, watchful Eye of Sauron from *The Lord of the Rings*! I'd hoped it was only a superficial comparison.

Making our way through downtown Washington, D.C., we finally arrived at our destination; a church and community center. The owners of the property had been kind enough to provide us shelter for our stay. We were all promptly checked-in by an sds-staffed welcoming committee and entered the vacant and generously provided establishment. Some familiar UCF sds'ers, including a fellow filmmaker and friend of mine Chris Walker, had already arrived and I happily engaged in some conversation with them.

Despite the general excitement and anticipation about the following day's event, it was nearing midnight and soon time to hunker down for a much-needed night's sleep. I used my backpack as a makeshift pillow and soon eased into a restful slumber.

The following morning, I prepped for a day of video recording and kept up with Chris. I joined him and other sds'ers for breakfast at a nearby restaurant. It would be our last stop before we would make our way to the National Mall, where all the demonstrators were set to gather for the march.

On our way to the mall, I started capturing video of my immediate surroundings but immediately began to feel uneasy about the form the footage would ultimately take. Frankly, I was overwhelmed by this new environment and the scope of the whole occasion. Could I hope to shoot and edit together something worthy of it all?

For some reason, Chris, myself and a few other sds'ers found ourselves needing to walk past the Vietnam Veterans Memorial in order to join with all of the other sds'ers and anti-war activists on the other side of the mall.

However, there was some trepidation in doing so. A group of pro-war veterans had been led to believe that the student protesters were planning on defacing the memorial. But a choice was soon made to simply storm through the crowd of angry, potentially violent veterans and hope for the best. So, we made our way directly through the throng. Their counter-protest signs read "Safe since 9-11", "Peace Through Strength" and, quite contradictorily, "Peace Sucks". I've never heard a louder, more crude barrage of insults and threats hurled in my direction. It was nerve-wracking! But I stuck close to my fellow compatriots and thankfully made it out to the opposite side of the memorial in one piece.

I soon joined the assembly of students and activists from a wide variety of progressive organizations - about 30,000 demonstrators in total! At once I observed many fond and good-natured interactions between the activists, many of whom seemed to be reuniting and recounting their activist experiences from their respective localities.

Casually recording the plethora of exciting sights and sounds around me with my video camera, I soon settled on a most fascinating spectacle! A group of sds'ers had large, red-and-black painted shields (some with the words "U.S. Out of Everywhere" on them); masks (including gas masks); and other makeshift riot protection gear. I inquired about this particularly well-equipped contingent of students and learned a new term that day - black bloc.

A black bloc is a tactic in which a group of protesters disguise their identities and form up to appear as one large unified mass. It is typically employed by anarchists and anti-globalization activists in occasions where conflict with riot police is expected.

The march soon began and the crowd of protesters toppled a flimsy picket fence boundary and made their way out of the National Mall and toward a bridge crossing over the Potomac River. The march to the Pentagon had begun!

My hands were freezing in the D.C. cold but I made my best effort to hold my camera as steadily as possible as I continued to acquire shots. Still overwhelmed by the bounteous visual and aural stimuli all around me, I persisted with my video chronicling. I simply aimed my camera at whatever piqued my interest in the moment and randomly alternated between using my wide-angle lens and fish-eye lens with nary a thought about what form the documentary short would ultimately take.

After passing Arlington Cemetery, the massive group began to split up into two groups. A vast majority headed toward a large stage area where a slate of speakers were expected to address the audience of less daring demonstrators. However, the valiant sds'ers, including those assembled in a black bloc, and other supportive activists were intent on marching right up to the Pentagon some several hundred yards away - if we were lucky enough to make it.

Without fear or doubt, I followed the latter group, numbering several hundred.

As we progressed past the path to the stage area, we encountered a lengthy row of pristine, white-plated police motorcycles seemingly arranged not necessarily to block our movement forward but to intimidate us wayward activists with this theatrical, outward show.

We soon found the street leading to the Pentagon blocked by a row of officers with gas masks and batons; lined up shoulder-to-shoulder and preventing any further travel toward the large, flat, dreary-looking headquarters visible from the distance.

The black bloc or front-most group of students walked right up to the line of policemen. There, they faced each other as protest chants rang out more spiritedly from the multitude of voices. The students decided to stage a sit-in which would last several hours.

Capturing as many shots I could of this dramatic stand-off, I was embedded among the students as they cried out repeatedly, "Who do you serve?! Who do you protect?!"

I found the repetition of those words so spiritedly defiant and fraught with implications of grave injustice that I shed a tear or two.

Chris Walker, the other filmmaker among us UCF sds'ers, was also busy filming the unfolding events. At times, we stood back-to-back recording the piping hot resolve on this frigidly cold day. A true comrade.

Some time later, police reinforcements arrived in the form of Virginia State Police officers wielding long, transparent shields and wearing full-on riot gear. On at least two occasions, the VSP officers violently grabbed and arrested several students who'd gotten too close to their impenetrable blockade formation.

"The whole world is watching! The whole world is watching!" the crowd then began chanting. Nearly everyone on the sidelines had a recording device out and aimed at the confrontation.

The students soon decided to hold a vote to decide whether to hold their ground before the VSP or return to the capital to plan their next course of action. As some of the officers behind the riot control officers prepared to disperse the crowd with chemical crowd control agents, the students voted to retreat. And so they did.

The march was over.

During the students' retreat back to the capital, a few more students were taken into custody.

I soon rejoined my fellow UCF sds'ers at a restaurant just beyond the capital to decompress. We would later re-assemble with students from the other sds chapters in our lodging space that evening to socialize and recount the experiences and lessons of the day's events - like none I'd ever known.

We then settled in for our final night in D.C.

The following morning, I boarded the same SUV I'd traveled to D.C. in and with most of the same passengers as before. Overall, it was a quieter trip back to Orlando. It seemed like the party I was with had all been changed by the whole experience in ways we couldn't quite process yet.

I had plenty to reflect upon during the trip back to UCF, including my earlier plans to make a short documentary out of the occasion. But I initially believed the footage I'd gathered was too haphazardly shot to make into something despite the highly dramatic confrontation. So, I decided not to put together a new documentary vignette upon my return to my student dorm.

However, a few months later, I would revisit the footage I'd shot and grow convinced of its potential. This march on the Pentagon was too important to abandon.

It had also made for one particularly memorable birthday!

36. Casting (September 2002)

The latest and final draft of the script for what would become my actual first short film *Mass Education* (initially titled *The Joy of Knowledge*) was now complete! I'd whipped the script into a definitive state at the end of summer and I was poised to get started producing it now that I'd settled comfortably into my junior year at Miami Killian Senior High.

In preparation for the production, I'd produced numerous storyboards and sketches to help me pre-visualize the more significant moments in the short film. I also kept a composition book filled with copious notes about story, character and craft, in general.

I also purchased a wide angle lens adapter for my Sony DCR-TRV720 Digital Handycam (no longer my dad's) as well as an ample supply of Digital8 tape stock. Ready for the incoming video footage, I had a bedroom computer equipped with a FireWire card and Adobe Premiere for video capturing and editing purposes, respectively.

In short, I was rearing to go. However, I lacked one crucial element: the actors!

Of a painfully shy and asocial disposition, particularly in high school, I had practically no friends to rely on for casting purposes. So, I endeavored to reach out to people I wasn't yet on friendly terms with from my school - students and teachers alike - to fill the required ranks. As the entire film was set in a fictional high school, it would be easy to recruit participants whose only major obligation would be having to remain in the school building an hour or so after classes had let out.

Even so early and untested in my self-initiated career, I appreciated the value of tying a script to available resources. For the two principal roles, I'd need to find a young man and an adult. Easy enough, I'd figured, in a school populated by countless students and many, many adults.

"Hi, I'm making a short film. Would you be interested in playing the main character?" I nervously entreated a fellow school bus passenger with a copy of my script in-hand, ready to share it.

The young man, who I'd thought would make a great lead for my short film gave me a curious look and replied, "Uh... I don't really have the time."

"Please!" I insisted, far from realizing how forward and undue my completely cold solicitation was.

"Sorry. I can't," he said, letting me down gently.

I accepted and retreated to my seat.

A few days later in the school library, I recognized a familiar student sitting and reading by himself much like my own routine habit. We'd both attended the same geometry class in summer school at another local high school the summer before last. We weren't friends but we had interacted at least once all that time ago.

Thinking him a suitable fit for the lead role, I approached him with a copy of my script in hand.

"Hey, we attended the same summer geometry class at Palmetto over a year ago," I started.

"Oh, yeah! That's right," he responded pleasantly.

Still lacking a degree of tact, I lept right into it. "Would you be interested in acting in a short film I'm planning on making?"

"Sure, I'd love to!" he said straightaway. "What's your name again?"

"Gabriel Rhenals," I responded. "Yours?"

"Sam Williams," he answered.

"Here's a copy of the script," I said as I offered up a pristine copy from my previously tense grip.

The other principal role would require an adult.

I initially reached out to an eccentric family friend who was willing to participate and seemed a perfect fit for the part. However, he was unaffiliated with the school and I wanted to avoid the potential challenge of acquiring the school's permission to allow a stranger on the school premises. So, I'd need to find someone else.

Over the course of the first few weeks of my junior year, I'd found myself in the kind graces of my English teacher Mr. Hill. I loved his class and participated in great measure. He greatly appreciated this as he was always willing to engage when I would often linger after class to offer some commentary on the preceding lesson and follow-up on some particular facet of the material I found interesting.

Given this mutual positive regard, I eventually popped the question and he was absolutely flattered. It was a resounding yes!

With my two principal parts cast, I was ready to commence production. The confidence raised by exacting the involvement of Sam Williams and Mr. Hill gave me all the confidence I needed to commence and carry out this inaugural production.

At the time I had no idea that in looking for participants for my first short film production, I'd be forging indelible friendships and mentorships. I would stay in touch with Sam for years. And Mr. Hill and I would continue to fortify our bond well into the future.

Unfortunately Killian would prohibit me from filming on school grounds for several months, delaying significant production work on the short film. But *Mass Education* would ultimately be completed at the start of the following summer.

37. Cavalry (December 2002)

I'd been making slow but steady progress on my high school-set first short film production *Mass Education* throughout the first half of the school year at Miami Killian Senior High. Filming mainly during after-school hours in mostly vacant areas of the school grounds, my activity had gone largely unimpeded.

But my fortune was about to change.

After classes one day, I entered the school library with my tripod and camera bags in tow. The student I'd enlisted as lead actor, Sam Williams, and a teacher who I'd also persuaded to act in my short film, Ms. Green, would be arriving in a moment's time. Seeing minimal activity in the library, I figured the planned filming would go off without a hitch.

I walked up to the main desk.

"Hi, I'm planning on filming a scene for my short film in a few minutes. Would it be possible to allow Ms. Green to stand behind the desk for filming?" I asked the assistant librarian.

The attendant librarian glared at me disapprovingly.

"I'm sorry but filming isn't allowed here in the library," the assistant librarian replied.

"What?" I fired back.

"Is this a school project?" she responded.

"No, but I'm a TV Production student," I replied.

"Well, why don't you use the TV Production studio instead?" she suggested sincerely.

I was livid out of rank offense. Tense and looking around, I spotted some ironic inspirational posters nearby.

"By not allowing me to film here, you're going against the purpose of this school!" I exclaimed, starting to make a scene.

"I'm sorry," the assistant librarian affirmed.

I gathered my bags and my cool and stormed out of the library. Encountering Sam and Ms. Green in the hallway outside, I told them the filming was off.

When I returned home, I told my parents everything. They urged me to speak to my TV production teacher Mr. McClendon about the matter.

As soon as I could, I spoke to Mr. McClendon. I explained what had happened and how insulting the whole situation was. He admitted he had no special influence to allow me to film in the library and advised me against pursuing the matter further, warning me about being a "flag carrier."

When I arrived home, I told my parents about Mr. McClendon's powerlessness and they agreed to raise the issue with the school administrators.

So a few days later, a meeting was arranged between me, my parents, Mr. McClendon and Curriculum Director at Killian, Mr. Brennan.

The meeting was cordial but went nowhere fast. Mr. Brennan essentially described a filming permit acquisition process involving submission of an application to a plant operations department and, if it was approved, then required the obtaining of liability insurance for all parties involved in whatever filming would take place.

A labyrinthine prospect.

Amazed at the brazenness of what Mr. Brennan had outlined as a course of action, my dad set to writing a letter to Killian's Principal Dawson the next day.

At two-pages in length, the firmly worded document encouraged that "the creation and production of short films by students of [TV Production I] and similar courses must be supported by the school" and that "failing to support such students' creative activities would put the school in the indefensible position of thwarting their legitimate educational objectives."

With regard to the meeting that had taken place, my dad described how "a quick inquiry about [obtaining a permit] revealed that the entire process would be so cumbersome, lengthy and costly that by the time it would be completed, the school year would have ended." He continued, "Mr. Dawson, it is clear from the above that the procedure suggested by your Curriculum Director is equivalent to 'killing ants with an atomic bomb.'" Way to wax poetic, Dad!

My dad closed his letter to the principal by writing, "On behalf of my son, I ask you to find - at your earliest convenience - an appropriate and reasonable solution to this small problem and grant Gabriel and his collaborators the authorization required to successfully complete this short but worthwhile film project."

The letter was delivered.

A few days later, I was informed that Principal Dawson wanted to speak with me in private.

I was excused from my class and invited to enter the principal's impressively spacious and furnished office. Invited to sit before him, the principal had an utterly friendly and open demeanor.

"Mr. Rhenals, good morning!" he said kindly.

"Good morning, sir," I responded.

"Thank your dad for his very thoughtful letter," he said.

He then told me what I'd longed to hear.

"I spoke with the librarians and you should be fine. Please let me know if you run into trouble anywhere else," he advised.

I now had my high school principal's express permission to film on school grounds.

"Thank you, sir," I said in a deeply appreciative tone.

I'd gained an invaluable ally.

Relishing this victory, I soon re-initiated production on my short film and was able to resume my independent filmmaking at Killian practically unhindered from that point forward.

Through his letter, my dad had faced down the cold, uncaring bureaucracy of my high school and found kinship in its office of greatest authority. It was a crystal clear lesson in the importance of having and defending your values and communicating them clearly to the right audience.

Thanks, Dad.

38. Clemency (September 2008)

Bang!

With great force, my mom threw her flip-phone down at the tile floor just outside of our kitchen. She was venting her stinging frustration over my adamance about re-shooting a particular scene on my latest short film. I'd rarely seen her this angry.

I had recruited my mom to play the lead character Linda in what would be my 11th short film. To be titled *The Nap*, it was about a woman who needs to pick up her sister from the airport after her husband has made some mysterious modifications to their car.

"No más!" my mom cried.

I picked up her phone, which surprisingly hadn't shattered into a thousand pieces given the violence of her throw, and offered it back to her.

"Mom, I need to re-shoot the scene!" I insisted.

"I said no!" she shot back as she snatched her phone from me.

"Mom, please!" I beckoned.

She stormed off, ignoring me.

I turned to see my dad, casually observing the drama from a couch in our home's sitting room. I approached him and pleaded, "Dad, please tell Mom that I need to re-do the scene!"

"You have to respect the limitations of your actors," my dad advised.

I sighed and collapsed onto one of the couches in the space.

"I need to re-shoot that goddamn scene," I vainly repeated.

I had recruited my mom, dad and aunt to act in the film; all non-actors. Filming, which had commenced that past May, involved rather intensive on-set coaching throughout the entire production. The resulting performances would then require careful dubbing in post-production to compensate for the myriad of shortcomings in my cast's line deliveries.

Taking a different tact than usual, there was no traditional script produced for the film. Instead, I relied on detailed notes to guide the filmmaking process.

Given the manageable size of the short film, I knew how every beat should be performed. I certainly didn't expect my parents or my aunt to prepare as any trained or even aspiring actor would. My immediate guidance on-set and right by the camera was all I felt was required to elicit the right emotional tenor for each scene. This approach would yield adequate, if not satisfactory, results.

Despite having considerable experience working with non-actors on several previous short films, working with my parents was a whole new test of patience and directing ability. My mom and dad found my particular level of quality control somewhat extreme and, as exemplified by the aforementioned flip-phone episode, intolerable to the point of refusing to continues. Luckily, my best persuasive (and sincere) rhetoric often allowed me to exact a few more takes from them, often proving pivotal, in desperate circumstances. This was best exemplified in the immediate aftermath of that flip-phone episode:

As I sat with my dad in the sitting room after my mom's dramatic show, I talked to him about how the film was turning out based on my viewing of an early assembly of the footage I'd shot so far. I was extremely thrilled about the results and the prospect of wrapping production on the film in a matter of weeks. Production had lasted for nearly eight months!

Despite my optimism about the project, my dad still saw my demands as excessive and unjustified. My mom's emotional tirade was merely the latest upcrop of what had been a growing resistance from both of my parents against a taxing and protracted filmmaking process. I had been pushing them too far for too long. Still, I implored my dad to trust me and urge my mom to do the same.

Although I doubted I was moving the needle much with my words, I soon turned our conversation to a certain visual effects shot I was particularly thrilled about. I explained to my dad how I was growing increasingly adept at using a piece of motion graphics software Adobe After Effects as a result of the considerable visual effects demands of the project.

I explained that the shot in question was a frontal close-up of Linda driving her car shot through the windshield. The shot, like virtually all of the short film's car-set shots, was achieved using what's known as "poor man's process" where a stationary car and some practical on-set effects are used to cast the illusion of a scene taking place within a moving car. Using After Effects, I would be overlaying slightly shifting footage of a cloudy sky on top of the windshield to add to the illusion that the car was traveling under a cloudy sky.

But the visual effect I was most excited about involved replacing the reflection in Linda's sunglasses with a first-person POV shot of the highway to hide the video camera involved in obtaining the head-on angle. A logically impossible shot!

Apparently, my enthusiasm and glee regarding this aspect of the film were so infectious that my dad relented in his earlier wariness and disapproval. It seems the joy I'd expressed toward my craft was enough for him to overlook the harrying overages of the process and realize that I was pushing myself just as hard as I was pushing them. Almost instantly he turned sympathetic and promised to talk to Mom about cooperating more generously for what remained of the production.

Some weeks later, production on *The Nap* was completed without further incident.

39. Co-Directing (October 2006)

Having heard a series of spirited knocks, I opened the door to my apartment located on University of Central Florida's campus.

It was Cris Mertens.

"Let's do this!" he exclaimed.

As we'd decided, he was cleanly shaved and donning baggy cargo pants, a form-fitting white crew neck t-shirt and his pair of top rim-only glasses. He looked properly calculating and up to some evil. Perfect, in other words.

Kyle and Reid, my two roommates, eagerly joined Cris and I and our merry band of four ventured out of the Lake Claire apartment complex toward the Nicholson School of Communication building, home of UCF's film school.

We'd all discussed making a short film about a school shooting but the particulars were still developing as we trekked to our decided filming location. It was a form of run-and-gun or improv filmmaking.

Cris would function as lead actor, director and editor. Kyle would be the Steadicam and camera operator as he was the owner of a professional and very impressive body-worn Steadicam apparatus. Reid would be a supporting actor and prop master, providing us with a terrifyingly convincing AK-47 replica. And I would co-direct with Cris and assist in formulating any needed dialogue.

When we arrived at the film school building, we jumped right into action. Cris had some very firm ideas about how to begin the short film and was able to swiftly coordinate with Kyle and knock off some shots of his character's entrance with great speed. A confident start.

For the opening shot, I lay hid in a hallway door alcove and allowed my arm to extend into the hallway on the floor like that of a slain student's. If you watch the background of the opening shot closely, however, I blunderously retract my arm before we cut to Cris's proceeding close-up.

Cris and I then spent some time working out what would follow. We decided to have an oblivious student, played by Reid, accidentally knock over a desk in a nearby classroom and immediately give away his presence. Cris added a beautiful touch of having a television in the classroom visible from the hallway and displaying static as if an entire class had suddenly rushed out in a panic and left the television running. I thought it effectively contributed to the unnerving atmosphere we were aiming for.

Although I was in favor of wider shots to help give a better sense of geography, my inclination was balanced by Cris's desire for tighter, more actor-focused shots. We butted heads about it a bit but we agreed to shoot various options and leave the final decision for the editing room.

Next, we continued our extemporaneous filmmaking effort in the film school building's large and completely vacant auditorium. Cris's gunman was to drag Reid's unlucky student past the rows of seats and onto the stage area at the back of the massive space where he would have some choice words before he let him go. The words that would be uttered by Cris's character was my primary contribution to the film.

"We don't have a lot of time so I'm gonna make this short," the gunman establishes. "There are business deals at this university that support the military-industrial complex," he continues. "The war machine, my friend!" the shooter states in exasperation.

The violent activist then beckons the student, "So, why are you not trying to stop it? Why are the students not trying to STOP IT!"

And with that dialogue, I imbued the film with a salient anti-establishment message about U.S. defense companies' ties to the university system; an issue I stood with fellow sds'ers (members of Students for a Democratic Society) to have addressed by UCF's own university administration around the time the film was made.

The penultimate line of the film and the accompanying close-up was also my touch.

Right before the shooter lets the traumatized student go, he commands, "Tell them this: Violence makes violence!"

Reid's character runs off with his life.

The film then concludes with the tragic suicide of the gunman. I opted for a calmer, more subdued approach to the cinematography for this final moment while Cris had a different idea. But after we'd shot my version, Kyle was in serious physical pain from having worn the Steadicam device for so long. So, we didn't get a chance to film Cris's more ambitious and inventive suggestion for the final shot involving closer staging and a dramatic upward pan to the ceiling of the auditorium as the gunman does himself in.

With the film in the can, so to speak, the responsibility now lay with Cris to spin the results of this exercise in impromptu filmmaking into a finely tuned short film. An editor-at-heart, neither Kyle, Reid nor I had even the slightest doubt that Cris would work his magic and it would be great!

Cris put pedal to the metal.

Several days later, Cris and I informed the leadership of UCF's film club that we had a short film ready to be screened.

12:03 was the title. Cris's idea.

We were summarily allowed a slot in the club's short film screening line-up and Cris, Kyle, Reid and I attended the meeting with great anticipation.

When the lights dimmed for the weekly showcase of the film club's members' work and the first shot of Cris's character toting the utterly convincing AK-47 replica appeared, there was a dramatic and sustained silence from the entire room. It's a tiresome cliche to say so but you could hear a pin drop.

12:03 had such an impact on its premiere audience that it prompted Professor Barry Sandler, the club's faculty advisor who rarely, if ever, spoke up about any of the screened short films, to say he was pleased my friends and I had made a film "with something on its mind." Barry Sandler was also a veteran Hollywood screenwriter. It was a major endorsement!

After the screening, many intrigued parties descended upon Cris, Kyle, Reid and I. Responses to our short film ranged from surprise to concern to shock to appreciation and more.

Although this effort flew in the face of my usual lone and premeditated approach to filmmaking, I was glad to share directing credit with one of my best friends Cris Mertens.

It was an evening to remember.

40. Contest (June 2005)

"Hope it works out and all, wortha shot, right? Good luck!"
-Jessica Maitre

So read the email from my friend Jessica and enclosed with the message was a link to a nationwide call for short film contest submissions. The contest was being held by an organization called the Youth Free Expression Network (YFEN) and the theme was free speech.

Intrigued by the prospect of producing a film with a strong political bent and the opportunity to gain a reward and some recognition for what would be my second canonical short film effort, I decided to produce an entry for the contest.

With a deadline fast approaching, I soon found myself performing some initial research in Green Library at Florida International University, where I'd completed my spring semester earlier in the year. Lately, I was a frequent visitor to the campus, or wanderer to put it more accurately, as I wasn't enrolled in any courses that summer but found the collegiate ambience generally invigorating as a writer. I was already working on another short film script that was going nowhere. I gladly put that aside.

Having acquainted myself with some of the basic liberal ideas behind the hallowed institution of free speech and its challenges in a current political climate of beating war drums, I started hatching some story concepts. One early idea involved a group of radical student journalists confronting an affront to their ideals. Another centered on a father's attempt to protect his son from a home-intruding Ronald McDonald (yes, the fast food chain mascot). And a third idea had shades of a horror film with a scene involving a large quantity of blood emerging from a family's bathroom toilet.

Ultimately, however, the father and son motif from the second idea survived my early brainstorming and led to the development of a simple story of a father becoming politically active on the eve of the second Iraq War in 2003. I proceeded to write the script with my brother Alonso in mind for the role of the father, Abraham Vanizetti, and my young cousin Samuel as Abraham's son.

Production soon began in a rather free-form fashion as I worked off a bare-bones script and played the scheduling by ear. Being only my second official short film, I was still very much a novice and found myself asking for more takes than necessary, feeling indecisive and rather unconcerned with how the footage would ultimately cut together. I also found myself filming a number of scenes that would ultimately be abandoned during production or later on in the editing room.

But in spite of my relative inexperience, I managed to complete the short film and mail a DVD copy of it to YFEN well ahead of the deadline.

Some months later, I was notified that my short film *Does Free Speech Matter?* was one of the ten semifinalists selected out of hundreds of submissions from across the country. Although I wasn't included among the three finalists selected soon after, the recognition I'd achieved was persuasion enough to continue writing, producing, directing, shooting and editing well into the future.

41. Counterculture (June 2004)

Some weeks after I graduated from Miami Killian Senior High, I learned that my aunt had a large box of surplus, blood donation-themed t-shirts from her job at a t-shirt and apparel printing company. At around the same time, I was aware that my friend and former classmate from Killian, Josh Rosenberg, had a connection with a local chapter of Food Not Bombs, a nationwide group of independent collectives formed to provide surplus food and other items to local shelters and other programs for the homeless. I'd met Josh in my senior year of high school and we'd always gotten along like two politically angsty peas in a pod. So, I informed him of the box of t-shirts and he gladly put me in touch with his FNB friends to arrange for their pick-up at my home.

While Josh's friends were on their way to collect the sum of t-shirts, I waited outside in the driveway of my home.

But why was I doing this?

Was it the punk rock I'd recently been introduced to?

Or politically progressive news sources like Alternet.org and *Democracy Now!*?

Or writings from intellectuals like Noam Chomsky, Howard Zinn and Michael Albert?

Or Marxist critiques found in books from local libraries?

Or passionate anarchist essays from CrimethInc.?

Or excerpts from terrorist Ted Kaczynski's incendiary, Luddite manifesto?

Or *The Daily Show with Jon Stewart*'s endless stream of political satire?

Or the rabble-rousing of Michael Moore's films and books?

Or the cautionary tale of a republic-turned-empire in George Lucas' *Star Wars* prequels?

Or the grim view of power in Stanley Kubrick's films?

Or the youthful irreverence toward the status quo in Richard Linklater's films?

Or the themes of more mature, late-period Steven Spielberg films?

Or political readings of literature and poetry from my last year of English?

Or analysis and criticism of the media by Marshall McLuhan and Neil Postman?

Or successful coup d'états in Haiti?

Or unsuccessful coup d'états attempts in Venezuela?

Or FTAA protests against economic injustice in downtown Miami?

Or a foolhardy war on terror in Afghanistan?

Or a war based on lies in Iraq?

Or generally incessant strife, famine and poverty in the Global South?

In any case, I waited for the members of FNB to arrive at my comfortable suburban surroundings that now sheltered, for whatever reason, a modicum of social consciousness and compassion.

When the FNB members arrived, I was initially startled by the manner of their conveyance - a beat-up sedan perhaps a month or two away from total breakdown. But where most others would see an unsightly lack of proper means, I saw uncommon nobleness.

I picked up the heavy box of t-shirts and handed them off to one of the young men of the raggedy-looking group.

"Do you want to come with us to drop this off?" they beckoned.

I was surprised by their offer but unsure.

"No, sorry. Maybe another time," I replied, letting them down gently.

They crowded back into their vehicle, backed out of my driveway and took off.

Although I'd refused the call to adventure this time, I would more fully embrace such an invitation through my involvement with radical student activists, including those in another FNB chapter, at University of Central Florida just a few years later.

For now, however, I had an obligatory summer job in retail to contend with and the first year of my college career at Florida International

University to look forward to. Acting on my spirit of rebellion would have to wait.

42. Dedication (August 2014)

At long last, the final draft! I'd been revising my latest short film script, *Leo's Love Letter*, for a month or two before I determined that it was finally time to begin production. At the time, I was a Communication Arts student at Florida International University and just about wrapping up my second summer semester at the school.

The script for *Leo's Love Letter* told a simple love story about a young man named Leo struggling to rekindle the lost spark between he and his partner Rachel. Inspired by a visual idea I'd hatched during my first year at University of Central Florida eight years prior, this would be my 15th short film.

On this production, I was particularly excited to get going because I'd be flexing my new DSLR video camera, the Canon T5i, which would be replacing my previous video recording device, the Canon HV20. I'd be saying farewell to MiniDV tapes as the footage from my camera would now be recorded onto tiny SD cards in the form of editing-ready files instead - and quite refreshingly so! Another exciting prospect on the production would involve use of a fresh subscription to Adobe Creative Cloud in order to use the latest versions of their video and image editing software.

Regarding the cast of the film, I recruited two young actors Emmanuel Franco and Stephanie Maltez, whom I'd met recently. They'd be playing Leo and Rachel, respectively. Production was expected to last only a few days but... there was one caveat.

As for that visual idea I'd conjured as a UCF freshman? It would require a wholly unprecedented quantity of concentrated manual labor I'd not committed to any of my short film work up to that point. But if I didn't do it, who would?

So, I visited my local office supply store and purchased about $100 worth of supplies for my ambitious endeavor. After that was done, I calculated the rate at which I would need to work and set myself to task at the start of the week. It was determined that the job be performed over the course of six days. There were many temptations along the way but I persisted, alone in my bedroom.

On Sunday, I turned down a casual hang-out with an amusing friend.

On Monday, I refused to chew out an inept group project member.

On Tuesday, I canceled an Asian buffet lunch outing with my family.

On Wednesday, I avoided a famed guest filmmaker event on-campus.

On Thursday, I ignored a young woman's transparent dinner invitation.

On Friday, I rejected a schoolmate's social marketing proposition and later that day, I completed my work and enjoyed some much-needed rest.

Over the six-day period for roughly four hours per day, I had turned $100 worth of notebook paper, or 20 reams of 500 sheets/ream, into 10,000 individually crumpled paper balls! My hands' joints had been worked to the point of wince-inducing soreness while the surface of my hands were covered in small nicks and scrapes.

Despite the cost in comfort, I had completed my self-assigned mission and all of the paper balls were now neatly collected in nearly 40 garbage bags which now sat in orderly rows in one of the bedrooms of my home. But even so, I wondered if the quantity of paper balls was enough to fulfill the visual I had in my head. At night on that same Friday, I decided to find out.

I closed the door to the vacant bedroom and began unloading the first garbage bag. My glee grew immediately and I quickly unloaded a second, a third, a forth, a fifth, a sixth, etc. As the paper balls came tumbling out of their confines and onto the bed and floor of the room, I felt a surge of ecstasy and joy unlike any other I'd ever experienced in my life up to that point!

As I emptied out the last of the garbage bags, I realized my initial concern about the amount was completely unfounded. I managed to submerge the room in paper balls to an extent I did not anticipate. The sheer volume of paper balls suggested the unreality of a dream. And so, with a knee-high layer covering the entire surrounding floor and a mountain of paper balls on the bed, the set was finally ready for production. After nearly a decade, the image I'd birthed during my freshman year at UCF was at long last realized!

In the coming week, I would film the short film's final scene involving this spectacle of inordinate effort which conveyed the main character's seismic devotion to remedy his relationship woes. After filming this scene, production would swiftly conclude on this 15th short film of mine, *Leo's Love Letter*.

It took several months to recycle all of the paper balls.

43. Denied (July 2006)

Earlier in the summer at University of Central Florida, I had partnered with a fellow UCF schoolmate named Joshua on a short film production. We had met on our housing complex's shuttle transport which ferried students to and from campus. Learning that I was an aspiring filmmaker, he had proposed working together on a short narrative fiction project with a salient eastern spiritualism theme owing to his interest in yoga and holistic medicine. As payment for my work on the film, Joshua would gift me a new video camera.

Seizing the opportunity, I pitched an idea to Joshua which he deemed acceptable and then I produced a script which both of us were excited about. The short film would center on a young man, to be played by Joshua, who is interested in eastern spiritual disciplines which later prompt a surprising outcome when he and his roommate's apartment is burglarized.

Unfortunately, the production of the short film only lasted a single day due to the admittedly tedious pace of shooting. I was mostly responsible for this particular shortcoming due to my relative inexperience as a filmmaker. After a pair of tense phone calls at the end of our first day of filming, Joshua and I ultimately agreed to dissolve our partnership and move on from the project.

There would be no video camera gift.

Although the yoga project had been a bust, I was determined to complete at least one short film during the summer before I had to vacate my student apartment at the end of its lease. So, I set about writing a fresh, new script.

Titled *Yeomans*, the 5-page script very efficiently wound a tale about a young man caught between his responsibilities as an employee of Yeomans, a fictional convenience store chain, and as a student of an unnamed university.

With a script as spare as it was in terms of characters, locations and staging complexity, I expected production to be a cinch. Who would stand in the way of such a simple and harmless creative endeavor?

For the film's casting, I recruited another fellow UCF schoolmate and recently made friend named Dustin to play the lead role. He had very little acting experience but I was accustomed to working with non-actors on my previous two short films. And following through with that particular predilection of mine, I also cast my oldest brother Alonso. He'd be making an hour-long drive from his home in Tampa for the shoot.

On the first day of production, Dustin, my brother and I gathered in the common area of my student apartment to rehearse before we set out to film on-location at a local convenient store. Despite many notes to both of my actors, I wasn't feeling too enthusiastic about the performances. I figured we'd nail it by being in the right environment. So, we soon concluded rehearsal and set out to the first location in my brother's car.

We arrived at a convenience store not too far from the UCF campus.

Upon entering, I spotted and approached an older woman at the check-out station. I assumed she was the manager.

"Good afternoon, ma'am. I'm a film student at UCF and I'd like to film some scenes for a short film project of mine. It won't take very long."

"You'd like to what?" she responded guardedly.

"Film some scenes for a short film," I stated.

"I'm sorry but I have to clear that with the manager," she shot back. She wasn't the manager.

"I really don't think that's necessary," I advised.

She grabbed the nearby phone.

"Sir, who are you again?" she asked with a nervous tremble in her voice.

"I'm a local film student," I responded.

"How do I know that?" she tested.

"If you'd like, you can contact the head of the UCF film school to confirm my identity and-" I was interrupted by Dustin.

"Gabe, I think you should stop," Dustin urged.

The manager grew increasingly flustered and irate.

"Sir, I'm going to call the police," she threatened.

I eased off.

"No, that's alright," I said in concession. "We're leaving."

So, Dustin, my brother and I left the store with my tail firmly between my legs.

Entering my brother's car, Dustin and my brother looked at me for further direction. I suggested we look for another store and make another attempt. So, we found a second convenience store nearby but the owner also denied my request - but in far less dramatic fashion.

Now it was getting dark and my brother had work the next morning in Tampa. So, we hunkered down to Lazy Moon, a popular pizzeria located across from UCF, where my brother ordered us some pizza for dinner. As we ate, I could feel the animosity churning behind Dustin's calm facade. Sensing this, I decided to call it a day and my brother subsequently dropped Dustin and me off at our respective apartment buildings.

After this most upsetting afternoon, I abandoned this short film project as well. The world had been unkind toward my humble filmmaking effort but the experience taught me an important truth: Sometimes the world doesn't open up for you despite your best intentions and gentlest demeanor.

In any case, I would still live to film another day.

44. Discovery (July 2005)

Over the summer, I'd managed to complete production on my second short film *Does Free Speech Matter?* Produced for a national short film contest, the production had a far quicker turnaround than my first short film *Mass Education* had, principally as a result of the constant availability of my oldest brother Alonso, who played the lead character, and the near-totality of filming taking place in my home.

The looming contest deadline was doubtlessly the primary motivating factor. Luckily, producing the voice-over narration as well as editing together the entire short film would also happen in fairly short order.

Over the few weeks the production had lasted, I was continually satisfied with my shot compositions and the mostly silent performance I had exacted from my brother. The script provided for a variety of scenes which kept up narrative and visual interest, making editing a satisfying experience. But even though the script remained somewhat in flux throughout production, I concluded filming confident in the footage I'd acquired and my abilities to weave together a compelling short film worthy of a panel of judges' consideration. The editing process would be far more exploratory than I'd become used to but I was more than up to the challenge.

When I deemed it time, I entered my bedroom, shut the door, hit the lights, closed the blinds and powered up my PC. For the next day or two, I would only emerge from my room for bathroom breaks or a kitchen snack. I'd seek alike periods of absolute isolation for editing purposes during my time at University of Central Florida and beyond but this was one of my first bites of the apple.

One of the first tasks in post-production involved finalizing the text I'd be reading for my part as the film's omniscient narrator and then recording it. The development of my one-man-band ethos which had defined my first short film and every subsequent production of mine, short or feature-length, was particularly salient in this instance. I relished the opportunity to provide the voice for the all-knowing entity which guides the film. I made sure the writing and performance were as good as I could possibly make it. I was my own domineering boss.

Once the narration was recorded, which clued me in on the necessary length of shots and scenes, I made the decision to have non-diegetic music accompany the visuals and narration. For most of the short film's musical score, I opted for fife and drum selections from authentic reproductions of American Revolution-era music to help link the main character's story with broader historical context. The music would lend a jaunty and propulsive quality to the proceedings. But I also had the mind to use a small selection of music from a modern Polish composer Krzysztof Penderecki. I'd first become aware of this composer's remarkable work through its inclusion in Stanley Kubrick's 1980 horror film *The Shining*.

This use of non-diegetic music would be the first instance of it in my canon. At that age, most of my favorite moments from my favorite films stemmed from the powerful synthesis of sound and image. It was a facet of filmmaking that had always been alluring to me but I was only beginning to explore it on my own terms.

With the various scenes carefully edited according to the voice-over narration and overlayed with my music selections, editing was soon concluded. So thrilled was I upon exporting a video file of the near-final cut of my short film that I immediately called out to the family member in closest proximity to my cave-like domain; my dad.

I eagerly played the film for him.

As it played, I felt exhilarated and quite proud. I'd never made anything that melded visuals, narrative and music so elaborately.

"What'd you think?" I asked my dad.

"Can you play it again?" he requested.

And so I did. After his second viewing, my dad asked to have the 4-minute video file replayed once more.

"Es excellente!" he finally opined after his third viewing.

Later that day, Alonso paid my home a visit and I showed him a more refined edit of the film. While he'd been lukewarm about my first short film, he was a smidgen more generous on this occasion. Ever the philistine, that Alonso.

Months later, during a fall film club meeting at UCF, I screened the film in an auditorium-style classroom and enjoyed a generally enthusiastic reception. In fact, one student lauded the "casualness of [my] compositions" while another thanked me for "making [my short film] look like it was shot on film." I would receive other encouraging comments in the days following the screening.

The experience of making *Does Free Speech Matter?*, particularly of finding it primarily in the editing process, led to some significant realizations toward my craft that I've not since forgotten.

First, I discovered the profound joy in wielding so much control over my hard-won footage and exercising the knowledge I'd gained of the advanced editing tools at my disposal. Few joys in my teenagerhood could compare to the forging of new audio-visual experiences by virtue of combining shots and sounds in effective ways, narratively or otherwise.

Second, I uncovered a strong preference for producing work that exuded density, intensity and speed. I grew sympathetic toward an almost maximalist mentality because I loved how relentlessly I could make a short film dance and sing.

Lastly, I became acutely sensitive to the use of music in films to the extent that it led to a somewhat anti-music attitude, particularly during my time at UCF, because I staunchly believed a film's visual offerings should be as strong as its aural ones. Although I didn't feel this second short film achieved this ambitious benchmark, it was a newly exposed criterion I would be intent on satisfying as I continued on my filmmaking journey.

For what was only a sophomore effort, the bounty had been staggering.

45. Earnesty (July 2006)

I had presided over two ultimately abandoned short film productions during the first half of the summer. The first was a yoga-themed drama that had only lasted one full day of filming and the second was a work-themed drama that also didn't continue past the first day of production. This was the summer after my first full year at University of Central Florida and confidence in my personal filmmaking aptitude was almost completely shot.

With a mental slate clear of any immediate short film plans, I packed up my belongings at the end my off-campus apartment's lease. I was going to be staying with my oldest brother Alonso at his home in Tampa for about a week before traveling back home to Miami for the remainder of my summer break. Much needed repose.

I figured my next production would be a class assignment carried out in the fall semester amid an abundance of film school resources (I'd learned of my acceptance into UCF's film program earlier in the year) and, along with that, assurance of actually being able to complete a new short film. But for now, I saw my stay in Tampa as necessary downtime.

My brother's suburban home was most spacious and quiet. It was the perfect environment to decompress after what had been a new experience of living independently while at UCF. For the first time in a long while, I would take life easy and relish a stillness of surroundings and mind.

But this stillness would not last long.

A few days into my stay in Tampa, my brother returned home from work one afternoon with exciting news. He'd won a giveaway at his workplace.

"What'd you win?" I inquired.

"It's in the garage. Go check it out!" he proudly replied.

I walked over to the garage door, opened it and laid my eyes on my brother's coveted prize - a generously sized, stainless steel barbecue grill.

Big things appeal to most men.

Moments later, I couldn't help myself and began considering the idea of filming a simple short film involving my brother and his new, hulking piece of meat-grilling hardware.

As my idea gained greater traction, I soon jettisoned my retreat mentality and returned to the familiar headspace of a working filmmaker. Given the simplicity of my idea, I would forgo a traditional script and instead opt for a highly detailed outline.

The short film would eventually be titled *Meat on a Grill* and tell a simple, cautionary tale about a man's ignorance of his doctor's better judgment regarding his diet.

I presented the outline to my brother and secured his participation. It would be our second collaboration after my second short film, the previous year's *Does Free Speech Matter?* So with the man and the grill locked in, I then began plotting a filming schedule.

Everything involving the main character's activity at his home would be fairly easy to shoot. The most difficult part of production, however, would be the opening scenes which would require location shooting at a local supermarket. I therefore decided to film the most difficult part of the film first. It's a habit I'd continue on all future productions to ensure peace of mind throughout the majority of production after an initial hurdle.

Without any degree of permission from the grocery store management, my brother and I nonchalantly entered the establishment and made our way to the meat aisle toward the back of the store. Thankfully, it was late enough at night that there wasn't too much activity in that area.

I then manned my video camera and jumped into director mode. We knocked off some shots but I soon felt an extreme low-angle shot was necessary for a key close-up. So, I lay down on the tile floor and pointed my camera up at my brother and gave him some direction.

That's when I sensed a potentially threatening presence in my periphery.

I turned to see a bald, heavy-set man with his hands on his hips watching my brother and me from afar.

"I think that's the manager," I suggested quietly.

My brother said nothing, likely expecting an abrupt end to our clandestine, late-night activity.

"I'll go talk to him," I proposed.

Getting up off the floor, I straightened my clothes and gathered myself. There had been a few occasions over the years in which I had to explain my filmmaking activity to curious onlookers but none prompted as much fear and nerves as this particular encounter. I didn't want to have to cancel yet another production this summer.

So, I walked over to the burly man, a store manager judging from his appearance, and desperately willed myself to disregard my encroaching fear and nerves.

"What are you doing?" he tested.

I entreated him with a firmness I rarely mustered.

"Good evening, sir. My brother and I are filming a scene for a school project of mine," I half-fibbed.

The man still looked on suspiciously.

"We're almost finished, though. If you could allow us just a few more minutes to finish up, we promise we'll be out of your hair (no pun intended)," I insisted.

Glaring at me, the man took a moment to decide the fate of our operation. Was he sympathetic to the arts or a common philistine?

"Okay," he decreed. "That's fine."

I was utterly relieved!

Having been granted permission to continue, I returned to my brother who hadn't been within earshot of the conversation. I exhaled a breath that had waited minutes to escape and shared the good news.

He was pleasantly surprised and we continued filming.

When my brother and I had wrapped up our business in the meat aisle, I actually had the temerity to find the same store manager and request use of the check-out counter for a shot of meat products traveling on the conveyor belt.

Thankfully, the man was most gracious enough to allow us to do that as well. And after I'd gotten all the needed shots, I thanked the manager and my party of two left on immaculate terms.

On the ride back to my brother's home, I recounted how nervous I'd felt during the encounter with the manager but how I'd unexpectedly risen to the occasion. Luck had certainly played a role that night but I imagine the manager wouldn't have been so generous and sparing had he not sensed my sincere, forthright temperament.

46. Economy (July 2005)

I was roughly halfway through production on my second short film *Does Free Speech Matter?* It had been a smooth process so far. Having cast my oldest brother Alonso as the lead, marking the first time I'd involved a family member on-screen in my work, I found working with him a different but pleasant experience. And despite W.C. Fields' famous advice, "Never work with children or animals," I also found directing my young cousin Samuel as Alonso's character's son an unfamiliar but enjoyable aspect of the production.

I intended the short film to be mostly dialogue-free as I was planning on dousing the majority of the proceedings with a voice-over narration I'd be providing. Given the relatively light emphasis on acting performance and line delivery, I didn't feel it was necessary to produce a formal script. Instead, I mainly relied on a detailed outline that was more suggestive than absolutely determinate regarding the content and direction of the scenes.

However, a key exception was a lengthy monologue that would be delivered by Alonso at his character's son's bedside about 2/3rds into the film.

On the night of filming that particular scene, I spent some time rehearsing the monologue with Alonso. The scene involved a father giving dire warning to his son about the threat of greater political repression. My brother had the lines memorized and gave it his best effort. I was mostly satisfied with the scene as we rehearsed and after sufficient practice, Samuel joined us in the U.S. flag-adorned bedroom and we filmed a few acceptable takes.

Afterward, when I sat down at my computer to review that night's footage and edit together the monologue scene in rough form, it soon dawned on me that there was a glaring problem. Alonso's performance felt awkward and forced despite a most earnest effort on his part. Despite the usual mitigative properties of effective blocking, framing and editing, the scene still wasn't working. I began to sense what the problem was. I'd faced a similar one before.

A few years prior while shooting the penultimate scene of my first short film *Mass Education*, I felt a similar uneasiness toward its next-to-final scene's amount of dialogue delivered by non-actors.

Confronted by a related predicament, I revolved the present situation in my head and was able to glean a major realization: I was freighting these scenes in question with either too much unnecessary dialogue or on-the-nose rhetorical point-making. In the hands of a seasoned actor, I could perhaps get away with it. But with non-actors, there was a lack of dexterous or strategic verbal and nonverbal communication. What could I expect from these enlisted individuals who'd never acted before in their entire lives?

So, as had happened on my first short film production, I ended up nixing the problematic verbosity in this second short film of mine and replacing it with something much more terse and suitable to the skill level of the performer. I re-shot the scene some time later with about 1/5th the amount of interaction between the two characters. I lost some of the verbal thematic relish but I realized it was worth sacrificing if it meant a greater feeling of cohesion, verisimilitude and flow.

With that done, my movie was back on track! And what's more, these sorts of measures toward greater leanness and efficiency would be continually exercised on future projects. I was definitely learning how to improve my craft.

Years later, I would read a biography on the legendary American filmmaker John Ford (one of my most favorite filmmakers) and discover that Ford used to throw out entire pages of dialogue in favor of economizing his storytelling.

With some of my choices, it seemed I was in good company.

47. Encouragement (April 2006)

Michael Hausman is an American film producer who's worked with the likes of filmmakers Ang Lee, Miloš Forman and Martin Scorsese among others on such films as *Brokeback Mountain*, *Gangs of New York* and *Amadeus*. He was scheduled to visit the film school at University of Central Florida for several talks and to meet with the film program's senior class about their capstone projects.

It would be my first interaction with a major industry name. One responsible for films I grew up with and loved.

On the day of his visit, I was seated in the film production hallway waiting on a friend. I was unaware that he was in the film building but soon gathered from the activity in the hallway that Mr. Hausman was busy meeting with the upperclassmen in the adjacent editing suites.

Sitting cross-legged on the floor, Mr. Hausman and a student soon emerged from one of the editing suites and Mr. Hausman saw me.

"Are you waiting for me?" he inquired.

I immediately responded that I wasn't and rather nervously began rambling about my status as a film student (my Film BFA classes wouldn't begin until the following fall). Coming off as rather overbearing and verbose, the student in charge of scheduling the meeting time slots intervened and directed Mr. Hausman toward his next appointment.

Mr. Hausman entered another editing suite with the next student in the line-up.

A few minutes later, the student coordinator popped a startling question to me.

"Would you be interested in meeting with Mr. Hausman?" she asked.

"I'm not a senior, though," I admitted.

The coordinator didn't see a problem.

"That's okay," she assured.

So, we scheduled an appointment in the immediate future and I soon found myself returning to the film production hallway later that afternoon for a one-on-one meeting with Mr. Hausman.

At the pre-established time, I met Mr. Hausman in the area I'd encountered him earlier (perhaps having slightly annoyed him) and joined him in one of the editing suites.

So, there we sat opposite each other in one of the film school's cozy dedicated post-production rooms. I immediately launched into a brief introduction and elected to show him my first two short films; the only two I had to my name at the time. The suite was equipped with a near-state-of-the-art computer loaded with all the essential post-production software. But all I needed was a simple media player to play some of the files stored on a USB flash drive I regularly wore around my neck at the time.

I showed him my first short film, *Mass Education*.

No perceptible response.

I fired up my second short film, Does Free Speech Matter?

Again, no perceptible response.

Feeling discouraged and hardly giving him time to offer any kind of feedback, I launched into an explanation of how my third short film production was going. In truth, it was halfway complete but far from ready to be shown. Despite that, I spoke excitedly about the film's pace and invoked a phrase coined by Robert Rodriguez. I said I wanted the film to "move at the speed of thought."

Mr. Hausman seemed particularly intrigued by what I had to say about this latest but unshown effort. Regaining my confidence, I then asked him frankly.

"So, what did you think of my two short films?"

His response was uncomplicated and direct.

"Keep going," he encouraged.

I nodded.

That was enough for me and with that, our brief meeting was concluded.

Later that day, I attended the weekly colloquium where he gave a general presentation about producing and then a separate event later in the evening where he offered a more detailed presentation related to the latest film he was producing for Miloš Forman, *Goya's Ghosts*.

During the colloquium, he was asked a question by one of the more enterprising students in the program.

"What's the best way to get a job in the industry?" the student asked rather bluntly.

"What's the hurry?" Mr. Hausman casually replied.

He of course elaborated but, to a degree, that shot from the hip was enough.

Mr. Hausman was a man of few words when it came to his engagement with aspiring filmmakers but I've never forgotten how impactful those two instances of simple advice were: to keep going and to take your time.

Coming from someone who'd accomplished so much in an industry most everyone yearned to be a part of, they were emblematic of a rare kind of sagacity.

48. Engineering (May 2007)

The sun was setting on my first year of film school at University of Central Florida. I was wrapping up two productions at the end of this spring semester: my seventh short film *Breakfast, Lunch and Dinner* and my eighth *Jesus Christ Goes to Mars*.

Breakfast, Lunch and Dinner was the result of an assigned Directing I project. Its requirements? No dialogue allowed and it had to be one minute in length (without credits). I'd enlisted a fellow acting class attendee Josh Rigdon as the lead actor and invited two friends Josh and Reid to also appear in the film. But I made up for such a sparse cast with a variety of locations to suit a growing propensity toward a feeling of travel in my films. With speed and a minimal footprint (no crew beyond myself), I was able to make use of such locations without needing to ask for permission. Asking for permission is often asking for denial as amateur filmmaking goes.

Settling on a thin, anti-commercial narrative based around the most ancient and universal sequence of events, I found producing the film wholly uncomplicated. It lacked anything resembling melodrama or the theatrical. It was an exercise in ordinary subject matter and simplicity. The most difficult work had been getting to this particular germ of an idea and then writing it.

Lacking only a few remaining shots which I knew I'd be able to acquire in fairly short order, I decided to export my latest cut of the short film to DVD in order to watch it on the sizable screen in my dorm's living room area, courtesy of my roommate Reid (who played a small role in the film). Up to then, I'd only watched what I had of my film on my computer monitor via the tiny preview window of my editing software. So with the help of my roommate (Reid again), his computer soon spit out a DVD player-ready copy of my movie!

Inviting Reid and my other roommate Kyle to watch this early cut, I recall Kyle's comments about my improving visual composition skills and the snappy pace of the film. At the very least, I was glad to see that something I'd made had clearly retained their attention for its roughly two minute runtime (I'd gone over the assignment requirements a bit).

After my roommates had had their fill of my short film, they left our dorm and I remained sitting alone in front of the television with my creation. I was proud of my work and watched it a number of times just to relish the effort that had gone into the piece. In between my rewatches, however, I noticed something quite intriguing.

The DVD menu template that had initially appeared and continually reappeared between playbacks of my short film involved a Mondrian-like array of differently sized tiles with each tile space containing a random shot from the video included on the DVD.

Seeing the visuals from my short film presented in this manner prompted a particular appreciation of their variety, cohesion and overall synergy. Confronted with this unexpected arrangement, I started to feel more like an engineer preoccupied with an intricate system of interconnected parts than an artist principally concerned with aesthetic or romantic ideas.

Admittedly, I had begun to grow somewhat weary of the banal emphasis on story and character in UCF's film school. It was a daring prospect as an eschewing of the storytelling tradition in filmmaking is practically verboten in film schools intent on grooming their students for work in the film industry. But I couldn't put away my increasing regard of filmmaking as a more structural practice and less rooted in emotionalism.

In any case, the impression made by this random DVD menu template would stay with me for a long time. But for now I kept it to myself. I had two short films to finish!

49. English (May 2003)

A number of 11th grade students gradually filed into one of the portable classrooms on the east side of the school grounds at Miami Killian Senior High. These students were there for their first period class of the day: English. As usual, I had arrived early and sat at my desk patiently waiting for our teacher to rise from his desk and begin his lesson. The school year would be over in a few weeks.

"Hey Mr. Hill, can't we watch a movie today instead?" one student casually proposed some minutes before the morning bell rang.

Mr. Michael Hill, our English teacher, sat at his desk looking over his notes for the lesson plan of the day.

"A movie? Don't you want to learn about the Madonna-whore complex in *Catcher in the Rye*?" he suggested.

"No, not really," replied the student as he slumped down into his chair and sighed in resignation.

The morning bell soon rang. In response, all the young people took their seats and quieted down. Almost Pavlovian.

Mr. Hill rose from his desk and approached the front of the class. But before getting started with his opening announcements and preview of the day's lesson, he began class on a different note than usual.

He pointed at the television fixed to the ceiling at the far corner of the room. "That... is a powerful thing," he stated. "Years ago, I was planning on showing a movie to one of my classes and its power was revealed to me," he regaled us.

We all listened intently.

"As soon as all the students entered the class from their lunch period, they quietly sat down and stared at the TV on the rolled-out cart," he explained.

"Dead silence," Mr. Hill intoned dramatically.

My present class was dead silent too as we all listened to Mr. Hill.

"All the kids were in a trance-like state, as if they were under a spell of some kind," Mr. Hill continued. "Just staring at the TV with the blankest expressions on their faces."

His students looked on mystified.

"What was on the television?" one of Mr. Hill's students ventured without raising his hand.

Mr. Hill slowly turned to him.

"Nothing," our teacher revealed. "Just a blue screen."

There was always a streak of social critique and no small amount of wisdom in Mr. Hill's occasional anecdotes and his teaching in general. As I'd later learn, he came from a family with a strong encouragement of personal values and social responsibility. He always welcomed discussion of weighty social and political topics but would tactfully steer their consideration through the prism of the literature we were currently exploring. The regularly robust engagement with classic novels, short stories and poetry in Mr. Hill's class appealed to me in particular because it felt like a close cousin to the intellectual and analytical energies behind so many of the film analysis content I was being exposed to in my personal reading pursuit at the time.

In Mr. Hill's class, we explored the distinctive use of color in *The Great Gatsby*, the audacious social satire in *The Adventures of Huckleberry Finn*, the prescient political themes in *The Crucible*, the bold characterization of youth in *The Catcher in the Rye* and the sheer majesty of language in Ernest Hemingway short stories and Robert Frost poems.

Those were the key subjects we delved into in Mr. Hill's class but there were countless additional works and topics discussed throughout the entire curriculum.

Throughout that junior year English class, Mr. Hill and I forged a close bond as teacher and student. So strong was our shared affinity for the material and its discussion in class that I'd eventually grow comfortable enough to ask him for some help with my first short film *Mass Education*. I asked him if would act in the short film as the story's particularly unscrupulous antagonist Principal Montag. He gladly agreed and his agreement to participate was testament to his desire to see the best in his pupils and support their potential if it was there.

After that 11th grade year at Killian, I would see him intermittently in the school halls between my senior year classes or after the school day. But after I graduated, I fell out of touch with him.

However, that was far from the last I'd see of Mr. Hill...

50. Exhibition (November 2003)

In the fall of 2003, I was a senior at Miami Killian Senior High and I had unsurprisingly fell into the good graces of my English teacher of that school year, Ms. Yolanda Muller. I say unsurprisingly because the narrative theory and criticism explored in English class was about as close as an aspiring filmmaker could get to film studies at Killian. Additionally, I was also a rather boisterous, outspoken pupil and gravitated toward many of the ideas introduced in her classroom.

In any case, Ms. Muller soon learned that I'd recently produced my first short film *Mass Education* and was interested in seeing it. So, I lent her a VHS copy of my short (yes, I hadn't mastered DVD authoring at the time). And consequently, she invited me to share it with the class. I suppose she saw some merit and curricular relevance to what I'd made. At any rate, I agreed but I recall being more nervously ambivalent than proudly honored. The occasion would mark the first public exhibition of my filmmaking work.

A few days later, Ms. Muller introduced the screening to the class and lowered the lights. That nervous ambivalence persisted. And as my short film played, I ducked lower and lower into my chair desk. I did not at all appreciate that this occasion involved the first audience I'd ever had beyond my family for the product of what was my fairly recent and very solitary venture into filmmaking.

Given the rather humorless and dour nature of the short film, I remember rapt silence - even through the credits. However, some applause from my classmates did follow at the very end of my short film.

When the lights were turned back on, Ms. Muller initiated a little Q&A and asked me to share a bit of insight into this amateur cinematic confection the whole class had just witnessed. I could only offer an awkward and vaguely pretentious musing on meaning and interpretation.

The lucid exposition and showmanship toward my work I'd later adopt was far, far from conception.

Nevertheless, the screening was an important stepping stone and it exposed me to the reality of artistic exhibition, particularly as it applies to filmmaking. You must always stand by your work and be ready to speak intelligently and confidently about it. And ever since that memorable but stomach-churning occasion, I've always tried to live up to that.

In conclusion, I am most thankful that Ms. Muller pushed me into the spotlight that day and helped me to grow as an artist, especially one who would later find himself as committed to the public as to himself.

51. Experimental (July 2007)

At home in the middle of summer and in-between semesters at University of Central Florida, I decided to make a short film that reflected my peculiar affinity for a household chore that was sometimes required of me - mowing the lawn. The short film would also represent the maiden voyage of my newly acquired digital video camera, the Canon HV20!

After some time writing and at least one initial production attempt resembling stop-motion animation, my idea began to take firmer shape. While it would contain a thin narrative throughline, it would have no dialogue or identifiable characters. It was an experiment to see whether I could create something wholly self-made and substantial enough without any of the usual narrative trappings. The narrative short films I'd produced in film school at UCF had either been totally silent or plastered with wall-to-wall voice-over narration so I was more than used to bucking convention and playing with form in a similar fashion.

As had become custom, I would write, produce, direct, shoot and edit the film on my own. And for the first time I would also appear on-camera - underneath bed covers.

In setting out to make the film, one of the earliest challenges I faced was acquiring a shot of the sun rising over a suburban community, dually indicating time and place in dramatic fashion. I figured I could wake up before sunrise, climb onto the roof of my house and from there capture what I needed. So I did that, giving my new camera its first scuffs in the process. Unfortunately, my vantage point wasn't as high as I'd imagined it would be to effectively create the shot as envisioned so its inclusion was ultimately scrapped.

To accomplish shots from a seeming grass-level POV, I applied numerous blades of grass to a length of tape, then applied the tape to the outside of the front of my camera so that the blades of grass circled around and protruded from around the lens creating the illusion of filming upward from amid a bed of grass when the camera was pointed at the sky. Many have been convinced that a GoPro camera was used to accomplish those particular shots. Nope!

Another challenge involved creating several freeze frame shots from the underside of the lawn mower as it violently chewed up the tall grass in the film. To accomplish this series of shots, I flipped over my family's push mower and filmed some gently hand-pushed blade movement at a low shutter speed. I'd take stills from this footage containing the motion-blurred blade and superimpose a random assortment of grass blades (motion-blurred using Photoshop) to complete the trick.

Another challenge on the film involved acquiring a shot of the lawn mower's actual under-workings as it passes over the camera's grass-level POV (also using the technique previously described). The process of getting this particular shot involved suspending my family's push mower, in operation with its blades at dangerously full rotational force, above my up-facing and very vulnerable camera using two elevated surfaces. The two elevated surfaces were wide enough apart to allow the camera to film upward between them while allowing the mower enough space to move an adequate distance over the camera. Getting the shot was tense! Do not try this at home, folks!

One of the more dramatic events which unfolded during the making of the film involved my need for a shot of white plumes of smoke emanating from the lawn mower upon ignition. Foolishly believing that adding water to the gasoline tank would result in the desired effect, I made a doubly stupid mistake of adding water to the oil tank instead. As a result, the mower jammed. And when my dad learned what had happened, I don't think I'd ever seen a more angry human being in all my life! Thankfully, one trip to the service center and $200 later, the mower was soon back in regular operation.

With the end of summer approaching, my short film was still missing a few complicated shots. They weren't necessarily challenging but they would require more time than I had because I was preparing to return to UCF for the Fall 2007 semester.

In any case, I put my short film on hold and got ready to return to school. I expected I'd be able to finish the film the following winter break but little did I know under what circumstances I'd be returning home prematurely that semester...

52. Expiration (June 2007)

When I returned home from University of Central Florida at the start of summer, my dad and I had already been in talks about starting a business venture together. My dad had an idea to offer a service wherein we would record and catalog all of the valuable property of area homeowners to be used for insurance purposes in case of hurricane damage, burglary or some other unforeseen calamity. The record would become the exclusive property of the homeowners, of course. Our company would be called ImageOnRecord.

My dad and I discussed the logistics of everything involved and we soon set out to create a website, print flyers and begin strategizing for our hopeful first client. We planned on using the same video camera I'd been using for my short film productions.

But there looked to be an issue with that.

My Sony DCR-TRV720 Digital Handycam had had a good run but after roughly five years in my possession, it was clearly showing its vulnerability to age and wear. The malfunctioning topside buttons made tape playback nearly impossible, the battery holding mechanism barely clasped attached batteries and the body of the camera was literally coming apart at the seams.

My camera was dying.

This dear machine had been with me since my first adventures in filmmaking. It was part of my most cherished memories related to this ongoing creative practice of mine. And now I now felt an odd sense of sadness over my once-mighty video camera's current state of degeneration and obsolescence.

It was time to move on.

Thankfully, my dad was willing to cover the cost of a new video camera with the expectation we'd be using it for ImageOnRecord-related activities, though not exclusively.

I was thrilled!

Consulting the internet, I immediately happened upon some interesting possibilities for a replacement video camera but found one of particular appeal: the Canon HV20. It was a sleek, diminutive, consumer-grade high-definition digital video camera that also shot standard-definition video. I appreciated the SD functionality because at the time I didn't have the means to edit HD footage. But with the HV20, I'd have that option readily available once I had a desktop computer capable of an HD workflow.

So, I ordered the Canon HV20 and anxiously awaited its delivery.

Once it arrived, I performed some simple tests to acclimate myself to the new technology. Due to its considerably smaller size compared to the Sony camera, filming with it felt far less obtrusive and conspicuous; in fact, less so than any video camera I'd ever used. I fell in love right away!

With this new, crucial piece of video equipment in my possession, my dad and I resumed our activity on ImageOnRecord. We launched a website and began distributing flyers around the neighborhood.

Then, we waited for a response.

And waited.

And waited some more.

No response.

Maybe this wasn't as great an idea as we'd imagined.

My dad and I soon came to grips with the more-than-likely misgivings area homeowners might have about letting two of their neighbors into their homes to record the location of all their precious belongings.

We soon closed up shop on our fledgling company and that was that.

But despite the turning of the tide against ImageOnRecord, I was glad about the bonding experience I'd shared with my dad and supremely pleased that I'd managed to get a new video camera out of the whole affair.

And so enamoured was I with my new digital video camera, I looked forward to giving it a proper baptism by using it on a fresh short film project.

But what would that project be?

53. Extremity (February 2012)

My nearly two-and-a-half-year-long creative slump had finally come to an end several months earlier and I was now on the cusp of production on a new narrative short film! From 2009 to 2011, my creative output had been significantly hampered by stultifying health and legal difficulties. I was still writing throughout most of that time but the reality of starting and finishing a full-fledged short film production was far beyond my grasp. My last narrative piece had been my 11th short film *The Nap*, completed in late 2008 - months before the unexpected hellscape that was 2009 to 2011.

But now, with my personal troubles cleared up and my motivation fully restored, I found myself putting the finishing touches on a near-final draft of a new short film script, titled *Semester of Madness*. This would be the 13th entry in my canon and I would begin filming in only a matter of weeks.

The idea for this short film was hinged on an extensive use of voice-over narration. So, I decided to record myself reading the narration using my dad's analog tape recorder; allowing me to produce a rough mock-up of the film in aural form to determine whether my idea worked on a fundamental dramatic level.

When I'd recorded my reading of the narration, I cued up the tape recorder and looked for my dad. I found him in our home's sitting room reading the newspaper.

"Hey Dad, I want you to listen to something I recorded," I said invitingly as I approached him.

He finished the sentence he was reading and gave me his undivided attention.

I hit the play button.

* * *

The idea for *Semester of Madness* came from an idea for a trilogy of short films I was interested in making. I dubbed it the "Crime, Madness and Love" trilogy because the three short films would each tackle one of those three themes. I'd written the script for the crime-centered one, titled *Corrections*, but I'd opted not to produce it in favor of the next one in the sequence; due mainly to logistical considerations. The last, love-themed short film would ultimately evolve into my 2014 short film, *Leo's Love Letter*.

Considering the rather rare position I was in of being a filmmaker with over 10 years of experience and having been afflicted by not just one but two episodes of breaking-from-reality psychosis, I was energized by the prospect of treating the subject matter as authentically as I could with the finest filmmaking my experience made possible.

The writing of the short film began to feel more like an obligation or duty given the considerable reserve of first-hand insight I had about the actual experience of mental illness and the crucial social need for greater understanding about the issue. And when the short film was complete, many would take notice. The film would end up garnering a number of mental health-themed film festival acceptances and ultimately lead to my association with the great folks of the Miami-Dade chapter of NAMI (National Alliance on Mental Illness). My film would also be well-received among my various doctors, including one who would use it for educational purposes at a local mental health hospital.

Regarding the formal aspects of *Semester of Madness*, the primary mode of expression for the almost clinical-like insight to be provided would be its wall-to-wall narration. I usually regard narration as a crutch in filmmaking because it's far easier to tell rather than to show. However, I thought if I could implement the narration in a distinctive enough way I could avoid that common pitfall. Therefore, I wanted the narration to be delivered breathlessly fast to command the audience's attention and have it be as factually based as possible to also help set its use apart.

To further satisfy my particular artistic criterion that the narration shouldn't be doing all the heavy lifting, I determined that the short film should have a matching visual scheme whereby the visuals flowed with as much consistency as the language in order to maintain visual interest and captivation.

When I began writing the script earlier in the year, I encountered a problem involving the usual way that action and spoken words are represented in the traditional scriptwriting format. This standard approach lacked a needed sense of simultaneity. Desperate to see image and language placed side-by-side to gain a more accurate feel for what I'd ultimately be editing together, I devised a two-column approach to my script document that allowed me to organize visuals and narration in the much clearer manner desired. The old way had to go (for now)!

Based on the length of my preliminary recording of the short film's guiding narration, *Semester of Madness* was expected to be my lengthiest short film. However, I felt its narrative and visual happenings would be constant and dynamic enough to not try anyone's patience. A criminal sin, in my view! And since the short film's completion, I've never once heard anyone complain about its length or pacing.

The production logistics would be fairly straightforward. I'd primarily be filming at two local college campuses (without permits) and at my home. Additionally, all that would be required in terms of casting would be two principal actors and a handful of other actors for some very minor roles. And for the first time in my filmmaking career, I would end up compensating and working extensively with individuals who had significant acting experience. Although my next short film *Proteus* would once again rely on non-actors (both human and animal), I was intent on moving past that previously cherished and Italian neorealist-inspired practice on this occasion. The production of *Semester of Madness* would also mark the first time I printed and posted practical casting notices to recruit cast members.

It is no mistake that *Semester of Madness*' most characteristic aspect resembles that of the 2005 short film of mine, *Does Free Speech Matter?* The relentless narration in *Semester of Madness* was borne out of my increasing affinity for the density, speed and intensity of my earlier effort. Such formal considerations were and continue to be as important to me as the more literal content of what I make. However, such an extensive and bold use of narration would be indefinitely discontinued after its inclusion in *Semester of Madness*. Worse than trying one's patience is re-using the same bag of tricks.

My recording came to an end and I stopped the tape recorder. "So, what did you think?" I asked my dad.

He took a moment to gather his thoughts.

"People are going to be shocked," my dad insisted.

"Really?" I stated somewhat incredulously.

"Not many people understand experiences like these," he added. "It's important that they do."

My dad would offer more expressions of confidence and trust in what I was doing as I finalized the script and proceeded to make the short film. He saw great social relevance in this particular piece and the substance of his early, encouraging appraisal would later be echoed by many at the short film's various film festival screenings and other instances of public exhibition.

Perhaps the response most indicative of the short film's social value came from a veteran clinical psychologist and educator Dr. Harriet P. Lefley. "[Your film is] a very powerful portrayal of the actual experience of psychosis," she wrote to me after viewing the short film. "It's certainly one of the best films I've seen on this experience."

Dr. Lefley would go on to use the short film as a teaching tool for doctors-in-training at Jackson Mental Health Hospital in downtown Miami where she worked.

54. Facebook (August 2009)

In the grip of a psychotic episode in 2009, I had used Facebook to regularly rant and rave against the perceived unfairness of University of Central Florida authorities and the Orlando legal system over a conduct infraction I'd been charged with during my time as a student in the spring semester that year. I felt small, attacked and utterly defenseless.

For nearly six months, I published a litany of increasingly cryptic, damning posts at every step of my involvement with UCF and broader Orlando authorities over my increasingly harrying legal predicament. On some occasions, I published multiple posts on the same day. I posted most of these cries for help while living alone in my student apartment off-campus. My friends and family expressed great concern.

"...the purpose of Law should be to protect what is valuable to a society, namely freedom and truth; and not allow a fear of punishment to overwhelm our muscular ability to be intelligent, diplomatic and understanding," I wrote on one occasion.

In another instance, I wrote that I hoped "the UCF Police Department is enjoying their time attempting to hide their bureaucratic ineptitude. At this point, I'm more willing to trust their canine unit with my case because at least the animals in those ranks don't have a choice in being so subservient and unthinking."

Out of desperation, I later wrote that "[Gabriel] is under direct attack from an uncompromising and hostile enemy, seriously threatening his future enrollment at UCF. But vengeance and deceit will never constitute his defense strategy."

As my agitation and derangement mounted, I wrote that "[Gabriel] doesn't exist. Nothing he says or does matters. All his most pure intentions and actions have led inexorably toward his destruction and dismantlement at the hands of an irrational, hostile and decidedly deaf world. Fear and silence are the reigning powers now."

When my psychosis reached its feverish, suicidal peak shortly after returning home to Miami, I was hospitalized. After two weeks interned at a local mental health hospital and with the crucial aid of certain psychotropic medications, the chemicals in my brain were restored to a healthy and balanced state.

During my recovery, I looked back at my particularly caustic bevy of Facebook posts as a symptom of an unsound mind. So, I deleted all of the posts I felt had been the product of my illness - virtually all of them related to my difficulties with UCF authorities. I also deactivated my Facebook account.

Since I'd first heard of "The Facebook" from a friend of mine Elsa Bolt during a chance encounter at a midnight screening of a *Star Wars* film in 2005, I'd used the platform extensively to interact and keep up with friends and classmates during my first years at UCF. I considered it a powerful tool to communicate with others, share experiences as well as store and exhibit all manner of personal creative content.

Some time after recovering from my serious bout of mental illness at the close of summer in 2009, I would reactivate my Facebook account with a renewed intent to use the platform for expressly constructive purposes as I gradually returned to filmmaking and reintegrated with society at large.

I was determined to use the social media platform primarily to spread word about every significant development related to my filmmaking projects. I would use it to announce casting calls, the start of productions, the conclusion of productions and festival acceptances. Beyond that, I'd also post retrospective commentary, accounts of screenings and other think-pieces related to my creative process. All of this would help set the stage for a major internet undertaking of mine - publishing a personal website.

Over a decade and countless posts later, I owe the preeminent social media tool with allowing me to grow and maintain a sizable audience for my work. It has also allowed me to connect substantially with other creatives in my field. While some ancillary content and navel-gazing occasionally makes its way onto my feed, I always try to ensure that my posts meet a high standard of quality.

While I'd had an unfortunate spell of using Facebook to air my mad ramblings in the past, I've never disavowed the fundamental good this tool is capable of. I continue to believe in the promise of social media if users exercise great care and responsibility in the curation of their content.

Like so much in life, it is what we make it.

55. Feedback (June 2003)

I considered many ideas for what my first short film would be.
I spent countless hours crafting my idea at a local library.
I produced a draft of my script using unfamiliar formatting.
I storyboarded my script using printed-out templates found online.
I scouted locations at my high school for various scenes.
I casted non-actors I didn't know too well.
I worked with my dad to make a home-made Steadicam device.
I made a makeshift boom pole using a microphone and broomstick.
I forgot to turn on the microphone on my first day of filming.
I lugged my camera and tripod to school on many, many days.
I overcame the trepidation of working with actors.
I carried and made use of heavy but superfluous lighting equipment.
I stayed after school frequently to film scenes.
I lost my cool when being prevented from filming on school grounds.
I gained permission from my high school principal to continue filming.
I revised my filming strategy during class lectures.
I recruited extras for an incredibly ambitious hallway scene.
I tossed out several scenes or refilmed them throughout production.
I ventured through my high school to record needed audio samples.
I edited my footage using Adobe Premiere extensively for the first time.
I rearranged several scenes during the editing process.
I solved dozens of editing problems, both large and small.
And finally, I exported the latest cut of my first short film *Mass Education* to share with my family.
When the end credits rolled, my gathered family members sat silently.

The short film ends on a rather grim note with the fate of the main character's precious domain of solitude, his high school library, fated for the chopping block by greedy and unscrupulous forces. Such a dour ending likely attributed to the muted response as I would later observe the same immediate response in subsequent screenings with other audiences.

"So, what did you think?" I asked, piercing the awkward quiet.

My dad soon spoke up.

"It's good but remember, it's only your first," he said.

"Sí, solamente es tu primer cortometraje," my mom reiterated supportively.

My oldest brother Alonso was far less diplomatic and bluntly stated that he didn't expect the short film to be so "corny."

A part of me expected ringing praise from everyone but I wasn't too hurt by the rather lukewarm reception. I was aware of many of my short film's flaws but I was generally proud of what I'd accomplished and that I'd finished my very first short film rather single-handedly. I wouldn't allow anyone's less-than-enthusiastic response obscure the potential I knew existed. Besides, there was really only one audience member I was interested in satisfying: myself.

But my parents were right. They understood that this was a first-time effort and that excellence or any degree of mastery in any field takes much greater time and toil.

I was ready for that.

56. Feminine (July 2014)

"Leo... did you honestly think that some chicken scratch letter of yours could make things better between us?" Stephanie asked of her remorseful counterpart with the exact right balance of caution and causticity.

"Well... you're right," she continued, gently altering her demeanor toward the titular character. "This is the sweetest thing you've ever done since we've been together."

Stephanie Maltez and I were in one of the vacant bedrooms of my family home, filming the final scene in my 15th short film *Leo's Love Letter*. The short film weaved a story about the titular young man's desperate effort to rekindle the fire in his relationship. And right at once I was astounded by Stephanie Maltez's earnest and delicate treatment of her lines in this simple yet pivotal scene. I expected a rough start as Stephanie acclimated to the part but she instantly introduced a disarmingly feminine quality to her performance I'd rarely included in my mostly androcentric work up that point.

No stranger to romantic relationships, Stephanie brought an authenticity to the brief but crucial portrayal of the crossed lover Rachel. As I would be increasingly witness to, Stephanie wielded an uncommon aptitude for the harmonious mobilization of her verbal and nonverbal expression. She always made the scripted material work and routinely asked the questions she needed to have answered in order to facilitate her highly effective process.

Our first collaboration was on *Leo's Love Letter*. We would then work together on my final short film *The Promotion* and then join forces once again on my first feature-length film *For My Sister*. Through it all, Stephanie would prove a stalwart ally and a crucial support beam. No person had ever had such a direct and practical influence on my creative output.

We first met at the 2nd Annual Florida International University Student Film Festival earlier in 2014. I had submitted my 13th short film *Semester of Madness* to the festival and it had been accepted along with the work of other filmmakers either attending FIU themselves or whose productions involved any participants attending FIU. The main event was the short film showcase and my film was set to close the night's program. I was thrilled that the evening of the event saw a packed house in one of FIU's largest auditoriums!

One of the other short films included in that evening's slate was *Mr. Williams*, written by FIU student Morgan Smart and co-directed by Morgan and a fellow FIU student Alexia Lue. It featured Stephanie Maltez in the lead role as a woman who has a tense encounter with a past lover. It was a straightforward single-scene drama but Stephanie's compelling performance was the star of the show.

Several days later, I attended the award ceremony reception event of the festival at FIU. I can't recall who initiated the conversation but I soon found myself chatting with Stephanie Maltez who'd greatly enjoyed *Semester of Madness*. And I of course dispensed no small amount of praise over her stand-out turn in *Mr. Williams*.

Stephanie and I spent a good half-hour or so discussing our creative experiences and aspirations. At one point, she expressed an interest in working with me if an opportunity presented itself. I told her I'd keep her in mind as I worked to determine what my next project would be. Our rather involved conversation came to a close when she excused herself to smoke a cigarette outside. I then met with several other filmmakers and festival attendees but Stephanie had made a strong impression and seemed like someone who was recovering from a rough patch and would greatly benefit from association with an earnest filmmaker.

Some months later with a complete script of *Leo's Love Letter* in-hand and pre-production in full-swing, I reached out to Stephanie about a part in my latest short film. She instantly accepted!

As I described at the start of this chapter, that instance of hearing my dialogue so deftly delivered by Stephanie on our first day of working together was all I needed to hear to know that our creative alliance would be a strong one. Although we spent no more than two days filming her scenes and a single day dubbing some dialogue, by the end of our collaboration on *Leo's Love Letter* each of us understood how serious we both were as purveyors of our respective crafts.

Shortly after the last day of filming with Stephanie had concluded, I received a call from her.

"Hey Stephanie, what's up?" I asked.

"You don't have to pay me for my work on the film," she stated. "But I want to be the lead in your next project," she insisted.

I was surprised by this unexpected proposition.

"Uh... sure," I responded. "Why not? I'd love to work with you again."

And with that, the stage was set for a second collaboration.

Over the next year-and-a-half, Stephanie and I kept in touch as I worked on the script for my next short film. I was encouraged by the outwardly imposed condition of having Stephanie as the lead. Indeed, it was a refreshing challenge to write a part with a particular gifted actor squarely in mind.

In early 2016, I finally completed the script for *The Promotion*, my 16th and final short film; about a young woman who's all about her career despite her father's warning. Another smooth and blissful collaboration with Stephanie, who delivered yet another sterling performance, followed.

While *The Promotion* was deliberately written as a showcase of Stephanie's acting talent, the demands of that film would pale in comparison to what would be required of her for our third collaboration - my first feature-length film *For My Sister*. But as I wrote in a social media post commemorating our five years in league with each other, "...since our first moments working together, I knew I'd scarcely find someone better to help shake the heavens and the earth, the sea and the dry land in the arduous but rewarding world of independent filmmaking done right."

I really meant that.

57. Festivals (February 2011)

In the summer of 2010, I decided to submit my 11th short film *The Nap* to a spate of film festivals and contests; ten in total. The promise of festival acceptances and screenings was an invigorating one as I gradually recovered from a dim period of my life characterized by a deep depression and creative paralysis.

Additionally, getting *The Nap* out in the open was long overdue as I'd completed the short film nearly two years prior but hadn't presented it anywhere except for a few screenings at my home for family guests and to whoever found it on YouTube. After this experience, I'd make sure to submit every subsequent short film I made to festivals immediately upon completion.

Months later, out of the ten film festivals I'd submitted *The Nap* to, I heard back from only one: Gasparilla International Film Festival in Tampa, FL. Their 5th annual edition would be host to my first film festival experience!

I would be traveling to Tampa via private shuttle to stay with my oldest brother Alonso and his fiancée Paola, who conveniently lived in Tampa at the time. I packed plenty of business cards I'd had printed earlier on.

The trip went smoothly and I was glad to be staying with a family member for the event. With comfortable lodgings and with the company of family, I would definitely try to make the most out of this maiden festival experience. The first order of business? The opening night event!

When I arrived at Tampa Theatre in downtown Tampa for the opening night festivities, I was immediately overwhelmed by the size of the crowd and the loudness of the event music.

As I wandered the heavily congested theater lobby among so many strangers, mostly older adults, I was expecting to find other young filmmakers to converse with. But not finding any, I kept to myself and roamed rather aimlessly.

At one point, I found myself momentarily walking behind M. Emmet Walsh, a legendary character actor I was familiar with from numerous films. He was being presented with a lifetime achievement award at the festival that year.

Foolishly believing that I didn't have the right credentials to attend the opening ceremony, I decided to leave the event prematurely. However, before I left, I recognized the president of the festival and prepared to greet him and introduce myself. I waited a bit until I found an opening to speak with him and soon seized my chance.

"Hi, I just wanted to thank you for the opportunity to screen one of my short films at your festival," I said.

"I'm glad you made it out. What's your name?" he asked.

"Gabriel Rhenals," I replied. "I'm a filmmaker from Miami."

I gave him one of my business cards.

As the president glanced at my card, he asked me, "When's your film playing?"

I told him the date and venue of my program.

"I think I'll be there for that," he suggested.

I smiled.

"Well, it was nice meeting you, Gabriel. Enjoy the rest of the festival!" he encouraged.

"Thank you, sir," I responded.

I walked away from that interaction feeling particularly proud of my courage and enterprising in the face of some social anxiety.

Upon arrival at the opening night event, I had received a lanyard and badge that identified me as one of the festival's attending filmmakers and provided for access to any film screening at the festival.

So, the following day I was all set for some time at the festival's main theater venue - a multiplex theater also in downtown Tampa.

At the multiplex and without any planning to speak of, I randomly strolled into a few feature-length indie film screenings that afternoon. Some of these long-form films featured major Hollywood names and some of the producers of these films were actually in attendance. It was an exciting, new experience for me!

I also partook in an exclusive and highly informative filmmaker's luncheon that afternoon. But all of this was, of course, in eager anticipation of my own short film's screening in a short film program taking place later that day in one of the multiplex's many auditoriums.

In between these earlier select screenings and events, I saw others with festival filmmaker badges. So, I challenged my hopelessly introverted nature by introducing myself, however awkwardly, and distributing business cards. I also accepted their business cards and collected many of them that afternoon. The filmmakers I interacted with were quite affable and generous, sharing plenty of advice and stories about their experiences at other festivals. One of the kindest fellow filmmakers I met that afternoon was Aaron Hose, who had close ties to University of Central Florida and who I'd later learn was programming director of Aruba International Film Festival.

After some schmoozing with other filmmakers, the time had finally arrived!

Alonso and Paola soon joined me at the multiplex and we entered the auditorium for the occasion I'd been anxiously awaiting.

The auditorium wasn't packed but it housed a substantial viewing audience (I didn't see the president of the festival in attendance, unfortunately). After several quality short films had played, *The Nap* finally made its triumphant theatrical debut! I was immediately thrilled by the flawless technical presentation of my short film. Its impact bolstered by the fact that *The Nap* was my first high-definition video production. I absolutely relished the experience of watching my work under such immaculate conditions and on a screen of considerable real estate.

After the short film program concluded, the attending filmmakers of the featured short films were asked to group at the front of the auditorium for a brief Q&A.

I was asked about the inspiration for my short film and simply cited the its origin as a contest entry with the mandated theme of technology. I recall responding well enough considering this was some time before I got involved with Toastmasters International.

With the screening concluded, I made my way out of the multiplex with Alonso and Paola. Just outside the building, a woman who'd attended the screening greeted me and complimented me on my film. She also told me that she'd recognized one of the exteriors in my film as she was a former resident of Miami. I was amazed that she'd recognized the location as it seemed fairly nondescript to me. In any case, I thanked her for her kind words and with that, my day at the festival came to a satisfying end.

A day or two later, I was back in downtown Tampa for more festival events: a closing night ceremony, including a screening of *Cocaine Cowboys* director Billy Corben's latest documentary, and an after-party at a neighboring warehouse.

The closing night film, Corben's *Square Grouper*, was an entertaining historical exposé on the Miami drug trade of the 1970s. It was my first time seeing one of Corben's films (I hadn't seen *Cocaine Cowboys*) but I actually had a connection to Miami's foremost cinematic raconteur. Several months earlier, I had volunteered to do some production design work on a local short film Corben had helped produce.

So after the screening, I decided to introduce myself to Corben.

"Mr. Corben, hello!" I started.

"Hey, what's up?" he replied.

"I really appreciate the important work you do shedding light on Miami's dubious past," I said.

"Thanks, man," he responded.

"I'm actually a filmmaker from Miami and worked on Jillian Mayer's Uncle Luke short film which you're helping to produce," I informed him.

"I've heard that's coming along great! What part of Miami are you from?" he asked.

"Kendall," I instantly replied.

"I once had a girlfriend from Kendall," he said.

I took out a business card and handed it to him.

"Well, I just wanted to say hello and introduce myself," I concluded.

Corben accepted my card.

"I appreciate that. Thanks, man!" he said.

Once more, I'd overcome my social trepidation and felt like I'd made a good impression and stretched those important interpersonal muscles. In the years since that interaction, I'd see Billy Corben a few more times and on each occasion hand him one of my business cards. He has like four of them by now.

The busy after-party in the next-door warehouse didn't hold my attention for too long. The affair was far too loud and I hardly saw anyone familiar but the gourmet finger foods were delicious and the burlesque-style entertainment was something I'd never seen in-person before.

Upon leaving the party not too long after it began, I happened to pass veteran actor Tom Berenger, who I was familiar with from his work in Oliver Stone's 1986 war drama *Platoon* and Christopher Nolan's 2010 sci-fi thriller *Inception*. He was being honored with the second of two lifetime achievement awards at the festival.

My time at Gasparilla International Film Festival would be the first of many, mostly South Floridian, festival experiences. I loved that my short film was presented in the way it was intended: as big as possible. But the festival experience also challenged me to buff up my social and self-promotional skills so I could engage with other film professionals in the future without my usual nerves and general uneasiness.

As I returned home to Miami via private shuttle, I felt strongly compelled to fight my present emotional funk and continue a spirited engagement with the world, particularly as it came to my filmmaking. I also realized film festivals like these are always waiting to accept and celebrate the kind of talent, creativity and hard work I want to live for.

Considering the numerous festivals my work would be accepted to over the next few years...

They wouldn't be waiting long.

58. Generativity (February 2017)

At another meetup with my former high school English teacher (at Miami Killian Senior High) and mentor Mr. Michael Hill at "the 3rd Place" (a local Starbucks), Mr. Hill told me about an upcoming film-related event taking place at Arthur & Polly Mays Conservatory of the Arts, where he now taught. I expressed interest and made plans to visit APMCOTA for the event.

On the afternoon of the event days later, the auditorium at APMCOTA was filled with students from every grade level (Grades 6-12). The film festival known as the All-American High School Film Festival was visiting schools across the country in a roadshow-style tour to introduce students to the festival, screen several award-winning short films and generally encourage students to submit their work to the festival. The presenters were true showmen and the energy in that auditorium was electric as they energized the crowd of youths about the opportunities they were offering.

After the event was over, I spoke with Dr. Devin Marsh, Entertainment Technology and TV Production teacher at APMCOTA. Introducing myself as a local filmmaker with a substantial short filmography, he proposed having me come in to talk to his students about my filmmaking and share some of my work. I eagerly accepted and soon set to do so.

Not too long after that earlier film festival presentation, I found myself at the head of the APMCOTA auditorium presenting to several groups of Dr. Marsh's media students. I opened my presentation with a screening of my first short film, 2003's *Mass Education*. After that, I spoke about the origin of my interest in and practice of filmmaking and highlighted my collaboration with my go-to composer Ben Morris. I proceeded to screen each of our short film collaborations: 2013's *Proteus*, 2014's *Leo's Love Letter* and 2016's *The Promotion*. Each short film was received with considerable vigor; a welcome surprise given the age range of the audience. And after *The Promotion* played, one student exclaimed, "She got her wish!" suggesting younger audiences are sometimes more receptive to my intentions than the older crowd.

Concluding my presentation, I stressed ideas over technology, emphasized the importance of practice and invoked my own festival triumphs with micro-budget films to illustrate that more money doesn't equal greater formidability.

After the experience of presenting to the youth at APMCOTA, I spoke about it to Mr. Hill at another one of our regular Starbucks meetings. Any attempt to encourage and perhaps inspire young people, particularly in the direction of filmmaking, seemed like a socially responsible complement to my work as a filmmaker. Mr. Hill thusly encouraged me to consider becoming certified as a substitute teacher in order to teach at APMCOTA. He stressed that the school is always in need of substitutes and I would no doubt benefit from the experience.

Some months later, I finally took up Mr. Hill on his suggestion and enrolled in a course at Miami Dade College to earn my permit as a temporary instructor (a substitute teacher). After successfully completing the course, I applied to Miami-Dade County Public Schools and was accepted!

I could now substitute teach at any K-12 school in the district.

Right away, Mr. Hill put me in touch with APMCOTA's sub coordinator and I immediately found myself in her good graces. This allowed me to land a near-full-time schedule of substitute teaching right off the bat!

I taught in a variety of classes at APMCOTA and I found the days mostly enjoyable. The role of facilitating the education of young people was new to me and I began to consider it in a light I never had before. I increasingly looked forward to each new day at APMCOTA.

However, the opportunities to substitute for Dr. Marsh in his entertainment technology and TV production classes were easily the highlight of my time as a substitute. On one particular occasion, I had to help a number of his classes with a storyboarding assignment. Here I was able to wield my extensive knowledge in pre-visualization for film. So active and invested was I in assisting my students with their projects that I plumb lost track of time and the hour elapsed in a seeming quarter of the time.

On another memorable occasion I was able to partner with Mr. Hill during one of his lectures. As Mr. Hill and I took turns addressing the class, I was able to flex my filmmaking chops as well as my film criticism muscles - and directly alongside my most valued mentor, no less!

Unfortunately, my time at APMCOTA would be fairly short-lived. At the start of the following year, I decided that I had to buckle down and get back to focusing on my ambition to mount and complete my first feature-length film production. So, I decided to leave APMCOTA as a full-time sub even though I'd occasionally return to keep my temporary instructor status active.

Despite its brevity, my time at APMCOTA had instilled in me a previously unknown appreciation for the concept of generativity. This new understanding would inform my motivation to speak out often about my experiences in filmmaking through various interviews and a great deal of content on my website.

Maintaining a special regard for the guidance and inspiring of young people would become a parallel objective as I continued my work as a filmmaker.

59. Guidance (March 2004)

"Ms. Mahoney?" an office staffer asked via the classroom PA speaker, interrupting my International Relations teacher's lecture.

"Yes?" my teacher responded.

"Could you send Gabriel Rhenals to the counselors' office?" the staffer requested.

"I will. Thank you!" Ms. Mahoney affirmed.

Moments later, I was excused from my elective class and walked to the counselors' office located to the left of the main office. Over two years ago, I first visited an assigned counselor to assist with my transition from New World School of the Arts to Miami Killian Senior High.

I was aware that seniors at Killian were being asked to meet with their counselors about their plans for college. It was now my turn.

Upon arrival at the offices, my counselor, an Indian-American woman, invited me to join her in her office and reiterated the purpose of our meeting. Nothing surprising.

"Have you thought about what kind of career you'd be interested in pursuing?" she asked.

"I want to be a film director," I replied out of pure reflex.

My counselor seemed surprised. "I don't really see that for you," she replied doubtfully.

I couldn't believe what I'd just heard.

But completely ignoring her alarming incredulity, I immediately launched into diplomatic, self-promotion mode. "I've already made a short film here at Killian. It's called *Mass Education*. I wrote, produced, directed, shot and edited it all by myself," I proudly relayed to the high school employee.

She was surprised and a touch intrigued.

"I can show it to you. I have a copy of it in my backpack," I explained.

"Okay, I'd like to see it," she replied.

"I'll be right back!" I said rather excitedly.

After a race back to my International Relations class, I briefly explained to Ms. Mahoney that I needed to get something from my bookbag. Ever since completing my first short film, I always carried a CD copy of it among my belongings.

I raced back to my counselor's office.

As the short film played on her office's desktop computer, I offered commentary on the most challenging aspects of the production. I also highlighted the thematic and satirical underpinnings behind the piece. She seemed captivated by the film throughout the entire 4-minute runtime and intrigued by my supplemental verbal content. After my presentation was concluded, I stressed my fervent interest in filmmaking.

"Then what school were you thinking of applying to?" she asked.

"I'm not sure," I replied.

"Well, you may want to look into a university that offers film direction as a major," she advised.

I sat pensive for a moment and with the meeting concluded, I returned to my International Relations class.

Although I'd appreciated the counselor's positive reception to my novice work, what her immediate skepticism said about the guidance counseling at Killian was upsetting to me. I'd been hurt by someone who, in their position, was supposed to encourage, support and facilitate the aspirations of the youth under their auspices.

The counselor's snap judgment may have been based on nothing more substantial than my usually timid and reserved manner of the time. But I showed her that beyond mere appearances, there was a rapacious and highly motivated creative mind at work.

I'm glad I was able to demonstrate how mistaken she was.

60. Handcrafted (August 2016)

After 14 years, my career making short films was coming to an expected close. After completion of my 16th short film *The Promotion*, I would set my eye exclusively on feature-length filmmaking. I'd always seen short films as a temporary but necessary stepping stone toward the principal currency of the professional film industry - feature films. Having dedicated ample time to my short films, I considered them as mere pencil sketches in anticipation of eventual graduation to longer-form films or, to continue my analogy, the much more demanding process of painting with oils.

Now in the thick of post-production on *The Promotion*, I was almost singularly responsible (my composer Ben Morris would be fashioning the original musical score for the short film at the tail end of post-production) for putting the final technical touches on this story of a young woman who's all about her career despite her father's warning.

With deft performances from the entire cast (Stephanie Maltez, Juan Iglesias, Cristina De Fatima and Emmanuel Franco) and expert sound mixing by Evan Burr, I now looked forward to honoring all the work that had gone into production by conducting post-production with the same high regard for quality. The short film's themes of workaholism and inspiration felt particularly apt as I turned my attention to tackling these remaining technical tasks.

When the main character Em, played by Stephanie Maltez, is promoted at the nameless company she works for in the short film, she soon experiences the unreal implications of her career advancement: She cannot leave the floor of her office and remains indefinitely trapped - or consumed - by her workplace!

Before Em realizes her initially terrifying predicament, she attempts to descend to the building's bottom floor via stairwell. However, after attempting to descend the flight of stairs from her current floor she appears to descend the staircase from the above floor in a moment of Mobius Strip-like spectacle!

As I described it to Stephanie in a text, I wanted the feeling of the scene's dramatic revelation to be both "scary and awesome." In order to accomplish this visual of a person descending a looping stairwell, I had to carefully determine what elements I needed and how I'd combine them using Adobe After Effects, a powerful piece of motion graphics software I had extensive experience with.

Through countless man-hours spent at my desktop computer and numerous instances of tossing out initial attempts at pulling off these few but challenging shots, I was testing the limits of my video compositing know-how like never before. Combining such techniques as re-timing footage, motion tracking and rotosplining in complicated ways, the process was slow and arduous. But over the course of many, many attempts I was soon arriving at practically seamless results (if you knew where not to look!).

If the trick was executed shoddily, the sense of verisimilitude built up over the course of the entire short film would be shattered for the audience. It was critical that the visual spectacle of this moment in the film be pulled off immaculately. The crux of this short film rested on this climax's nakedly upfront visuals.

Taking a break from working on those highly demanding shots, I turned my attention to a different but equally necessary task. I needed to perform some on-location sound recording of footsteps, doors opening and closing, elevator sounds and general indoor ambience. I'd acquire all of them from the same building on the Florida International University campus I'd filmed many of the scenes.

In characteristic DIY (Do It Yourself) fashion, I set out to FIU with my tripod, DSLR camera and an external microphone (attached to the camera via hot shoe) to record my needed sound recordings. I performed the sound-producing actions myself and allotted for numerous takes in the interest of variety and safety to be absolutely sure I acquired what I needed.

Despite the fact that the sound work I was performing would be practically invisible to any audience of the film compared to the more attention-grabbing, infinity-stairwell shots, I was proud of regarding no detail as too small to engage my full energies.

After completing those complex stairwell shots and carefully applying the gathered sound effects I'd grabbed from FIU to the edit of the film, I handed off a practically complete version of the film to my composer Ben Morris, who'd be producing the short film's original score as the final stage of post-production dictated.

Whether major or minute, important or seemingly insignificant, I absolutely relished my involvement with virtually every aspect of the filmmaking process. I lived for it.

Bill Watterson, author and illustrator of *Calvin and Hobbes,* once said something about his work that bears some relevance to my own creative strivings: "There is great personal satisfaction in attending to detail and quality, and I remain very proud of the standards the strip met day after day. I also liked the responsibility of knowing that, succeed or fail, it was all my own doing... I wrote every word, drew every line and painted every color. It's a rare gift to find such fulfilling work and I tried to show my appreciation by giving the strip everything I had to offer."

Ditto for me.

61. Hijacking (April 2005)

The end of the spring semester was approaching at Florida International University and the Myth, Ritual and Mysticism course I was enrolled in as a freshman at FIU was concluding with a series of group presentations based on nearly semester-long group projects.

My group, tasked with exploring deep-rooted traditions of attempting to divine the future, would be presenting after the current group. We had a 22.5-minute video to play for the class.

My fellow group members were waiting patiently but as the presenting group shared some generic video clips with the class, I was concerned that they were going to step on our time. So, I spoke to one of their group members off to the side who insisted that their presentation was nearly done. They couldn't see the gritted teeth and rising anger behind my calm and polite facade.

After the presenting group finished their comparably tame show but before they properly vacated the front of the classroom, my group stepped up to bat. My group introduced our video with a few choice words about the topic we'd been assigned as I summarily cued up the video playback.

I made sure the classroom speakers' volume level was near its maximum, hit play and then shuffled to the back of the darkened classroom to sit among my fellow classmates as we watched the result of a video project I'd essentially hijacked from the get-go.

A dreary synth soundtrack soon emanated from the classroom speakers accompanied by the visual of a dark blue-tinted maze on the front projection screen. This is how my group's video, titled *The Predictors of the Future*, began...

When our group first met, I stayed rather quiet and simply observant as everyone else tossed around presentation ideas. All rough, all tentative.

Later that evening, I started brainstorming ideas on my own for a potential video presentation that was partly inspired by one of Lydia's ideas; Lydia was one of the more involved and motivated members of the group. I came up with an idea for a story-driven video that would incorporate all of the facets of our assigned topic.

On the next occasion my group convened, I shared my idea. It would involve Lydia playing the part of a student who has a series of encounters with each member of an unusual, unlisted student group called The Predictors of the Future. The narrative would neatly and elegantly incorporate all the different topics each group member was assigned by having each of them present their distinct angle on predicting the future to the journeying protagonist.

I immediately gained unanimous consent for my idea and started drafting a loose script shortly thereafter. Only the segues between the members' presentations in the video needed to be scripted. Each member would need to script their respective segment.

As soon as the script was complete and approved by the group, we decided that I would be the director of the video as I, by and far, had the most experience in video production. We would film on weekends on the FIU campus.

Over the course of a few weekends, I filmed the scenes of Lydia meeting with each of the other group members:

- Samantha the Dream Doctor interpreted dreams.
- Billie the Tarot Card Reader conducted the art of Tarot.
- David the Medicine Man read palms.
- Junior the Numerologist found significance in numbers.
- Danny the Prophet offered cryptic prophesying.

The presentations were serviceable and satisfied the project guidelines but Danny's presentation was particularly special to me because in his case, he wouldn't be responsible for the verbal content of his presentation like the others were. Instead, I would take the reins and write virtually every word of his part in the video.

I introduced Danny's prophet character as a student "unaccounted on any attendance roster, living in desolation and alone on the 13th floor of the Green Library since 1989" and, with a touch of absurdity, this 13th floor (FIU's Green Library only has eight floors) is described as being "made accessible by the simultaneous selection of the 6th and 7th floor." Lydia is then shown pressing the two elevator buttons at once and then the two buttons appear to blink simultaneously in confirmation of her selection (accomplished using motion graphics software)!

I wound up writing a nightmarishly grim narration that Danny would launch into following a brief bit of dialogue between him and Lydia. The narration would be accompanied by a bevy of images culled from exhaustive Google searches and all put to a selection of intense electronic music. I considered this portion of the videos its centerpiece, later dubbed the "Heart of Darkness".

Starting off with some dramatic footage of the 9-11 terrorist attacks shown to illustrate a highly dubious but nevertheless intriguing example of Nostradamus' prognostications, Danny soon spins his own precognitive vision for Lydia.

Danny describes a society (not ours surely!) wrapped up in imperialistic oil wars, ensconced in entertainment, entranced by moral absolutism and unwittingly given to an over-reliance on nuclear power. All oblivious to an alluded-to dark fate. As Danny levels a rather dim view of this nameless society, he intermittently points out that a population located a world away in a vast desert has been waiting patiently, gaining greater discipline and determined to "make their move."

Before long, the blue-tinted images of revelry, consumerism and tall cityscapes give way to blood-red images of nuclear explosions, mutilation and mass death against a soundtrack of blaring siren-like instrumentation. The intense cascade of devastating imagery stops at a shot of earth floating in space as Danny describes our home as a "now desolate, dry, ashen husk of a planet in an empty and indifferent universe."

The video concludes shortly after Lydia makes her way off-campus and has her thoughts about the series of strange encounters with the odd student group soon displaced by a pressing essay assignment for one of her classes.

After spending several days editing the video together, I screened it for my group on the media floor of FIU's Green Library. My first cut was generally well-received but some of the group members felt uneasy about the extensive use of 9-11 footage. So, I agreed to edit that portion of the video down. I also edited down some other parts of the video to conform to a mandated video presentation time limit of 25 minutes.

Once these changes were made, my group and I were finally ready to unveil the fruit of our labor to the class on our pre-established presentation date. Although this particular project wouldn't count as a canonical second short film of mine, I was just as proud to share it as though it were.

Throughout the video, many laughed at the bits of humor, both intentional and unintentional. While the required presentations that took place in the video were definitely pace-killers, I felt the creative segues between those parts compensated for those unavoidably slow spots. But one thing's for sure: The room fell utterly silent for Danny the Prophet's intimations about the future and its harrowing audio-visual illustration.

At the close of the video, our group received a hearty applause. Later, an older adult student told me that she appreciated "the framing" of the shots. It felt great to have my inordinate focus on camerawork acknowledged in that way. Later, I randomly polled another student about the video who gave a huge smile and remarked that she found the video "really funny."

As our grading went, our professor rewarded my group with an A for our effort or a 90/100, to be exact. But it was quite clear that many of us got so much more out of it than high marks. My group and I were exceptionally proud of what we'd accomplished and the time we spent working on the video together. To wit, the experience has continued to be a memory recalled with considerable fondness among those group members I've managed to keep in touch with over the years.

And nine years later, I did it again! When I returned to FIU to complete my undergraduate career as a Communication Arts major, I once again insisted on taking over all writing and directing duties on another assigned group video project; this time, for a course focused on intercultural communication.

I was quite proud of the resulting video and, like the take-over nearly a decade earlier at the same university, it was just as enthusiastically well-received by both classmates and the professor.

"He's the next Scorsese," one student quipped. Ha!

62. Idealism (September 2006)

Near the start of my first semester as a bonafide film student in University of Central Florida's limited-access film program, a man by the name of Mike McNamara showed up at our weekly colloquium to address the gathered film students.

The occasion for his appearance was promotion of his startup networking initiative based in Orlando and a major event his organization was putting together, involving a short film contest and talks by film industry figures, to be held in a few weeks at a local convention center. His newfound organization was interested in providing support, through said events and Mr. McNamara's pre-existing print publication, to us fledgling filmmakers. He was received well enough and, for my part, I listened intently to what he had to say.

Some time after that colloquium, I ran into Mr. McNamara in one of the film school building's hallways and told him a bit about myself and expressed my appreciation for his efforts to support wet-behind-the-ears filmmakers like myself. He seemed glad to engaged with me for a few minutes.

A week or so later, several of my friends and I made our way to Orange County Convention Center for the aforementioned event.

Famed *Clerks* filmmaker Kevin Smith was headlining the event and was expected to give a talk and take part in a Q&A that afternoon. Beforehand, however, a panel of Hollywood producers responsible for films like 2006's *Miami Vice* and 1990's *Teenage Mutant Ninja Turtles* (considered an independent film). I had learned that one of the producers who'd be participating in the panel was the father of a fellow UCF film school student with whom I'd interacted with on a few occasions. My friends were dead-set on seeing Kevin Smith live but I knew where I'd be investing more of my interest and attention.

The producers' panel was a fairly intimate affair and I found a seat fairly close to the row of panelists. Each of the four or so producers talked about their experiences in the film industry and generally had a great deal of insight to share.

After the panel was over, I approached Wayne Morris, father of the UCF film student I'd met and who'd been an associate producer on Michael Mann's crime drama *Miami Vice* earlier that year. *Miami Vice* had been one of the first major Hollywood films to be shot entirely digital. I wanted to have Mr. Morris' ear about how important such a choice meant to me.

So I approached Mr. Morris.

"Mr. Morris, hello! My name is Gabriel Rhenals and I'm a filmmaker and UCF film student," I announced.

"Thanks for coming," Mr. Morris replied.

"I just want to say that I really appreciate the decision to shoot *Miami Vice* digitally," I said. "I'd really like to see more Hollywood filmmakers push the change from analog to digital."

Mr. Morris was pleased to hear this.

"Maybe you'll be the one to inspire them to," he suggested.

I blushed.

"By the way, I happen to know your daughter Megan. She was a producer on a student film I worked on."

"Oh, is that so?" he said.

"I'll let her know I spoke with you," I replied and concluded, "Thanks for your time, sir."

Mr. Morris was charmed.

Despite the brevity of the conversation with Mr. Morris, I left the panel room feeling full of validation and encouragement from on high. Mr. Morris' daughter Megan would later tell me that I'd made a good impression on her father.

After the producers' panel, it was time to regroup with my friends for an audience with filmmaker Kevin Smith.

All I care to say about the Kevin Smith event was that it took place in one of the largest spaces I'd ever entered and among one of the largest crowds I've ever sat amongst. Kevin Smith is an incredible speaker with no shortage of anecdotes about his experiences in filmmaking and in

Hollywood. He told a countless many of them in an exhaustive Q&A that lasted hours longer than expected. As much as I enjoyed it, that was enough Kevin Smith for a lifetime.

Some time before the convention center event, I had written an email to Mike McNamara where I introduced myself at greater length than our in-person counter. I described how my approach to filmmaking involved "basing stories/content around available resources, adopting visual styles that maximize the use of very elementary tools, having very thorough pre-planning to greatly minimize time spent in production and having a hope to encourage and promote a local, bottom-up movie production/distribution/exhibition center somewhere in Florida. I also cited my current preoccupations as a filmmaker being "interested in getting to know the business of more ambitious productions, retaining a love of thrifty maneuvering and wanting to keep it all local."

Mr. McNamara wrote back soon after. He was pleased to have heard from me and wrote, "The experience you have over the next few years are going to be whatever YOU make it. Nothing is inherently good or bad, right or wrong. It is all subjective. Take water - it can either quench your thirst or drown you. Same with school, the film business, film festivals, events, etc. The ones who go above and beyond make it while the ones who feel entitled or just skate by the are the ones left complaining and making a bad name for the industry."

I appreciated Mr. McNamara's candor in response to my email and my perhaps overzealous self-regard. But as with my encounter with producer Wayne Morris at the convention center event, I never forget when someone far ahead of me career-wise is willing to level with me and share kind words of wisdom and encouragement.

It makes a difference.

63. Indecisive (January 2007)

My moviemaking momentum was at a peak upon return to University Central Florida following a several week-long winter break spent at my family home in Miami. I had managed to complete a (now non-canonical) still image-based experimental short film, titled *House Divided*, during my brief stint in South Florida. Its completion was a major confidence boost and I now felt ready to tackle a much more ambitious narrative short film.

Settled back into my on-campus apartment at UCF, I quickly set my sights on realizing the script for *Yeomans* which I'd attempted but failed to make over the previous summer. I would perform a substantial re-write on the script and re-title it *Back to School*.

To play the short film's lead role, I recruited one of my closest friends at UCF, Cris Mertens, a fellow Film BFA classmate and a highly motivated filmmaker in his own right. He also loved acting.

I didn't map out an entire shooting schedule or lock down every location right from the start. My plan was to manage the production day-by-day seeing as how the location and talent demands were fairly minimal.

It'd be a cakewalk, I believed.

The first day of production began at my apartment with an opening reverse-tracking dolly shot of Cris's character walking up a flight of stairs and entering his apartment. This shot was accomplished using my roommate Reid's office chair which Reid would wheel me backward in as I sat upon it with my camera. This makeshift approach worked well enough but getting the timing and movement to my satisfaction took an exorbitant amount of takes. Luckily, we landed on a few usable ones.

Moving right along!

The next few scenes we'd shoot on this first day of filming took place inside my apartment and included a simple dialogue scene between Cris and another roommate of mine Kyle, who agreed to participate as an actor. The scene was shot fairly easily as was another brief one which took place in my bedroom.

A successful first day!

Cris and I then scheduled to film in Millican Hall, one of UCF's administrative buildings, a few days later. The requirements were simple: two short, stationary dialogue scenes. In the first scene, Cris's character would be taking a call in the building's foyer and then a second scene involved a phone call in one of the building's elevators. We thought we'd be out of Millican Hall in a half-hour.

A cinch, I thought.

Everything Cris was asked to do he did perfectly. It was my performance behind the camera that quickly became an issue on this second day of filming. For the first scene, Cris need to walk a distance, respond to his phone going off and take a call while leaning against a wall. Easy enough except I couldn't for the life of me decide on the best angle to capture the proceedings. So, I asked for more takes than even I felt comfortable with until I settled for a less-than-ideal angle and composition. My doubts about it followed me into the next scene on the elevator.

Oh, boy...

Cris had his lines down for this short scene and was ready for direction. But at once I was unsure about where to put the camera. Too far back and the opening and closing of the elevator door between my camera and Cris would ruin takes. Too close and I wasn't sure the composition would clearly indicate that Cris was in an elevator. My indecisiveness, coupled with the sinking sensation that had carried over from the filming of the previous scene, was paralyzing and I struggled to give Cris adequate direction and begin recording takes. On top of all of this, I was concerned about essentially restricting building patrons from using the elevator. As I constantly readjusted and tinkered with my framing, I was being consumed by many doubts and pressures.

It was too much!

After what felt like an hour or more, I managed to film a few takes with

Cris but they were far below an acceptable level of quality in my mind. Overwhelmed and dissatisfied, I called it a day and apologized to Cris. I'm sure he detected some creative turbulence but he definitely couldn't see to what extent my self-doubt was devouring me.

As with a number of productions before this one, it was discontinued and eventually scrapped completely.

My mentality at the time was that every piece of a film production I embarked on had to be exactly right, particularly when it came to cinematography. There had to be no question whatsoever that I was making the best choices. But this extremely high standard of quality was as much a liability as an asset; a double-edged sword. If I succeeded, I was infinitely proud. But if I failed, I suffered a feeling of deep inadequacy.

This experience was yet another failure, to be sure. But a failure that would gradually prompt me to grow more decisive and accept a degree of healthy compromise when it came to the practice of my craft. I would need some more experience behind the camera with less complicated scripts before I was ready to climb back onto a steed of greater demand.

But I wasn't going to give up.

Never.

64. Ingenuity (April 2007)

A long night of editing lay before me as I settled into the editing lab in University of Central Florida's film school building one late afternoon toward the end of the Spring 2007 semester.

It was the end of my second year as a film student at UCF but I found myself prepared to put together a senior thesis project, or capstone film, of all things. I had gathered all of the necessary assets (i.e., footage, voice-over narration, visual effects shots, music, sound effects, etc.) I'd spent the past few months acquiring and was ready to give this post-production process a full night's attention with nary a break beyond necessary trips to a nearby restroom.

But why was I putting together a capstone film despite neither being a senior nor being enrolled in the respective capstone course?

Robert Grant.

Earlier on, Robert, a senior in the film program, had started production on his senior thesis project, titled *Jesus Christ Goes to Mars and Hitler Was Innnocent*. Robert had also been playing the title role. However, during production, some bizarre and aggressive behavior on the part of Robert led to a major falling out with his roommate and many of his friends during the filming of his project. Apparently, Robert was suffering from bipolar disorder and alcoholism.

After this dramatic turn of events, Robert was ostracized by his former circle of friends and stories about his unruly behavior reverberated throughout the film school.

Some time later, I encountered Robert on-campus and we soon found ourselves in conversation. He seemed rather despondent. I would later learn that he had started to take medication for his bipolar disorder diagnosis around this time. But having been friendly with him in the past,

I inquired as to how his capstone film was shaping up.

That's when his manner grew in desperation and he told me he needed help finishing it. He didn't mention what had happened between him and his former cohorts but I felt sympathetic to his plight. So, I questioned him at some length about his project's current state and at the end of our conversation, I took up his invitation to review what footage he had.

Later on, Robert showed me all of the footage he'd shot. It was made up of wholly disparate scenes with little connective rhyme or reason. But there was one clearly unscripted moment where Robert appeared to lose control of his emotions and breakdown in a fit of frustration and anger. As crazy as I am, I saw great potential in the material being shown to me! Before long I agreed to help Robert finish *Jesus Christ Goes to Mars and Hitler Was Innocent*... we'd axe the Hitler reference in fairly short order.

I immediately set myself to re-writing the film to allow for certain pieces of the already-shot footage to work alongside brand new elements I'd be filming and producing with Robert. More than up to the challenge, I would work with Robert in secret beyond the auspices of the capstone course or any of its professors. What would they think of a second-year film student essentially taking the reins of an upperclassmen's capstone film? I wasn't going to take any chance being prohibited from making the most out of this unique opportunity. I had utmost confidence!

The aforementioned re-write took several weeks and involved long nights wandering the campus mostly at night. I decided that an elaborate voice-over narration to be performed by Robert would be the key to combining new and old footage.

Before I started to work on the narration, however, I laid out a basic synopsis of the re-worked short film and presented it to Robert. The story basically followed a post-crucified Jesus Christ who travels to Mars with his dog Julius. Taken into Martian custody shortly after his arrival on the red planet, Jesus is once against prosecuted by the state. But this time, he's exiled to the vast Martian desert where he lives out the remainder of his human life with Julius at his side.

Robert was immediately charmed by my brief synopsis and with his approval, I set about writing the actual script, narration and all. Many of those lonely campus-wide walks involved writing and refining the narration that would be the key to making this Frankenstein creation work.

Drawing from other cinematic depictions of Jesus Christ, namely Martin Scorsese's 1988 film *The Last Temptation of Christ* and Pier Paolo Pasolini's 1964 film *The Gospel According to St. Matthew*, I was able to fashion a vision of this tragic messianic figure informed by the past and also imbued with a contemporary political twist and my own personal views. But more importantly, my writing granted connective, narrative logic to the otherwise random pre-existing scenes and set the stage for a series of new scenes to smooth over the patchwork. This short film would later join my short film canon as my 8th entry. I would become that proud of it.

After the long process of writing and refining the script, it was time to jump into production mode. With Robert's full cooperation, I filmed a series of new shots with him around UCF's campus and at Robert's off-campus apartment - still set-dressed from his initial attempt at the film. Using a blend of close-shots and clever angles, I was able to transform mundane locations into those of my fantastical take on Mars in this highly anachronistic tale.

When it came to recording narration, Robert was completely cooperative despite a lethargy likely the result of his medication regimen. In any case, with a little elbow grease we managed to record everything in a few sessions.

After this step, I would employ my visual effects know-how to produce a series of matte paintings and other elements involving a bit of 3D modeling and some animation work.

With all of the footage, voice-over narration, visual effects shots, music and sound effects gathered, I was now ready to fuse everything together in holy cinematic matrimony.

Upon entering, the editing lab was near-vacant with its last few occupants on their way out of the space for the night. I settled in before one of the iMacs and plugged in my external hard drive containing all of my assets.

I got straight to work. No visitors, no distractions.

As with an Editing I assignment earlier in the spring semester, I would become so engrossed with the job at-hand that I barely realized I'd worked all through the night and into the following morning; re-emerging from the film school building well after sun dawn - exhausted but fulfilled!

I was immediately thrilled by the results of my night-long endeavor and was able to have *Jesus Christ Goes to Mars* accepted by the capstone professors for screening at the end-of-year showcase a week or so later. The professors had asked to review a copy of the film prior to the decision so I guess they were rather impressed by the resurrection of this project once-presumed dead.

The evening of the capstone screening, the house was packed! Nearly all of the upperclassmen were represented along with many of their family members. Robert's family was in attendance and in an endearing gesture of gratitude they invited me to sit with them for the night's program. When they expressed their appreciation over what I'd done, I modestly suggested that I only wanted to make a good movie; a half-truth hiding a more compassionate sentiment. Sitting with Robert's family, we waited for *Jesus Christ Goes to Mars* to emerge in the line-up.

When our film finally played for the audience, the response was generally enthusiastic but the climax of the film, involving the unscripted scene of extreme emotional disturbance (the chief motivation behind my signing on to help Robert), received unexpectedly booming laughter from the near-entirety of the audience. Likely owing to this extraordinary moment, one of my roommates later described the short film as having been "a hit" with the audience. After the reaction I'd observed, I would be hard-pressed to disagree.

Owing to my reticence to discuss the conditions for the completion of the film with anyone except my close friends, the film professors at UCF were mystified by Robert's apparent surge from being behind his class. Some professors had their suspicion that Robert had been assisted by someone but no one knew the full story.

Allegedly, the film school chair Steve Schlow remarked that *Jesus Christ Goes to Mars* was one of the best short films he'd ever seen come out of UCF's film program. A staggering compliment, to be sure!

But whether this was true or not, what truly mattered was that I proved to myself that precious, glittering gold could be spun out of relatively worthless bales of hay.

Anything now seemed possible.

65. Initiative (January 2006)

At the start of the Spring 2006 semester, I was comfortably enrolled and ensconced at University of Central Florida but waiting to hear from the school's film program about my admission status. I had submitted my application and creative portfolio at the end of the previous fall.

Envious of the students who would be either starting their education as proper Film BFA students, I resolved to assign myself a project expected of them as part of their Directing I course.

From what I could gather, these first-year film school students were instructed to produce a narrative, dialogue-free and one-minute-long short film; the first of two major projects expected of them over the course of the semester.

I would be following similar parameters in producing a one-minute short film of my own. Although I'd proceed with none of the informed guidance and support provided by a class specializing in film direction, I was ready to prove my metal with this audacious self-assignment.

The one-minute time limit appealed to me despite the fact that my previous short films had been much lengthier. It seemed a sensible allotment for educational and training purposes. I also postulated how a filmmaker can entertain an audience for longer than a minute, let alone the runtime of a feature film (the ultimate destination), if they can't do so in only a minute's time?

The dialogue-free or silent rule was also intriguing. Since my interest in film began, the notion of pure cinema had always appealed to me; that visuals and editing should carry a film more than speech or dialogue. Taking narration or inter-character dialogue out of the picture also served to mask my perceived weakness in that area.

With these basic formal parameters in place, I needed to decide upon a subject for my short film.

It took some time but I finally landed upon...
Procrastination.

While I'd recently demonstrated ample self-discipline and time management skills enough to make Dean's List for the first time in my college career during my first semester at UCF, I was intimately familiar with being in the throes of deathly unproductivity and felt it would make for a universally relatable drama.

With the appropriate title of *The Procrastinator*, my short film would focus on a college student burdened by a lengthy paper assignment. I relished the ironic edge to focusing on a time-wasting protagonist when my previous two short films' main characters had demonstrated highly productive and effectual resolve. But as with most earnest art-making, there was intended to be more subtly at work than simply school and paper-writing. In any case, I completed a page-long script and set myself to produce it.

Throughout production, I found myself needing to complete a wide variety of odd jobs including but not limited to: Walking several blocks off-campus to purchase a roasted chicken to be included in a single shot; search for the tallest staircase on-campus; stand through the open sunroof of my roommate Dieri's SUV to record a bus traveling down one of the university area's busiest roadways; gathering up to 20 student extras for two separate scenes involving complex camera work; and gaining access to the top floor of a student apartment at the perimeter of campus in order to capture an elevated, wide shot of the UCF campus. For that last detail, I had a friend keep a backdoor to the tower ajar using a small plastic bottle so I could gain entry in the early morning hours required of the shot. Them's the breaks!

An overarching directive for the short film was to make every visual count with deliberate cinematography. In other words, I wanted careful compositions with absolutely no shooting from the hip. Additionally, I felt no color grading would be needed because the constant cascade of different locations, lighting and staging provided adequate visual interest.

With regard to editing, I wanted as fast a pace as possible despite exclusive emphasis on a single character ruminating, devoid of almost any interaction with others. My intent was to cram as much visual information into my one minute as possible. As a result, the average shot length of the short film would be no more than a few seconds.

A curious habit developed as I spent more time editing the short film. I would export the film in a low-resolution video file and scrub through it (i.e., drag the timeline marker to access different parts of the video) rapidly to appreciate said visual variety. Through this scrubbing, I also felt an uncanny sensation of watching my beleaguered character trapped within my aesthetic but confining construct.

When the *The Procrastinator* was completed, I screened it at UCF's film club to generally enthusiastic but somewhat muted reception. Perhaps some felt that the storyline was too trivial. However, the responses from some of my friends who watched the short film on separate occasions were interesting:

Sean, a UCF schoolmate partial to certain old masters, remarked, "It's edited like a trailer" and found its pace offensive.

Sam, a UCF classmate and fellow film program hopeful more acquainted with my peculiar artistic sensibilities, said, "You have a vision."

Dustin, a UCF schoolmate and also a fellow film program hopeful with whom I shared a similar sardonic attitude with, saw straight through the superficial trappings of the short film and declared, "It's about predestination." A most incisive observation!

But regardless of how others regarded my latest piece, I had my own share of self-criticisms: I had overstepped the boundaries of my self-assignment by going over the runtime limit by half-a-minute. Also, I was dissatisfied with the ending which, unlike those of most of my productions, was determined in detail fairly late into production.

Despite these fair, personal knocks against what was my 3rd short film, I experienced a high yield of creative and artistic takeaways. First, I had conducted the creation of a short film with a mind bent on greater economy and efficiency of expression. Also, I had further proven my commitment to my art by wearing so many wildly different hats. And beyond that, the experience of filming so extensively in a wide variety of public places and managing cast under those circumstances added to a sense of increased confidence and worldliness.

In view of everything, I'm glad I got my feet wet early with this Directing I-inspired short film production. However others or I felt about the final product, the principles exercised or originating throughout its creation would no doubt find purchase in future work.

What grade would I give myself?

I'm not sure but I'd definitely give myself extra points for initiative.

66. Inspiration (May 2008)

"Yeaaaaaaaaah!!!" screams a commentator, joining a chorus of exhilarated media correspondents from their reserved stands in the massive, Grand Prix stadium.

Speed Racer, having recovered from a dislodged main conductor by putting the car into fifth gear and jump-starting the engine, desperately races to catch up with the leaders.

"It doesn't matter if racing never changes," says Racer X in a flashback as Speed skillfully drifts down a length of track at top speed. "What matters is if we let racing change us," Racer X keenly advises.

We then see Speed Racer as a child, amusing himself with a flipbook animation fashioned out of the corner of his grade school test booklet. In it, two race cars collide into each other and explode. Speed provides some vocal sound effects as he flips through his crude animation.

"When I'm in a T-180, I don't know. Everything just makes sense," Speed recalls as he continues to fly past the competition.

"No hesitation! Nothing fazes him! No one seems capable of stopping him!" says one of the two official announcers as Speed's intense dash continues.

"He's on a mission," intones the other announcer with curious discernment.

"With a quarter lap to go, Speed Racer is back!" the first announcer exclaims as Speed closely trails the two leaders. "Two cars between him and destiny," the announcer adds.

The villainous Mr. Royalton, standing to lose everything if Speed proves victorious, cries out in agony as he watches the final moments of the race on a jumbotron, "Stopppppp himmmmmm!!!"

As Speed nears the lead, he is flanked by two cars and the trio of racers soon engage in some car-fu. But this is child's play for Speed.

"Here we go again!" utters one of the leaders.

Having toyed with them for a bit, Speed then backs off for a moment as the two drivers stay ahead. He then prepares for a final move as his family and all of the media personnel rise from theirs seats, everyone in anticipation of a major coup de grâce!

In a stunning move, Speed drives onto the adjoining, slanted track wall reserved for advertisements and gains a lead over the two remaining drivers. But he's not finished with them yet!

Not a moment later, Speed engages his car's spring feet and uses the fantastical, hook-like feature to grapple each of the two cars and slam them into the left and right barriers, respectively.

With tremendous inertia, the two launched vehicles tumble over and over along the track barriers until both twisted heaps of metal collide into each other and explode! By the force of the explosion, Speed is launched into the air through the mess of airborne debris and at such incredible speed that it warps our aptly named protagonist's very perception of space, causing the red and white checkered floor of the finish line area to bend around his car in an utterly sublime and unforgettable peak moment!

With the laws of physics soon restored, Speed's race car screeches to a stop atop melted tires - to the cheering and flashbulbs of thousands!

Speed Racer had won the day!

I left my solo weekend matinée screening of the Wachowski sisters' *Speed Racer* a changed person. In the wake of a serious mental health crisis that had me recovering at home in Miami after being withdrawn from University of Central Florida, it was the perfect antidote to my unfortunate slump and retreat from the world.

Beyond *Speed Racer*'s compelling story and characters, the film's bold, aggressive visual style and its inspiring, intensely cathartic finale had super-charged my creative drive (no put intended) in a way that few films ever had. The film immediately shot up to the number one spot on my list of favorite films of all-time!

It is no coincidence that days after that screening I set my sights on a new short film production. This return to filmmaking after my grave mental health woes was also spurred by the announcement of a short film contest being held by an online forum dedicated to owners and enthusiasts of my model of video camera, the Canon HV20. The assigned theme was technology.

I immediately began my writing process.

This new project, later titled *The Nap*, would be a simple yarn about a wife's harrowing experience using her car to pick up her sister from the airport after her husband had made some mysterious modifications to the vehicle.

Inspired by anxieties about a potential peak oil crisis, the film would touch upon themes of clean energy and oil scarcity, in addition to the requisite theme of technology. Even though my previous short *Rough Cut* had been a far more experimental effort, I decided to apply a more conventional narrative form to this project. While *The Nap* was initially intended to be a silent film constituted of visuals and music alone, weeks into production I would re-work the film to include spoken dialogue.

The Nap would be the first short film of mine to be shot in high-definition. So taken was I by the unabashedly digital nature of *Speed Racer*, I experienced a newfound appreciation for the dramatically improved crispness and dynamic range afforded by HD video. With this new format came a new frame of mind: I wanted my new short film to have an immaculate HD digital sheen and proudly flaunt it!

In keeping with my tendency to cast non-actors, I recruited my parents in the lead roles and began a production that would last about six months.

Despite a challenging mental health episode that had left my life in shambles, *Speed Racer* had worked its magic. As Speed's father Pops expresses earlier in the film, "...something just clicked. Like a light being switched on inside of me. After that, I never had trouble remembering how I liked my eggs."

67. Kindred (March 2006)

"Wait a second," Cris Mertens alerted me as I approached the passenger side of his parked sedan. "I have to open your door from inside."

The front passenger door handle was broken on Cris' worn but trusty transport.

Cris Mertens was a fellow University of Central Florida film student whose acquaintance I'd made during my second semester at UCF. He'd watched some of my short films and now he'd invited me to his off-campus apartment to view some examples of his own filmmaking.

It was uncanny. Cris' vehicle, a beige late-90s Toyota Camry, was the same make, model, color and almost same year as the one I'd left back at home when I came to study at UCF. I didn't need my car because I wouldn't be working while studying at the Orlando university and my apartment had a regular shuttle service to and from campus. For any travel off campus grounds, I regularly carpooled with friends and roommates.

During this latest carpool trip not a mile away from campus, Cris described a lease-related snafu due to a water leak in his apartment and inadequate action taken by residential management. He was flustered and incredulous over the issue but he described everything with remarkable clarity and detail. I would soon learn that this impressive degree of lucidity and exactitude were highly characteristic of Cris.

When we arrived at his apartment, Cris led me to his bedroom and I spotted some DVDs and DVD cases casually strewn about his personal living space. A telling sign of an obsessive film lover in my midst.

Cris gathered an additional chair for me and we both sat down in front of his desktop PC in the corner of his room. I noticed he had a desktop wallpaper from the *The Elder Scrolls* game series. Ever the gamer.

After showing me a few videos of which all were short, sleek and well-edited, Cris introduced a five-second video (believe it or not) he'd made for a short film contest.

I thought, what on earth can you do in five seconds?

Cris played the brief video.

After it played, my question was hanging out of my mouth. My mind was left reeling from the video's raw energy and bold form. It combined frenetically edited visuals of an athlete runner with a car speedometer put to the soundtrack of the revving-up of a powerful engine. I'd never known anyone capable of producing anything with such a degree of visual heat and intensity. To put it simply, I was blown away!

Cris explained how he'd achieved some of the video's most impressive effects but had been sorely disappointed by the outcome of the contest; not that his clearly belabored video hadn't won but that the chosen winner had been a single-take video of a baby doing something cute. C'est la vie.

I had admired how dexterous Cris had shown to be with his editing software and when I inquired about his NLE of choice, he shared that he'd edited everything he'd shown me using Adobe Premiere, the same software I'd used for all of my own editing. Cris explained further that he'd made a deal with his parents: Help me pay for the software and I promise to learn how to use it and take full advantage of it. And that's exactly what he did.

Seeing these early examples of his work and learning about his from-the-start dedication to the art and craft of editing, I knew great success was an inevitability for Cris.

In the two years we spent together in the limited-access film program at UCF, Cris and I sat in many of the same classes, worked on numerous sets, kept active with our own extra-curricular short film projects, attended many theatrical film screenings (seeing Zack Snyder's 2006 film *300* in IMAX was a particularly memorable highlight) and geeked out on countless occasions.

We were constantly in touch throughout our ensuing time at UCF and there existed a constant cross-fertilization between our ideas about film and filmmaking. We also shared a fervent interest in mainstream filmmaking which seemed like anathema to our fellow colleagues at the time but which we joyfully relished. On top of that, we seemed to share a certain eye for greater speed and intensity in our craft - and perhaps even in life.

But one of the qualities I most admired about Cris, very likely owing to his military base upbringing in far-off places as Saudi Arabia and Japan, was his worldly character. Such a personality type allows seamless integration with practically any group of people and a high tolerance for ambiguity. Therefore, Cris was always ready to blaze a trail in any social situation and with plenty of humor along the way, I might add.

Not long after that late night visit to his apartment during my second semester at UCF, Cris remarked about it in the following way on Facebook:

"Yo Gabriel. Thanks for watchin my stuff. I enjoyed your films, so now itll be cool to possibly work together in the future, seeing as how we have the BFA program ahead of us. Ahoy!"

And I in turn:

"Oh man! Thanks for showing me your work the other night. Your proficiently in Premiere is astounding! I await next semester with great anticipation. I know I'll be seeing great work!"

I couldn't have been more right.

After graduating from UCF, Cris moved to L.A. and unsurprisingly worked his way up the film industry food chain. He is currently employed as a full-time editor at Warner Bros. Animation and occasionally works as a freelance editor on indie projects. He no longer has to open his car's passenger side door from the inside. He is also a father.

Cris has remained one of my closest friends.

68. Learning (May 2012)

It was the first day of University of Miami's 15th Annual Canes Film Festival and I found myself sitting comfortably on my own in the school's spacious but sparsely-filled Cosford Cinema auditorium.

The Canes Film Festival is the end-of-year showcase of student films from UM's film program. The event programs about 120 short films over the course of three days and culminates in a ritzy award presentation on the evening of the final day.

The first day's program consisted primarily of first-year students' work and didn't draw too much attention from the local community. But I took the occasion to explore the caliber of work being produced at UM, perhaps to see how it compared with the output from University of Central Florida's film school, where I'd studied for several years. I was also interested in seeing the work produced by several students I'd gotten to know over the past several months working on some of the films that were also now seeing exhibition at the festival.

But after several hours of mostly freshman student short films, I badly needed a break. I enjoyed the exposure to so many different short films but I was painfully reminded of how difficult it is to make a good short film. In my experience, it's an ability few seem to reliably possess and I know I suffered long and hard with each entry of my own canon to escape that most dreaded fate - mediocrity.

So in need of some relief from the relentless cavalcade of novice filmmaking, I ventured out into the terrace lobby to stretch a bit and give my scrutinizing mind a rest. There I found another festivalgoer who was also in need of some repose from the endless stream of noble but ill-fated creative efforts.

Engaging in some friendly conversation, I'd soon learn that this kindly fellow festival attendee was a UM graduate named Kenneth Rubi. He offered up his take on the common pratfalls of UM's starting-out student filmmakers and I did the same. Kenneth and I shared the view that some of the work that seemed to have been produced as an in-class project in doubtless committee-like fashion were the worst offenders to our taste. And we generally agreed on a point that I'd later learn is called Sturgeon's law: Ninety percent of everything is crap.

Properly refreshed, I bid Kenneth farewell and returned to my seat in the auditorium. Despite my tested patience with the first day's programming, I would return for the second and third day of the festival.

The more intermediate and senior-level projects that made up the remainder of the festival's offerings were somewhat better for obvious reasons. However, I was struck by a recurring dichotomy among the films: The student films that were more comically-inclined were mostly unpolished technically while the films that were technically virtuosic lacked a matched level of comedy or charm. I guess it's just as hard to show refinement at a jamboree as it is to spread whimsy at a suit-and-tie affair.

But this was just one of the many insights about the art and craft of filmmaking I gleaned throughout this immense student film screening tear; a unique opportunity to truly reflect on the nature of cinema.

While the programming logically improved as the event wore on, nothing prepared me for *Beyond Duty*, directed by a film student named Eric Taggart. *Beyond Duty* was a contemporary military thriller that confounded all of my expectations about the achievable heights of the students in UM's film program. It was narratively engaging, deftly directed, visually appealing, tightly edited and absolutely worthy of its unquestionably expensive production design. Although I'm never one to heap too much praise on films of such jingoistic themes and sentiment, the film was met with an ecstatic reception once the credits rolled and that's nothing to sneeze at. When a good film is made, everyone wins.

On the third and final night of the festival, it was time for the Canes Film Festival's closing night event - a lavish award ceremony! The lobby was transformed for the event and featured a red carpet, live DJ, refreshments and decorative movie paraphernalia. In the stage area of the auditorium was a table upon which were numerous coconut-shaped trophies for the winners of the many categories. Not even UCF, the second-largest university in the country, expended as much money and resources to celebrate the creative accomplishments of its students. I was quite impressed.

Throughout the award ceremony, I took the opportunity to greet my fairly new UM friends and share some words of appreciation about the work of theirs I'd seen over the past three days. They were happy to hear it.

After I had engaged socially and wore my extroverted side out, I left UM's campus that night as I had arrived three days earlier: by myself and nursing a zeal for film and filmmaking. I would end up attending the next few years' Canes Film Festivals and having a similar experience each time.

For me, it was an invaluable learning experience.

69. Limitations (July 2015)

After working on it for about six months, I'd completed a 23-page first draft of a short film script I'd titled *Alumna*. It was expected to be my 16th and final short film. The writing process had been long and difficult. I'd spent many hours at a Florida International University computer lab in-between my classes hashing out the script.

A rather stark drama and love story with a supernatural twist, *Alumna* presented the tale of a female university student who becomes closely involved with a mysterious, university-dwelling young man. As the story progresses, stakes run high and some degree of violence erupts as we discover that not all approve of the bond formed between the two young people. It would have been shot entirely on FIU's campus.

Alumna was and remains my longest and most ambitious short film idea. It featured the most multi-dimensional characters I'd yet written and dialogue scenes in far greater length and quantity than I was used to at the time. I fully expected to tap the services of an on-set sound mixer for the production in what would have been a first (excluding a classmate's brief stint as one on my first short film *Mass Education*).

About a week after completing my first draft of *Alumna*, it was the night before an event I was interested in attending the following day. FilmGate Miami would be spotlighting local filmmaker Kenny Riches and he'd be giving a talk about his experience making his debut feature film, 2015's indie comedy *The Strongest Man*, and getting accepted into Sundance Film Festival.

That same night, Lucasfilm/Disney released a brief behind-the-scenes video to promote the year-end release of the first of the new *Star Wars* films under Disney. The excitement and enthusiasm from the cast and crew of the film was utterly infectious. I couldn't sleep.

As I sat at my computer in the wake of viewing the video (multiple times), I wanted to feel an alike level of gusto toward my latest creative work. Although I had a complete script sitting idly by and waiting to be produced, I soon realized that *Alumna* wasn't cutting it. My confidence in the project fell to zero that night.

Back to the drawing board that same night, I began to entertain vague new ideas about what a totally revamped final short film script could be. I immediately pictured something far shorter, more economic and far more propulsive. I'd still involve Stephanie Maltez, of course, but this new idea had to have fire!

Clearing the slate - again, on the same night - I soon established some new parameters to determine the bounds of my brainstorming process. I decided that I wouldn't pursue another love story so as not to repeat what I'd done with my previous short film *Leo's Love Letter*. This impulse toward not repeating my earlier successes in an attempt to reinvent my approach to my art with each new project would become a greater consideration moving forward. For this new idea, I determined that a fervor for work was just as alluring a theme to me as one celebrating love.

So, Stephanie Maltez and work!

I also decided that, as in *Alumna*, I'd retain the idea of localizing the entire short film story to a single place. I rather liked this peculiar feature of my earlier script.

So, now it was Stephanie Maltez, work and a single location.

Challenged to maximize the potential within these basic parameters, I set out to develop a new idea for what would still be my final short film script and production.

On that night before the Kenny Riches event, the ideas flowed and I didn't sleep a wink. My mind reeled with possibilities and in the days to follow, I would come up with one of my most irreverent and bold ideas yet - *Monsters Now Hiring*.

Intended as a comedic horror film, *Monsters Now Hiring* told the story of a young woman looking to get her start in the corporate world by interviewing with three potential employers. However, these three employers would curiously resemble the starting line-up of classic movie monsters: Dracula, the Mummy and the Wolfman. After these initial interviews prove unsuccessful, the main character is contacted by and meets with a seemingly normal employer - but that couldn't be further from the truth. In an explosive revelation, we learn that the interviewer and interviewee share something secret and extraplanetary in common.

Stephanie was stoked about the idea and I was so encouraged by my latest creation that I actually began filming the opening scene of a university graduation during FIU's commencement ceremonies later that year.

But despite this initial momentum, production on *Monsters Now Hiring* was soon discontinued when the logistics of the climactic scene proved far too challenging to pull off effectively. I would later turn the short script into a one-page short story.

I would explore other ideas in the space between abandonment of *Monsters Now Hiring* and coming up with the idea for *The Promotion*, the short film idea which ultimately became my 16th and final short film.

While it was a tough climb to realize my short filmmaking swan song, I thank my decision to impose boundaries on what would otherwise become a process of near or very much infinite creative gestation. Sometimes deliberately choosing to fight with one arm tied behind your back can motivate you to exercise greater craftiness and skill.

Pow!

70. Madness (October 2007)

"Then a few weeks into the semester, I began to feel different... It's difficult to explain and I don't know exactly why I began to feel this way... but something triggered a chemical imbalance in my brain that propelled me into something I've never experienced before in my entire life."
-Max, Semester of Madness (2012)

No response.

Professor Harris beckoned his class once more.

"So, no one can tell me what the paintings in the background throughout the film say about the filmmakers' overall visual strategy?" he asked with a characteristic frustration mounting in his voice.

My Film Theory I class at University of Central Florida had just finished watching Rainer Werner Fassbinder's 1972 German-language drama *The Bitter Tears of Petra von Kant* and my fellow classmates seemed particularly paralyzed by what they'd just seen; a lurid five-act film about a torrid lesbian love affair confined to a single location.

Professor Harris looked disappointed.

But I knew.

I knew precisely what the paintings in the background throughout the film said about the filmmaker's overall visual strategy. However, I thought my ideas must remain a secret due to their profoundly provocative and disturbing nature.

So I kept my thoughts to myself but chuckled audibly in amusement as the professor presided over his mystified class.

Perhaps in response to my chuckle, the professor's tone changed to one of admonishment, though not toward me directly. He expressed his disappointment with the collective lack of response and moved onto a new topic - an upcoming essay assignment.

After class let out, I felt on top of the world! It seemed I alone was capable of deciphering esoteric foreign films where no one else could. I even thought my ideas were far in advance of the professor's own. I began to feel as though I had an incomparably preternatural understanding of all films and filmmakers.

Those secrets I was nursing in class? They were growing increasingly vivid and indicative of how I was beginning to see almost everything just over a month into the Fall 2007 semester at UCF.

My madness was slowly taking hold.

In general, I grew increasingly fearless and uninhibited socially. I felt as though I could see through anyone I encountered; as if only I could pierce through their poised social veneer. I would lock eyes with almost anyone and proceed to speak with them volubly, assuming a great deal about their underlying motives.

Beyond that, I entertained grandiose and messianic ideas about myself. I believed myself to be a prophetic figure with a cosmic link to the greatest minds, leaders and pioneers throughout history.

These delusions were accompanied by a phenomenon known as ideas of reference wherein I found special personal significance in unrelated and irrelevant things. I felt as though there were coded messages and patterns in my professors' lectures, the films I'd watch in class and in the casual conversations among friends. I mostly kept this unusual experience to myself but I accepted the seeming reality of it all without any resistance.

One evening upon returning to my apartment from a routine swim in my apartment complex's pool, I began to feel unsafe. Walking the distance from the pool to my apartment building, dressed only in swim trunks and a towel strewn about my body like a poncho, I felt like I was being watched and stalked by several random bystanders in the area. So, I rushed home.

As I dressed into my casual wear, I heard some voices outside my second-story apartment window. I believed the strangers who I'd suspected of quietly stalking me were deliberately meeting just outside my apartment building and conspiring against me.

I stormed out of my bedroom and called out to my roommates Josh and Reid. They soon emerged from their respective bedrooms.

I immediately broke down into tears and confessed my fear that I was going to be destroyed by strangers just outside our apartment.

Not killed. Destroyed!

In the midst of an ensuing, seismic panic attack, I settled into a living room chair and admitted to a litany of truths I felt I'd uncovered over the past few weeks. Although from my roommates' perspective, it probably sounded like the most extreme paranoia - which it was. As I continued to explain, I felt as though my mouth was attempting to close itself involuntarily, preventing me from revealing more to my cohabitants.

And they were absolutely terrified! Reid was wide-eyed and Josh was hyperventilating.

As my panic attack wound down, I asked Josh and Reid not to tell anyone about what had happened. They agreed, if only to help quell my alarming condition.

I was eventually sufficiently calm to return to my bedroom for my night's sleep. Josh and Reid also retired, the two both undoubtedly shaken and concerned.

The following morning, I woke up to an eerie calm.

When I accessed the internet on my bedroom computer, every article headline on my slate of regularly visited websites seemed to be referencing me. The world was finally recognizing my cosmic importance, I thought.

I had received an email about an event being put on by a student political organization I was affiliated with. A guest speaker was intended to give a talk but I assumed that I would be the genuine guest of honor. So, I departed for campus.

I left my apartment and upon approaching the shuttle stop nearby, I felt oddly protected by what I believed was vehicular traffic under control of my favorite filmmakers. When the shuttle arrived and I boarded it, I made comments to my fellow passengers suggesting that I suspected they were local actors hired to appear as students as a sort of charade; a charade I could see through.

All three symptoms were at play on this strangest of strange campus visits: delusions, ideas of reference and paranoia. When I arrived at the site of the guest speaker event, there were only two or so students at the event site. In actuality, I'd arrived after the event had taken place but in my illness I believed that the event had been set up as a sort of ruse to summon me to campus.

As I left the Student Union, the campus felt unusually vacant. Perhaps, I thought, authorities were clearing out the campus grounds so no one would be present for what the authorities had planned for me.

It soon dawned on me that the campus was likely being evacuated in preparation for my assassination. I held too many vital secrets to be allowed to live.

When I made this realization, I soon encountered Kyle, my former roommate. I joined him at a table with two of his friends and felt as though they were cryptically referencing me and my dire situation. I felt resigned to imminent doom but had one last request for my friend.

"I was here," I told Kyle.

"What?" Kyle responded.

"So someone knows in case something happens to me," I intoned quietly.

Kyle and his friends seemed perplexed and I soon got up and left.

Believing I was being tracked by the police, both UCF's and those of a broader government agency, I made a dummy trek around campus and even hopped on a shuttle for a ride back to the apartment complex where I used to live when I first started attending UCF. After my feeble attempts at some sort of fake-out, I decided to return to my actual apartment.

When I finally arrived, my roommates were nowhere to be seen.

I went to my bedroom and accessed my computer. As in the morning, it seemed as though my news sources of preference were aware of my existence. What sick game was this? Why hadn't the police killed me yet? What were they waiting for?

I heard the front entrance door of my apartment open and two men announce themselves.

"UCF Police!" they shouted.

As my heart beat began to race, I gradually exited my bedroom and approached the living room area to confront the officers.

"Are you Gabriel?" one of them asked.

I immediately raised my arms and came to tears. However, they didn't pull out their weapons to finish me off. Instead, they asked me about what had happened the previous night. My roommates had apparently contacted campus authorities about my dramatic unraveling.

I shook and trembled as I explained; my explanation no doubt freighted with all the strange and unrealistic ideas I'd shared with my roommates during the previous night's panic attack.

Experiencing another but somewhat milder emotional breakdown before the officers, the pair of uniformed men soon explained that they were going to take me to a place where I would receive the right care and attention.

I regained my calm and completely believed them.

I believed I was going to be taken to meet privately with luminaries of the motion picture industry who were interested in meeting the great, prophetic and all-knowing Gabriel Rhenals. The right care and attention indeed! I had too many secrets that could upend civilization as it was known so I acquiesced as it appeared the police and Hollywood-at-large were now clearly more interested in taking the diplomatic route with me.

I left my apartment with the police without resistance. They placed me in handcuffs and loaded me into the back of their squad car. I assumed this was common protocol even for extraordinarily special circumstances like these. I expected to be taken to a ritzy hotel meeting space in downtown Orlando; either that or a dirt ditch out in the middle of some remote central Florida field for my execution.

I couldn't have been more wrong.

In police custody, I was driven miles away from UCF. Hotel or ditch, I kept thinking.

My police escort soon arrived at some sort of clinical processing station. Upon entering, I was asked a few identifying questions and was then asked to be seated in a small waiting room with a few other individuals. I was disappointed that I hadn't been taken to a 5-star hotel but relieved that I hadn't been taken to a remote ditch.

Made aware of this establishment's medical function, I assumed this station was intended to isolate extremely important persons from the general population for questioning and, if deemed necessary, some form of identity and memory erasure.

Called into meet with a doctor of some sort for a brief interview, I was convinced that my circumstances were related to my special identity and secrets I believed I alone possessed.

"I just want to know if what's happening to me has happened to great artists and leaders," I implored the doctor as he concluded the interview. It soon became clear that I would not be returning to my apartment anytime soon.

After my meeting with the doctor, I was led into a second waiting room and told that I'd be transported to a hospital in the morning. Despite the kindness and politeness of the staff, I knew my number was almost up and barely rested that night.

When morning came, I was transported by shuttle to Lakeside Behavioral Clinic; not too far from the assessment center.

As I was processed for internment at the clinic's in-patient unit, I became emotional; fearing not for my life - but for my ideas and identity.

I found the living quarters an unnervingly quiet place and populated by other men mainly, both young and old. Some friendly, others suspicious. But retaining the lack of social inhibition associated with my condition, I soon found myself in conversation with some of them and even impressed the whole floor with my construction of a house of cards using an available deck of playing cards.

When I was given a chance to phone someone, I called my oldest brother Alonso who was living in Tampa at the time. When I explained to him all that had happened, he was shocked and responded with a term I'd never heard before.

"You were Baker Acted?" he asked with great concern.

The term, unique to the state of Florida, means involuntary commitment to a mental health institution if one is deemed a threat to themselves or others.

Despite having never heard the term before, the tenor of my brother's remark said everything. In that instant, I felt like John Nash in *A Beautiful Mind*, the renowned mathematician who is suddenly slapped in the face (along with the audience) by the fact that his paranoid, conspiratorial fantasy is just that. Similarly, my entire reality had been flipped inside out and I then realized I was clinically insane. However, my own paranoid and delusional ideas persisted in an adapted, less intense form.

Later on that day, I was told by the doctor that I'd be placed on a particular medication regimen to restore my brain's chemical balance. However, my first and only interpretation of those plans was that the medication would completely erase my memories and my very identity! I would emerge from this treatment lobotomized, essentially; a hollow husk of my former self.

As the evening approached, I was counseled by a doctor about my fears and concerns. The doctor tried as best as he could to allay my apprehension and he ultimately persuaded me to accept the treatment. I did and part of me braced for the worst.

The next morning, my memory and identity were still intact. Over night, the worst of my psychosis had subsided. But I still felt lingering symptoms in the form of television programs seemingly referencing me and conversations between doctors and clinic employees seemingly doing so as well. But I began to increasingly accept that my condition was the result of a psychological abnormality. It was a mental health emergency and I wasn't the Second Coming.

My parents arrived the following day. They had received word of my predicament hours after I'd been Baker Acted and took off from Miami as soon as they possibly could. They were relieved to know I was safe and in proper care.

I was discharged soon after their initial visit to the clinic.

Withdrawn from my classes at UCF, I returned to Miami with my parents for my recovery at home.

The medication I'd been prescribed had some uncomfortable side effects but I knew how important the drugs were in treating the serious chemical disorder in my brain. My trust in the science of treatment would never falter despite my grievances with certain medication.

For a number of weeks at home, some of the psychotic symptoms persisted. I believed there were snipers outside my home, I was convinced visiting relatives were spies, I was certain my parents were secretly defending me against outside enemies and I still believed television programs were aware of my existence.

Thankfully, over time these paranoid and delusional ideas gradually dissipated and my brain's chemical balance was eventually more-or-less restored.

Did I need to continue taking medication, though? I still bemoaned the existence of certain side effects and I dreaded the idea of having to take anti-psychotic medication for a longer time than absolutely necessary. So, when the psychiatrist I was seeing in Miami floated the suggestion that my crisis at UCF was possibly the result of an acute episode of psychosis (occurring once and never again), I jumped on that most attractive view of affairs and gradually eased off of my medication. I would still continue to see a psychiatrist as a precaution but I would no longer be obligated to take any more medication.

I was relieved.

But seeing my crisis at UCF as an acute episode would prove to be the single biggest mistake of my life upon resuming studies at the Orlando university in Spring 2009...

71. Mentorship (May 2016)

At some point in the mid-2010s I came across a former high school English teacher's profile on the website of a local magnet school, Arthur & Polly Mays Conservatory of the Arts.

The design of the profile was spare and presented in elementary HTML-style formatting. The profile featured a tiny portrait photo, a selected biography and a link to the teacher's email. I wrongly assumed that APMCOTA was farther away than it was and put away any thoughts of potentially reconnecting with this English teacher. Despite this teacher having meant a great deal to me during my penultimate year at Miami Killian Senior High, I felt it'd been too long and it appeared he was no longer local.

However, my initial apprehension about reaching out would soon evaporate after a certain wholly unexpected encounter some time later.

One afternoon, as I was exiting a doctor's office after an appointment, I happened to run into Ms. Muller, another high school English teacher I was quite fond of and with whom I'd gotten on well with during my time at Killian. We hadn't seen each other since my time in high school either. We exchanged a few kind words but the most significant takeaway from our brief encounter was her encouraging me to reach out to my other former English teacher, who she confirmed was teaching at APMCOTA and, contrary to what I'd initially believed, was not too far away at all.

The teacher in question was the inimitable Mr. Michael C. Hill, who I'll forever regard in both formal and informal terms as "Mr. Hill."

Not too long after that chance encounter with Ms. Muller, I crafted a brief email message to Mr. Hill and sent it off.

I hoped he would respond promptly and with the same elation over reconnecting with a past pupil as Ms. Muller had shown.

And he did!

Right off the bat, Mr. Hill suggested meeting up for coffee and catching up at a local Starbucks. I was totally game.

I arrived earlier than Mr. Hill to the coffee house and waited somewhat nervously. So much time had transpired since we last saw each other. What kind of a reunion would this be?

Soon, a tall and familiar presence soon appeared at the entrance of our set meeting place. I immediately stood up from my seat as Mr. Hill spotted me. As he approached, we warmly acknowledged each other and then we embraced. Mr. Hill's familiar, open-armed disposition and comforting, Southern-accented voice was as it had always been! This was exactly the same Mr. Hill from memory.

We settled down into a pair of seats and spent the rest of that Starbucks' store hours chatting most enjoyably!

My effusive respect for him as a disciple of great literature was always matched by his utmost belief in my abilities as a budding storyteller.

There was no acclimation required of either of us. The nearly 15-year distance that had separated us seemed to collapse in an instant as though we were simply picking up from where we'd left off years ago.

Since our reconnecting at that local Starbucks (dubbed by us "the 3rd Place" owing to it once being Mr. Hill's 3rd most often visited location after his home and workplace), Mr. Hill and I have enjoyed countless long and deep conversations about such topics as literature, film, pedagogy, family, politics, relationships and, quite frankly, life itself - all at that very same Starbucks where we continue to meet up as often as we can. He is always willing to take the time to listen and offer his guidance, support and insight without hesitation in the face of any difficult personal or creative challenge.

Additionally, Mr. Hill has attended virtually all of my most significant public film screenings since our reconnecting and he has also invited me to others of mutual interest. In 2017, Mr. Hill was instrumental in my finding employment as a substitute teacher and being able to teach at APMCOTA, where he himself spent the last years of his career as a teacher (he is retired as of 2021, after over 30 years of teaching in the public school system). One day we were even able to partner as lecturers in the same class on a film-related topic!

Not counting my dad and his pervasive influence, I've had a number of other mentors enter my life primarily through an educational context: Mr. Hill at Killian, Mr. Steve Schlow at University of Central Florida and Dr. Andrew Strycharski at Florida International University during my second wind as a student there. I have always tried to keep and nurture these special bonds ever since my first taste of that rarest of elixirs... wisdom.

Indeed, I cannot easily imagine pursuing my craft as a filmmaker to the extent that I have without the moral support of elder, sounder minds to check in with from time to time.

72. Moniker (April 2013)

After my 14th short film *Proteus* was completed I felt it was high-time to select a meaningful banner name for my growing short filmmaking operation. I was uncomfortable using my name with the tag "Productions" to represent my work and the substantial depth and breadth of my creative collaborations, new and ongoing.

A list of approximately 300 potential production company names was compiled over the course of several weeks and reflected the wide variety of images and ideas I associated with my short film work up to then. I was looking for something simple and dramatic even if some of the above names are somewhat lengthy and esoteric. I was simply allowing my ideas to spill out with limited filtering.

The whittling down of names to arrive at a single one was a very difficult process but I ultimately landed on the term "hard edge" and affixed the tag "films" as my resulting decision on the matter.

Hard Edge Films.

The name spoke to an attractive sense of severity (hard) and extremity (edge). I was also inspired by the hard edge painting style characterized by flat areas of color with abrupt transitions (Piet Mondrian is a favorite example of mine); that abruptness not too unlike the forceful cutting in my short film work. Indeed, the name was far more evocative of the formal side of my work than their literal themes and content.

For the logo design, my choice also followed a directive of simplicity. White text on a black background with the three words on top of each other in a vertical, square-like orientation. The font of choice? ITC Avant Garde Gothic. Unquestionably modern, efficient and uniform.

I would also produce a video bumper to be attached to the opening of all of my short films, both future and past. The bumper involved three brief shots, each representing each part of the name Hard Edge Films:

- Hard - A brawny prisoner lifting weights in a chain link fenced area. Audio of labored breath.
- Edge - The edge of a cliff with a bird of prey soaring high above. Audio of a bird cry.
- Films - A man riding a horse from Eadweard Muybridge's 1878 film experiment *The Horse in Motion* (considered the earliest motion picture ever produced). Audio of a flickering film projector.

After the three shots, the Hard Edge Films logo appears accompanied by a deep, reverberant electronic sound!

P R R R R R R O O O O O O N N N N N N G G G G G - WWWWWAAAAAAAAAWAAAAAAWAA!!!

However, despite my satisfaction with the production company name and its fetching video bumper, the active use of Hard Edge Films would only persist for about three years as it was only ever intended as a banner for my short film work. I would retire the use of Hard Edge Films after the completion of my final short film *The Promotion* in 2016. After that my focus would turn exclusively to feature filmmaking.

Hard Edge Films certainly served its limited purpose and I definitely miss the dramatic impression it engendered on quite a few occasions but it'll always remain associated with my years as a short filmmaker; years that I will forever hold most dear.

73. NAMI (May 2017)

All of a sudden I found myself in a whirlwind of activity involving a media appearance blitz and a screening of my 13th short film *Semester of Madness*; all as part of a local mental health-themed film festival, the 2nd Annual Reel Minds Miami Mental Health Film Festival, organized by NAMI (National Alliance on Mental Illness) Miami-Dade.

NAMI Miami-Dade is a "part of the nation's largest grassroots mental health organization" whose mission it is to "offer free, confidential and safe information, support, advocacy and resources" to those affected by mental illness. It's a great organization that does valuable work across the country where there is a surprisingly marked deficiency of such services through federal, state and local governments.

My mental health-themed short film *Semester of Madness* is a narrative fiction film that follows the harrowing account of a college student's experience of a particularly severe episode of mental illness. It's based on true events. I had made the short film five years prior and it had already been exhibited at multiple film festivals and been enthusiastically received by the general public and certain mental health professionals.

NAMI Miami-Dade first heard of my short film when I teamed with the Florida International University chapter of NAMI (I was a student at FIU at the time) to screen the short film and hold a panel afterward consisting of two mental health experts and myself. About a year after that event, I was contacted by a family friend Beatriz E. Mendoza who was working with NAMI Miami-Dade at the time and informed me that NAMI Miami-Dade's board had heard of the FIU event, seen the short film and was interested in having it featured at their second annual film festival. And knowing fairly well what NAMI was all about by then, they had me at hello. A most welcomed honor!

About a week before the festival, it came time to promote the event and the first instance of that would be through an interview with the *Miami Herald*.

In preparation, I tried to anticipate what questions I'd be asked and prepare accordingly. Soon enough, I received a call from a most professional, young reporter Janette Vazquez and responded to her incisive and thoughtful questions. It's safe to say that the interview went supremely well and a few days later, the article featuring my interview and advancing the upcoming film festival went public in both online and print versions. Not my first published interview but a thrill all the same!

Some days following the *Miami Herald* interview, I was informed that NAMI Miami-Dade had managed to secure a spot on the local PBS station program *Your South Florida* and I was invited to be interviewed along with Director/Vice President of NAMI Miami-Dade Susan Racher.

The opportunity came as a surprise but, more than that, an inviting challenge! Let's see how I'd fare on live television flexing my impromptu speaking skills! Thankfully, my years of experience as a Toastmaster prepared me for such an occasion and I can say that I experienced virtually no nerves or trepidation during my live, in-person interview. I think I did a fairly decent job for my first-ever televised appearance. It was a novel experience and I absolutely relished the opportunity to express myself on such a platform. And long-time journalist and host of *Your South Florida* Pam Giganti was such a professional and skillful host and facilitator. I was in awe seeing her in action on the set.

Then, on Saturday, May 13th came the main event!

I had been asked to speak immediately following the screening of *Semester of Madness* at the festival so I prepared a few words and spent the run-up to the event rehearsing quietly on my own.

But I've got to hand it to the NAMI Miami-Dade organizers and volunteers big-time. They had to weather a last-minute location change due to an unexpected electrical issue. But upon early arrival at the location where the event ultimately took place (University of Miami's Fieldhouse at Watsco Center), you'd have thought nothing had been up-ended in any way. Color me impressed!

A total of about 600 people had RSVP'd (the maximum amount) and nearly as many, if not more, ultimately showed. It was an astounding turnout!

Prior to the film program, local band FogDog treated early-arrivers to some soulful original music that was a real pleasure to take in.

And then came the films!

I'd been privy to the selections prior to the event so I knew what was coming but I must once again commend the organizers for finding a wonderfully varied and remarkably insightful selection of films. They all focused on separate but equally important aspects of mental illness. Their topics and themes included depression, eating disorders, bipolar disorder and how race and family play into treatment and the prevalent stigma associated with mental illness. And there was a speaker programmed after each film which provided greatly informative context and perspective on the aspect that had just been illustrated cinematically. It was a great format!

As for my own turn at the podium, it went well considering I was addressing a massive audience of roughly 600 attendees. Approaching this opportunity with some small measure of confidence owing again to my experience as a Toastmaster, I spoke about my own story of recovery from mental illness and described how, with the support of loving family members and an unwavering trust in the science of treatment, a complete recovery is indeed possible.

At the conclusion of the event, Miami-Dade County Commissioner Aide J.C. Garrido presented an official proclamation that named May 13th (the day of the festival) "NAMI Day"! And with that, the festival came to a decidedly historical close.

I am deeply grateful to NAMI Miami-Dade for the tireless work of all involved in putting together such an extraordinary event and for giving me an opportunity to share my short film *Semester of Madness* and my personal story. NAMI is a remarkable organization that aims to advocate for the understanding of the complexity of mental illness, dispel myths, educate the public and provide support for those affected by mental illness.

I was thrilled to collaborate with them.

74. Occupy (December 2011)

Across the UNITED STATES OF AMERICA, hundreds of cities and towns have joined the Occupy Wall Street movement. But the movement is facing a difficult time. Hundreds of activists have been arrested and evicted from public spaces.

In Washington, D.C., Occupy activists from around the country are gathering for the first-ever National General Assembly to determine the future of the movement.

Today, a small group of Occupy Miami activists, who have stayed behind, take part in a National Day of Action to address the foreclosure crisis, protest corporate excess and call for an end to record-high economic inequality....

Despite the continuing burden of a mental health crisis and resulting legal quandary that had characterized much of 2009 for me, I never once considered forfeiting my filmmaking aspirations and continued to gather ideas for potential short films in the years following those calamitous events. However, the more hands-on creative process beyond that idea-gathering activity was continually stymied by an unrecovered mental state; the few productions I managed to commence were abandoned within days of starting. The emotional toll of a damaged reputation, a dashed film school career and a persistent depression continued to heavily bear down on me like nothing I'd ever known. I was simply unable to keep the motor running.

But that would soon change.

Toward the end of 2011, I suppose I'd simply endured enough creative stagnation when a familiar energy at last returned to me!

I gradually found myself with greater motivation and confidence about new projects. In turn, my creative process became less mired by immobility and began to result in ideas that engaged my long-dormant cinematic faculties. I was ready to wield my trusty Canon HV20 once again!

My new plans? To venture out into the world to add yet another short film entry to my professional canon. It would be another documentary vignette made in the style of the three I'd made while attending University of Central Florida. I'd be executing a fairly free-form project where I was simply operating as cameraman and editor, rather than any of the far more demanding roles typical of a traditional narrative project. Easy stages.

The subject chosen?

Occupy Wall Street protests or, to be more precise, those of the local off-shoot Occupy Miami, taking place downtown. A nationally coordinated day of action was coming up and I thought the occasion would make for a compelling and highly relevant mini-documentary.

Accordingly, I requested a ride to the Metrorail from my parents and they obliged.

Hopping off the Metrorail, I arrived at the Government Center plaza to find an encampment perfectly reflective of the occupational mentality behind the entire movement. Tents everywhere.

I began roaming the area and collecting shots.

The general shape of the documentary soon started to come together in my mind as I continued to explore and document "Peace City".

Soon, a group of about 30 activists began to collect in the area. They were planning on marching throughout downtown with stops at the Miami-Dade County Courthouse and various banks in the area.

I set off with them.

The sights and sounds of a grassroots protest like this one were familiar to me as a result of my involvement with student activist groups like sds (Students for a Democratic Society) during my time at UCF. But unlike those past experiences, I knew virtually no one among these Occupy Miami activists and, despite my insistence on being a sympathetic documentarian, some regarded me with a degree of suspicion.

In any case, I continued my filming mostly unfettered and enjoyed flexing my compositional muscles as I captured a variety of subjects from various angles as the rally progressed.

During a stop at one particular building, I happened to capture a group of anonymous businessmen exiting the building. One of the men noticed what I'd done and stomped over to me, fuming.

"Give me the tape!" he growled.

I was immediately unnerved but attempted to be as diplomatic as possible.

"I'm sorry, sir. I won't use any footage of you," I stated. "I swear."

He insisted on the getting the tape from me.

I changed tact and explained how I was going to rewind the tape and record over the footage of him. I even performed the rewinding action in front of him.

At that point, he began to relent.

"Again, I'm sorry, sir," I repeated.

Appeased but contemptful. He walked away.

After the man was out of sight, I returned the tape to its original position. Fuck that guy.

Our day of action soon came to a close as the sun began to set across the city. The activists and I returned to "Peace City". I bid farewell to those who hadn't greeted me with too much suspicion and shared the link to my YouTube channel where my video vignette would eventually find its home.

I then boarded the Metrorail and returned home.

When it came time to edit what I'd gathered at my computer, I found myself in familiar circumstances. With ample material to choose from, I eagerly selected the best shots and began shaping the piece. It was a practice I hadn't engaged in for over three years and it felt great!

Following through with what I'd decided early on, I'd be intercutting the live-action shots with some informative intertitles. So, I spent a good deal of time gathering some primer-like facts about economic inequality and the current housing crisis in the U.S.

For the music, I had had in mind "The Flower Duet" from the Léo Delibes opera *Lakmé*. The idea for its use came to me very early on in my conception of the piece. I felt it fit like a glove.

The turn-around for this brief short documentary, titled *Occupy*

Miami!, was quite fast and I immediately shared it with my family to fairly encouraging reception.

Having given my confidence as a filmmaker and as a person a much-needed boost through the completion of this project, I now set out to further develop my next and 13th short film as the year came to a close.

It would be my most complex up to that time and my most personal to-date.

75. Ostracization (April 2007)

The bully, as I shall refer to this particular person for the length of this chapter, maintained a reputation for caustic, insulting remarks and other scandalous behavior for as long, it seemed, as he was a film student at University of Central Florida. So insufferable were his actions that at one point he had to be reprimanded by the chair of the film program in private. I'll never forget the change in his demeanor, albeit temporary, following the alleged closed-door dressing down. But the trait of the bully I found most offensive was his general carelessness and lack of effort he put forward as an aspiring filmmaker. For someone who could admittedly be effectively charismatic at times, here was a glaring example of a young man spoiling his gifts and privilege.

The drama between the bully and me began on one afternoon after a film school colloquium at the start of the Spring 2007 semester. I was invited to dine at a local restaurant with the seniors in the film program, who were all concurrently working on their capstone films. I'd grown increasingly close with most of them since my arrival at UCF.

While I was enjoying a pleasant time with the group, I revealed that I would be taking the reigns of Robert Grant's failing capstone project that semester. My involvement with Robert, a fellow classmate of theirs who'd had a major falling out with several of them after a dramatic episode involving mental illness and substance abuse, was met with immediate opposition from... the bully.

He made his objection clear right away and insisted that it was "a shit thing" I was doing to be helping the likes of Robert Grant. Despite the bully's outspoken contempt for my decision, I was immutably determined to complete a short film worthy of presentation at the film school's end-of-year showcase.

Several weeks later, I encountered the bully and several of his classmates just outside the film school's production hallway after one of the capstone class sessions had let out. Here, the bully levied a number of insults at me. But instead of sinking to the bully's level with returned viciousness, I simply asked him to accept that I simply saw an opportunity to make something worthwhile and that he not be so mean-spirited. He laughed derisively at me and dispatched another barrage of crude insults. With none of the other upperclassmen coming to my aid, I soon left but not humiliated at all. In fact, I was more determined than ever to see Robert's capstone through to completion.

Toward the end of the semester, I received an unusual voicemail message from the bully as my work on Robert's capstone was reaching completion. He began his message by admitting his enmity toward me and recognized my unwillingness to return it in kind. But when he mentioned the fallout between Robert and him, his voice quivered and he became emotional in the recording. I was extremely surprised by the sheer outpouring of emotion but kept the voicemail message to myself in keeping with those nobler instincts.

The following day, the bully found me in one of the film school building hallways and asked to speak with me outside. I didn't mention the voicemail message and obliged him.

Outside and away from any other students, the bully immediately launched into a tirade of insults and threats unlike anything I'd ever experienced in my entire life! He was relentless in his verbal abuse. However, I stuck to my rather stoic constitution and attempted to be as diplomatic and pacifying as possible. It didn't work.

In the middle of the bully's venom slinging, one of his classmates appeared and the bully stopped his verbal assault. Sensing the explosive conflict between us, the classmate offered some kind but ineffective encouragement for us to settle our differences and left.

The bully started right back up again!

Despite my insistence that we involve the capstone professor or the chair of the film program himself as a mediator to calm this raging disagreement, the bully was soon out of patience with me. He summarily told me to "go fuck [myself]" and stormed off. I never spoke with the bully ever again.

Following that explosive incident, I began to feel a rift gradually form between the other upperclassmen and myself. The bully, despite his brutish and immature behavior, was still capable of persuading his classmates that my collaboration with Robert was utterly reprehensible. Through the grape vine, I'd heard the echoed view that my facilitation of Robert's graduation per the completion of his capstone project somehow invalidated the value of his graduating class's degrees. So, those upperclassmen's friendliness toward me turned to indifference and avoidance. I never spoke with many of those upperclassmen ever again.

Before long, the end-of-year showcase took place. I'd successfully completed the capstone with Robert and was very proud of the result. However, when the short film, titled *Jesus Christ Goes to Mars*, screened to a full house in one of UCF's auditoriums, a walk-out was staged by the bully and about ten or so students closest to him joined him in the act. At the start of my short film, the group made their way up the aisle and out of the venue and sat out for the duration of the film's screening.

I didn't mind too much, however, because the remaining sizable audience seemed to respond quite enthusiastically to the misadventures of Robert Grant as Jesus Christ. And the general audience that night wasn't the only group who'd reacted positively to the work. As far as I know, the short film also enjoyed a favorable reception among the UCF film school faculty who were present at the screening that night. Honestly, that's all I had hoped for.

Bullies be damned.

76. Outbound (July 2005)

Although I found some degree of purpose and direction in deciding to make my 2nd short film *Does Free Speech Matter?* for a national short film contest during the first half of summer, when work on that short film was concluded I found myself living the same disconnected and aimless existence I'd experienced after finishing my spring semester at Florida International University in the latter half of that summer.

Toward the end of spring, I'd missed the deadline to register for summer classes at FIU out of a deep ambivalence toward my college career. As my teenage years were drawing to a close, my life lacked a clear sense of direction and, truth be told, the idea of another semester at FIU as a philosophy major was far from the booster shot I needed.

But soon enough, my fortune would change.

Shortly after completing *Does Free Speech Matter?*, my mom hatched an intriguing idea. She suggested that I inquire about the film program at University of Central Florida in Orlando and perhaps take a trip to visit the school and take a tour. Considering how cloistered my life had been up to then, my mom's idea sounded outlandish at first. But she insisted.

After graduating high school, I had outright dismissed the idea of attending film school as I considered my ideal choices too distant and too expensive. However, the idea of attending a more modest program at UCF was a compromise I hadn't at all considered. Its cost was far less exorbitant than the out-of-state schools and its limited-access film program championed microbudget filmmaking as opposed to the industry-skewed focus of nearly every other film school. Plus, the idea of moving out on my own for the first time in my life became an increasingly alluring prospect.

Upon hearing that UCF would be hosting an open house at the end of the month, my parents and I agreed to make the trip and give UCF a fair shake. My excitement only grew.

After a nearly 6-hour long drive, my parents and I arrived in Orlando and checked into a hotel in the area around UCF on a cloudy afternoon. Then, we made a short drive from our hotel to the UCF campus.

Upon arrival at the university's welcome center, we took part in a general tour of the campus grounds and then headed off to UCF's Communication building where the film school was housed. Here, we filed into an auditorium and watched a presentation about the film program. What the film program representative had to say was so encouraging that toward the end of the presentation, my dad turned to me with a look of sheer delight and said, "This is the place for you."

I didn't say so at that moment but I completely agreed.

After this elaborate preview of UCF and its film school, my parents and I quickly made the rounds to learn what we had to do to ensure my enrollment in the upcoming fall semester. Thankfully, we managed to speak with the right people at the right time before the end of the open house event that day would shutter the opportunity.

When I returned to Miami, I hit the ground running! I quickly sent along all required documentation and bashed out an admission essay that expressed my passion for filmmaking with no small amount of words about the two short films I'd already produced on my own. My dad also fashioned a firmly worded letter to further persuade the administrators to grant my later-than-usual request for admittance.

A few weeks later, I heard back from UCF.

I'd been accepted!

Not too long after I'd received word of my acceptance, my parents and I were on our way back to Orlando but after a few days my parents would be driving back to Miami without their beloved son. With the lease of my student apartment arranged and all of my belongings packed into our car, we soon arrived at Pegasus Pointe, one of UCF's affiliated off-campus apartment complexes.

I immediately relished my new, clean and spacious living quarters where I was determined to work harder than ever as a student, prepare a stand-out creative portfolio for the upcoming film school application process, maintain good relations with my roommates and generally enjoy the comfort of living independently for the first time in my life. It was incredible freedom and an incredible responsibility. I knew what I needed to do.

The following morning, my parents and I made a short trip to UCF for an orientation event the weekend before classes were set to begin. Here, I registered for my classes, had my student ID card printed, signed up for a year-long meal plan and generally took part in a variety of activities intended to guide new students over the threshold of this grand experience!

Despite some nerves, I was far more excited and optimistic about what lay before me. I knew that my penchant for order, organization and self-discipline would serve me well.

Later that day, I bid farewell to my parents and watched as their car disappeared in the distance. We'd of course keep in touch via phone and email but I wouldn't be seeing them again in-person till the following spring.

When the first day of classes took place the following Monday, I found great joy in seeing a campus so brimming with life despite the punishing heat of the late-summer Orlando climate.

I showed up to my classes on-time, paid rapt attention to my new professors and took copious notes. I'd never taken to the role of a student with as much dedication and enthusiasm. But beyond the strictly academic dimension, I also exercised interpersonal strengths I never knew I had. I'd rarely been more social and completely at ease being so than during my time as a student at UCF!

While my time at the Orlando university would be characterized by remarkable flourishing and achievement in a variety of areas, it would also be the site of some severe challenges and trials far beyond the imagination of even this precocious 19-year-old...

77. PBS (July 2017)

South Florida PBS's 'film-maker' project offers our region's aspiring storytellers a unique opportunity for mentorship and broadcast distribution. The 'film-maker' initiative will serve 40 filmmakers from the Keys to the Treasure Coast and reach an audience of over 6.3 million.

So read the promotional description of *film-maker* on a call-for-entries posting I encountered during my routine perusal of social media.

Regional focus?

Broadcast distribution?

Professional mentorship?

I was totally game!

With the application period closing the following day, I instantly accessed the submission requirement information and prepared accordingly. My 16th and final short film *The Promotion* would be the elected work for consideration.

After sending all of the asked-for material, I waited.

A month passed.

Then, I learned that the judging status had changed on the submission tracking website...

I'd been accepted!

Over 100 submissions had been received by the local PBS station, out of which only 40 filmmakers had been selected. Overjoyed, I learned that the next step was preparing *The Promotion* for televised distribution and taking part in some filming at their studio for a brief profile which would accompany my short film's airing.

Some weeks later, I traveled to the PBS studio building with my friend and fellow filmmaker Tony Mendez, who'd also applied and been selected to be a part of *film-maker*. Having visited the building earlier in the year to appear on a news program highlighting the NAMI (National Alliance on Mental Illness) film festival I was involved with at the time, I was immediately familiar with the establishment's lengthy corridors and stage facilities.

Upon arriving to the set where the profile segments were being filmed, Tony and I sat quietly some distance away as we awaited our turn before the lights, camera setup and professionals running the shoot.

When it was my turn, I was mic'd, sat down on a waiting stool and directed to look at the person to the right of the camera. I would be asked a series of questions and expected to respond in an impromptu manner. Thanks to Toastmasters, I was more than ready to tackle anything thrown my way.

The questions were delivered in a steady, almost rapid-fire manner and invited responses about a variety of topics, including my short film, my influences, my criteria for great films and my experience. The entire interview took about ten minutes. My responses would later be condensed into 90 seconds for an online supplement to the *film-maker* program, titled "9 Questions in 90 Seconds".

During my interview I was glad to be asked about the best piece of advice I'd ever received about making films. My response was: "The best advice I ever received about filmmaking was to start quickly. Start with a hook. Get people engaged and then you can start with the more nuanced, more subtle facets of what you're trying to do." I answered this question with a smidgen of greater confidence because my answer honestly referred to a bit of advice I'd carried with me since my freshman year at Florida International University.

In the Spring 2005 semester, I met a fellow schoolmate and filmmaker Yecid Benavides whose acquaintance I'd made while filming a group video project I'd essentially hijacked. Seeing me in my element, he later invited me to his on-campus apartment so we could share our work with one another. During our meeting, he imparted that simple piece of advice which spoke to my then-dormant but eventually roused propensity toward speed in my filmmaking. I've always been grateful for Yecid's helpful push in that direction and my sharing it with the PBS folks was, to me, a way of memorializing it.

Some time after the profile shoot, I learned that my short film would be included in the very first episode of *film-maker*. I was ecstatic!

On the night of *film-maker*'s debut, I gathered with my family in front of the television to watch. I had made some noise about the short film's airing on social media and encouraged many of my friends to also tune in.

It was a thrill to see such a personal film of mine granted such great public exposure. Although my family and I were already quite familiar with my short film, we also appreciated the rather eclectic combination of pieces featured in the show's maiden episode.

In touch with Stephanie Maltez, the lead actress of *The Promotion*, she had been overwhelmed by the good fortune bestowed upon the short film through *film-maker* and would later report that she had tears streaming down her face during our short film's airing.

Some time after the broadcast, I along with the other *film-maker* filmmakers were invited to a brunch at an independent theater venue in downtown Miami. Here I met many of the other participating filmmakers for the first time and also was audience to a presentation by a group of local film experts, including documentary filmmakers of some notoriety and area film commissioners.

Months later, another event was arranged for the filmmakers associated with *film-maker*. This occasion invited a talk from senior PBS documentary filmmakers who shared their background and advice for possible future collaborations with the local TV station. At this event, I spent more time with my fellow filmmakers and continued to express my appreciation for the work of theirs I'd seen on the show. I didn't just watch my episode!

At the same event, I also met my assigned mentor Melissa Harmon, Supervising Producer at South Florida PBS. It was my first time meeting her in-person and she had no shortage of praise for my short film. We would keep in touch as I proceeded with feature-length films later on in my career.

In view of the show's positive reception, a nationwide roll-out was planned for *film-maker* and a whole slew of markets opened up for the program. Nearly 100 cities were announced, including New York City, Los Angeles, Chicago, Houston, San Francisco and Boston! I quickly spread the word to friends residing in the selected regions.

All of these tidings, however great in number and nature, were mere foothills in comparison to the tall mountains which lay beyond them. All during the *film-maker* experience, I knew I needed a greater challenge; to move past making short films and graduate to feature-length filmmaking! What was I waiting for?

Honestly, I felt a bit like Em, who at the conclusion of *The Promotion* says to her co-worker, "We have a lot of work to do... Let's get started!"

Let's get started, indeed.

78. Philosophy (March 2004)

The time had come.

As my time in high school was drawing to a close, I had to select a major for the application to my post-secondary educational institution of choice, Florida International University; a local university previously attended by my two older brothers.

What major would I choose?

Although I'd failed to successfully launch and complete a follow-up to my first short film *Mass Education*, I still considered myself an aspiring filmmaker. But in the absence of any significant filmmaking activity, another fervent interest had taken root during my high school years.

After leaving New World School of the Arts, a prestigious arts high school, I was in a dismal state. Freshly enrolled in a regular high school Miami Killian Senior High, I felt like my life had been reset upon transfer to Killian. I had no familiar sense of direction and purpose. It was a situation I'd never faced before. I'd always had visual art to cling to in the past but it now no longer centered me as it had before.

But there was hope.

Before I'd left New World, I knew film would be my new heading but while it would be about a year before my interest in filmmaking coalesced into actual practice, the semblance of a foundation did exist.

So what did I do?

I read.

What did I read?

Film and political books from Killian's library, mainly. My interest in politics had grown out of the reality of a post-9/11 world and was in no small part due to my dad's influence as a local political activist himself. At the same time, I also became an avid reader of critical film essays which I found in plentiful supply online. All told, these readings gave me more than my bearing as a developing film fanatic and, to some degree, a citizen of the world. But more importantly, they served as a gateway to an area of interest I'd never explored before: philosophy!

Indeed, I soon found myself branching off into books and online texts about the ideas of some of philosophy's most renowned contributors: Aristotle, Plato, Nietzsche, Marx, Sartre and many others; mainly on account of frequent references to them and their work in the film and political writings I was being exposed to. I was particularly interested in existentialism and post-modernism; their themes often found expression in the films I was exploring as a budding film enthusiast.

Another experience that galvanized my relationship with the love of wisdom was an occasion in which I volunteered to give a short presentation about a film I liked in Killian's own philosophy club; in essence, a fusion of these two developing interests of mine.

The film I chose to speak about was Andrei Tarkovsky's 1983 Soviet-Italian drama *Nostalghia*. The deliberately paced and highly meditative film follows a Russian man who travels to Italy to learn more about a famed but suicided composer. The climax involves a mad, self-styled prophet immolating himself in a city square to a recording of Beethoven's Ninth Symphony. It's a sequence rife with meaning and implication!

For my presentation, I played two clips from the film (including the climax) and talked about the themes of the film and those in the filmmaker's broader filmography. With this presentation, I had confidently delivered the most extensive public speaking performance in my life up to that point. My audience of fellow club members and the club's faculty advisor, Ms. Farnsworth, seemed particularly captivated by what I had to say and show, even if it teetered on the edge of absolute esoterica.

Later on in my senior year at Killian, after so many films had been watched and writings had been read, I came to strike up a rather idyllic friendship with fellow senior, Joshua Rosenberg. He was bright, well-spoken and we engaged daily on matters as mundane as what happened during our respective lunch periods to those as as profound as considering the greatest pleasure imaginable. We were inseparable, particularly during our International Relations class where we sat side-by-side throughout the entire year. Soon enough, Joshua and I realized we were both fairly avid readers and soon began trading books. One particular publication he shared with me was a small manual-sized book seemingly made from recycled material. It was about the history of philosophy but treated like an extremely user-friendly sampler of every significant school of thought in the entire philosophical canon of Western civilization.

Over the spring break of my final year in high school, I devoured Joshua's book and finished it just as my choice of major for attending FIU had to be made.

I would be applying to FIU with philosophy as my intended major!

When my dad learned about my choice, he was supportive. But that didn't keep him from attacking what he believed were my overly impractical, romantic and unscientific ideas about life on one occasion after I returned from school one day.

In any case, I greatly looked forward to continuing my education at FIU. Thankfully, my orientation experience the following summer was a positive one and I was able to register for intriguing courses in logic and sociology right off the bat. It felt more than appropriate.

Although a year after first enrolling at FIU I'd be transferring to University of Central Florida in Orlando to officially study film, I think back to my more intrepid first choice of major with some fondness. Many years later I'd learn that two of my most favorite filmmakers, Wes Anderson (*The Fantastic Mr. Fox*, *The Royal Tenenbaums*, *The French Dispatch*) and Terrence Malick (*Days of Heaven*, *Badlands*, *The Tree of Life*), both claimed philosophy as their college majors. While I didn't fully consummate my selection like they had, I believe my early liaison with philosophy expanded my mind and encouraged me to approach life with a greater sense of critical thinking and self-definition. Despite my dad's understandable reaction, I'm glad I was a bit impractical, romantic and unscientific about my aspirations all that time ago.

I think you have to be sometimes.

79. Prequels (December 2005)

May 1999

After years of anticipation, I was now counting down the hours till the early evening as the school day wore on at Southwood Middle School. I was in 7th grade. At the end of the countdown, I found myself with my younger brother Daniel, my oldest brother Alonso and Alonso's girlfriend at Sunset Place shopping mall on a rainy evening lined up at its theater for an opening day showing of *Star Wars: The Phantom Menace*.

May 2002

Having kept up with the latest news and media about its production via the internet, I was excited to finally catch the middle chapter of the tragic story of Anakin Skywalker. I was in 11th grade. Initially, neither of my two older brothers - my only transports to the theater - were too interested in seeing the film. However, my older brother Juan eventually showed a modicum of generosity and took me to The Falls shopping center for an opening weekend showing of *Star Wars: Attack of the Clones*.

May 2005

Lured by the abundance of leaks and spoilers for the third and final prequel of this most beloved cinematic space opera, my active membership on two online forums dedicated to the films supplanted my earlier online sources for the latest in pre-release content. Freshly concluding my first year in college, I could now drive so I no longer relied on my elder brothers for a lift to the theater. Nevertheless, I elected to attend a screening with my oldest brother Alonso, who expressed interest in joining me. So, there we both were in Sunset Place for a midnight showing of *Star Wars: Revenge of the Sith*.

A turning point in my *Star Wars* fandom occurred months after AOTC came to theaters in 2002 which would ultimately led to an encounter with one of the most fascinating and intelligent people I've ever known - despite never having met in-person. His impact on me and my filmmaking is almost incalculable.

After the theatrical release of AOTC, my enthusiasm toward the property had waned as I embarked on my own filmmaking. Also, the generally negative reception toward AOTC among fans online didn't help matters either. However, two events would help keep the flame alight.

The first was receiving AOTC on DVD as a Christmas gift from Juan. The second was happening upon a favorable critical essay of AOTC which re-contextualized the film for me in a politically and aesthetically appealing way. Now able to peruse the film at my whim on my bedroom PC and with viewings newly infused with an intriguing intellectual coating, my affinity for the second prequel film increased tenfold and made the wait for the final prequel film unbearable!

With this resurgence of interest and fascination with *Star Wars*, I found myself hungry for any and all rumors related to ROTS. This relentless hunger led me to the world of online movie forums where I quickly developed a compulsion toward their use.

The Jedi Council Forums was my principal virtual stomping ground. The forum, one of the largest on the whole of the internet, was teeming with activity and I greedily consumed as much advance knowledge of the 2005 film as I could even if most of it was unverified and based in speculation.

As the months progressed, I found myself not only reading about the films but also interacting with other members on Jedi Council Forums in addition to dispensing with short, irreverent and often humorous postings. And months ahead of the release, I also joined another forum at Millenniumfalcon.com and enjoyed its more adult and anarchic atmosphere.

After the theatrical release of ROTS, I couldn't kick the forum habit and I continued my routine of regularly reading and participating on both the Jedi Council Forums and the MF.com board.

At the start of winter following the release of the film on DVD, I had finished my first semester at University of Central Florida but opted to not return home to Miami and instead remain at my student apartment complex for the duration of the seasonal break. Throughout those few weeks, I spent an inordinate amount of time in my bedroom, at my computer and on my precious forums among other online destinations.

It was around this time that I made a most curious discovery.

On the Jedi Council Forums, users were participating in a scene-by-scene analysis of ROTS made possible by its recent home video release. In this regularly active thread, I came upon the intriguing posts of what I soon realized was a singularly brilliant user without equal. His username was Cryogenic.

Cryogenic was uncannily knowledgeable about George Lucas and his films, particularly his newly completed *Star Wars* prequel trilogy. Cryogenic's argumentative skills were unparalleled and he offered up his infinitely wise, poetic analyses and interpretation in great quantity; almost daily from time to time. Defending this oft-derided trilogy of films with uncommon intelligence, grace and wit, I'd never seen anyone talk *Star Wars* in quite the same way. It was also refreshing to see a mutually shared regard for proper grammar and punctuation.

I kept up with Cryogenic's posts for days, then weeks, then months and it has since been nearly two decades.

Although I lost track of him for a few years after the sale of Lucasfilm to Disney engendered an unfortunate challenge to his involvement on the Jedi Council Forums, I was most pleased to find that he had relocated to a smaller, out-of-the-way forum called Naberrie Fields at the end of the 2010s. And it was here at Naberrie Fields that I was able to express my fond admiration for him and his invaluable contribution:

"Sir Cryogenic," I addressed him reverently.

"Your deeply thoughtful, critical, insightful, elaborate, witty, lyrical and always eloquent commentary about these films and much more were (and still are) a masterclass lecture series unto themselves. If Lucas provided the almighty text, you provided the irresistible and just-as-essential subtext or reading between the lines. Your posts exposed me to a new dimension of artfulness and profundity in [the prequel films] that not only morphed my view of Lucas' work but my own active conception of creativity and filmmaking. And to the filmmaker I was at the time, struggling to find his footing in film school and early short film projects, it was literally life-giving breath."

Meaning every word, I continued, "So, thank you! Thank you for years of intellectual and creative stimulation that even my real-life mentors would fall short of being able to provide! You're one of the brightest stars and if this pandemic just happens to claim this life, I'm infinitely relieved I finally got to say my piece directly to you."

Cryogenic was most pleased and most humbled to receive my tribute but I can never fully repay him for the light he has provided.

We occasionally engage in some back-and-forth on Naberrie Fields and it's always edifying. I've scarcely known such joy in online interactions.

May the Force be with him.

80. Preserved (January 2007)

Beyond the boundaries of international law, the UNITED STATES OF AMERICA's violent occupation of Iraq rages on. Three thousand U.S. troops have died since the start of the war.

While the new Iraqi government prepares to ratify a new hydrocarbon law, which will give unprecedented control of the country's vast oil reserves to foreign oil companies, President Bush has ordered a new surge in military forces.

Opposing these foolhardy plans, a group of young college students, calling for an end to the Iraq War and any further plans of military aggression, unite in protest....

On a drearily overcast Thursday afternoon in the spring of 2007 at University of Central Florida, I made my way from my on-campus apartment to the Student Union courtyard with my video camera. An anti-war rally was currently underway and I was intent on recording the proceedings. If all went well, my footage would provide for the making of what would become my second political short subject.

Upon arrival, I saw a crowd of students surrounding an elevated platform where John Barry, a legal advisor to several progressive student political groups at UCF, was leveling a fact-filled indictment against the U.S. government's continuing war in Iraq. Several UCF police officers watched from afar.

I quickly jumped into videographer mode and began capturing the happenings from various angles. I didn't want to miss a beat.

After Mr. Barry spoke, Patrick DeCarlo, a highly active member of sds (Students for a Democratic Society), took the stage to deliver an even more impassioned renunciation of U.S. intervention in the Middle East.

When Patrick concluded his speech, a young woman was handed the microphone and began reading a long list of names. As she did so, two large, black cardboard coffins were carried into the courtyard by several students all dressed in black. The names that the young woman read were the names of the college-aged students who had died in their Iraq tour of duties.

In this mock-funeral ceremony, a number of participating students approached the coffins one-by-one to deposit rolled-up sheets of paper, or fake diplomas, representing the unfulfilled promise of the deceased servicemen and women.

After this stage of the rally, a march was announced. The coffins would be taken to a nearby U.S. Army recruitment office.

The coffins and a group of about 50 students, with many carrying anti-war posters, soon made their way out of the Student Union area and toward Alafaya Trail, the six-lane street between UCF and the mall plaza where the recruitment office was located. All the while, the students chanted such protest slogans as "One, two, three, four; UCF will end this war! Five, six, seven, eight; Iraq was a big mistake!" and "No war, no way, no fascist USA!"

As the group of students approached the large roadway, Matt De Vlieger, another highly active member of sds and head of the procession, made a bold move and led the group onto one of the northbound lanes of Alafaya Trail.

"We are keeping this lane! We are keeping this lane! It is a minor convenience for them! They'll get over it!" Matt confidently advised with the help of a megaphone.

Many cars beeped at us in either annoyance or support as we obstructed traffic. Unfazed by any hostile motorists, we trekked onward.

Arriving at the Armed Forces Career Center, the students huddled together for a sit-in and several more speeches were given with the aid of a megaphone. The office soon announced that it would be closing for the day.

A coterie of local law enforcement soon arrived and watched our group from some distance away. One of the officers was video recording us.

At the conclusion of the rally, march and sit-in, the coffins were laid against the door of the recruitment office and left there. The group of students soon dispersed and the event was over. We had raised enough alarm for the day.

Feeling I'd captured the events rather well, I soon returned to my apartment and began the more cerebral work of editing the footage together into far more condensed form.

Several days later, with my short documentary complete, initially titled *War Dogs' Dirge* before I would change it at the end of the year to the far less condescending *3,000 Too Many*, I shared it with various members of sds. The response was encouraging and the view ticks of the initial YouTube upload were the highest I'd ever had.

But Matt, who'd led the march, used a particular word to describe the manner in which I'd depicted the persons of that day. His comment sent me down an odd path of thought:

The eagle-eyed officer watching over the Student Union courtyard during the event? He'd always be doing so.

The young woman who narrowly avoids the mock-pallbearers as they approach the heart of the rally? She'd always be doing so.

The service member who walks past the camera moments later? He'd always be doing so.

The female announcer who reads the names of the deceased U.S. service members during the mock-funeral? She'd always be doing so.

The student who deposited one of the fake diplomas dejectedly (it is rumored that his father was killed-in-action while serving in the Middle East)? He'd always be doing so.

The various students and non-students observing the mock-funeral? They'd always be doing so.

The drivers of the vehicles that neared and honked at the marching students? They'd always be doing so.

Matt leading the procession up Alafaya Trail and announcing that "We're crazy for being here!"? He'd always be doing so.

Matt's comment prompted a feeling that I'd essentially fossilized everyone who'd appeared in my documentary vignette. They were permanently fixed in this digital historical video record I'd put together;

their existence saved and stored for posterity. Nothing about them really known, for the most part, except that for a moment in time they existed in relation to this elaborate expression of anti-war sentiment. Now, their trace of existence preserved for all time.

And the word Matt had used which prompted this peculiar feeling?

"Timeless."

81. Principles (September 2006)

Fall 2006 was my first semester as a full-fledged film student in University of Central Florida's limited-access Film BFA program. And one of the first courses in my initial slate of classes was Professor Lori Ingle's Cinematic Expressions.

As described in the syllabus, Cinematic Expressions was "an introduction to the expression of meaningful cinema through a detailed exploration of the visual principles of design and the elements of art, with parallels drawn to narrative theory..." Given my extensive visual arts background, I greatly looked forward to this particular offering in the film school curriculum.

In fact, so intrigued was I by the premise of Professor Ingle's class that I had actually sat in on the introductory session of her class the previous spring semester before I'd been accepted into the film program.

As my classmates and I filed into one of the classrooms now accessible with our new, film student key cards, I relished every moment of this new experience. As soon as Professor Ingle entered the classroom, she introduced herself and made everyone feel right at home in our new classification as Film BFA students.

After some basic orders of business like reviewing the syllabus and the professor addressing her expectations of us throughout the semester, Professor Ingle surprised us by asking us to clear our desks of everything but a pen and paper. We were going to do some drawing!

Professor Ingle guided the class through a simple, contour drawing exercise in which we were to sketch our free hand without looking at our sketch marks and without lifting our drawing utensil from our sheets of paper.

More than familiar with these sorts of exercises from my time in art schools, Professor Ingle walked by my desk and found my resulting sketch an ideal example to share with the class. So, she picked up my sketch and showed it to all of my classmates. They seemed impressed. What can I say? I'd had a generous head start.

After several more exercises and some theoretical discussion, Professor Ingle introduced our first take-home assignment. Our class was to use Photoshop to produce a simple, black-and-white abstract design using four lines and three of the same shapes. None of the edges of the elements could touch, overlap or drop off the page and we were to employ the Theory of Thirds.

Simple enough, I thought, and got to sketching out some ideas at my earliest convenience.

However, I did not anticipate how seriously I'd take the assignment. I ended up filling numerous pages of a sketchbook I kept with countless variations of line and shape enclosed in a rectangle divided into sections according to the Theory of Thirds. Most of my sketches governed by the principles we were exploring in class. The work quickly became an obsession as I continually played around with these few basic elements during any available free time.

Before long, I was approaching the assignment with the alike rigor of a short film project. I even began seeing if it was possible to convey political ideas through the simple use of line and shape. Needless to say, I wanted to come up with something exceptional and I certainly didn't hesitate to furnish my creative process with the necessary amount of time and mental effort to breach such lofty ambitions.

About a week later, the due date arrived and I eagerly submitted the result of my inordinate noodling. All of the abstract designs would be presented to the class for review at the following class session.

My fellow classmates' work was certainly fascinating to behold but when my design was shown, I heard gasps! My design had done something quite distinctive. About 7/8ths of the composition of my design had been taken up by one of the allotted shapes. It was a bold choice which made a strong impact. The professor spent some time praising my design and I felt like I'd done the utmost possible with a few lines and a few shapes. Although none would ever divine the political sentiment which powered my approach, I still felt rather satisfied with the design's reception.

After class let out that day, one of my fellow classmates Marco Cordero stated frankly that my design had been "the best one." That simple comment meant more and more to me as Marco's reputation as an incredibly talented cinematographer grew over time.

Unfortunately, my experience working on subsequent abstract designs for Professor Ingle's class would suffer from increasing frustration and indecisiveness. While several of my later designs would receive favorable attention during in-class review, I struggled with deadlines as the requirements of the projects grew more complex and demanding. Professor Ingle was patient with me but my performance toward the end of the semester left a great deal to be desired.

Despite my latter faltering in the course, I absolutely loved Cinematic Expressions and everything that Professor Ingle attempted to instill in all of her students. She passionately defended the idea of design, as opposed to chance or happenstance, as critical to the success and development of a filmmaker. She wanted us to live and breathe a codified language of grounded principles and theories that could guide us to higher and higher planes of artistic creation.

For this and so much more, I will always be grateful. Thank you, Professor Ingle!

82. Professors (May 2014)

Intending to finally complete my undergraduate education and earn a bachelor's degree, I tied up some loose ends at University of Central Florida related to my conduct-related severance from the university four years ago and set my sights on resuming my college career at Florida International University. I would be enrolling at FIU in the earliest Summer 2014 semester as a Communication Arts major.

Having matured a great deal since my initial stint at FIU (I spent my first year in college at FIU as a philosophy major from 2004 to 2005), I'd grown particularly sensitive to the potential for the facilitation of a student's moral, practical and intellectual development by a quality professor.

Over the course of my two years in my undergraduate program at the Miami university, I would come into contact and develop relationships with numerous standout instructors who'd leave an indelible mark on me in and beyond class. What follows is a recounting of several of these professors (by no means a comprehensive listing):

Professor Daniel Blaeuer was my professor for two courses, Artistic Expression in a Global Society and Communication for Effective Leadership in my Fall 2014 and Fall 2015 semesters, respectively.

On the first day of my first class with him, his lanky and informal appearance betrayed a deep and rare erudition. For someone so young (he was 36 at the time), I was amazed.

Some of the most resonant themes explored in his classes included the extremes of acceptable artistic expression, the self-organization potential of social groups and wicked social problems (i.e., problems without any evident solutions). He was heavily influenced by systems thinking and approached most topics through that lens. I also appreciated the salient skeptical and iconoclastic streak to many of his opinions. He was never afraid of being a firebrand.

Outside of class, he was generous with his time and I once spent an hour or so in his office deep-diving with him into some of the ideas brought up in class. Besides many other instances of extracurricular interaction, I also received a warm hug from him immediately after taking the stage at my undergraduate commencement in 2016.

Professor Antoine Hardy was my professor for Persuasion in my Spring 2015 semester.

Early on in his class, Professor Hardy made references to a range of varied teaching and research experiences he'd enjoyed. Some of them involved branding and public opinion; highly relevant to a class about changing or manipulating attitudes in an attempt to win over an individual or groups of people. He had a novel perspective I greatly appreciated.

On one memorable occasion, he wrote atop a paper I'd written, "This is genius!". The paper I'd submitted was a script for a spoof of a Victoria's Secret advertisement which, instead of describing visuals of scantily clad women, described a series of courtship displays by organisms at different points in our evolutionary lineage. I'm glad I impressed him with that as I had a great time conceiving of the idea and writing it up.

But the kindest and most encouraging gesture Professor Hardy ever offered was screening my 15th short film *Leo's Love Letter* to one of his classes (I wasn't in attendance) to illustrate a class topic. According to him, it went over quite well. He did this without my consent or any fanfare and when he casually mentioned it some time later, I felt the warmest gratitude.

Professor T.J. Aiken was my professor for Rhetoric and Public Address in my Spring 2016 semester.

Professor Aiken had a style all his own. Highly irreverent, filled with anarchic humor and often resembling a sports team meet owing to his role as a debate team coach for FIU. I was also fond of the breakneck pace of his lectures and leading of discussions.

One of the most surprising, though relatively insignificant, revelations in his class was his partiality toward the *Star Wars* prequel trilogy over the original trilogy of films. As a die-hard prequelist and apologist for the oft-maligned series of films, my jaw hit the floor when he mentioned his particular preference and I stayed after class to express my amazement. I'm such a geek!

However, Professor Aiken offered up a memorable piece of deadly sincere (surprisingly enough) encouragement when he recommended that I pursue some type of career in writing. He must have been impressed with a recently submitted essay of mine and felt I had ample talent for such an enterprise. I never forgot that and it may be one of the reasons I often describe myself as a filmmaker and writer in the same breath.

Professor Orly Shuber was my professor for Communication in Film in my Spring 2016 semester.

A film class in college.

Familiar territory.

My involvement in the lecture discussions was characteristically spirited and even boisterous at times. I was always eager to exercise my extensive practical and theoretical bearings in the class. At times, I was overzealous but I couldn't help it - I lived and breathed virtually all of the presented terms and concepts. Thankfully, Professor Shuber was tolerant and was more often appreciative than annoyed.

Some time after the semester wrapped up, Professor Shuber invited me to present my two latest short films *Leo's Love Letter* and *The Promotion* to a few of her classes. I jumped at the opportunity and prepared extensively. I brought archived production material and helped give my audience of young people a look into the creative process of an independent, micro-budget short filmmaker. On these occasions I was able to give my teaching skills a first-time stretch and my presentations generally seemed a success owing to the evident captivation of the students.

Related to the making of my 16th and final short film *The Promotion*, Professor Shuber kindly lent her support for a request made to an FIU administrator about making use of a library location for filming purposes.

Professor Shuber was willing to back up my effort by according it relevance to the objectives of her class. When my request was granted, I was most grateful!

Professor Dr. Andrew Strycharski was not a professor for any of my courses but we met at a local filmmaker showcase in 2015 and continued our interaction at FIU. He is also Director of Film Studies at that university.

Unlike the other professors I've written about, I never took a class with Andy (as I now affectionately call him). Our paths met under circumstances beyond the university setting. Andy happened to be a judge at the aforementioned local short film showcase in downtown Miami in 2015. My 15th short film *Leo's Love Letter* was being screened and in contention for an award or two. At the end of the event, I spoke with Andy upon learning that he was a professor at FIU where I was actively enrolled. We hit it off immediately and soon found ourselves enjoying coffee together on campus. Our conversations touched upon media, culture, politics, family, film theory, pedagogy and mental illness. I was continually intrigued by his half of the dialogue.

During my time at FIU and after, Andy offered some integral support to me as a filmmaker. He had me interviewed for the official FIU Film Studies newsletter. And he, like Professor Shuber, lent his sanctioning help in my petition for filming location access from an FIU administrator for the making of my last short film. And I also reciprocated such generosity in turn by authoring a recommendation letter for him for a senior lecturer position he intended to get.

Knowing Andy, you'd rarely see a professor who was a more nourishing and flowing river to their entrusted pupils. His interactions with his students and teaching assistants were always congenial, intelligent and substantial. There was also a cool edge to Andy no doubt spawned from his great wisdom and ceaselessly critical eye. And there was never a more dedicated and hard-working fleet of interns as he commanded. It was always a sight to see and I respected Andy for all of these attributes.

* * *

I graduated cum laude with my Bachelor of Arts in Communication Arts at the end of the Spring 2016 semester with a pristine 4.0 GPA among all of the 16 courses I enrolled in as part of the program. I was as committed to excellence as I was because I was in an environment populated by the kind of professors who embodied that charge through and through. I loved most of my professors and all but one of whom I've previously highlighted are always a phone call, text or Facebook message away.

The one professor who is no longer available to interact with, however, is Professor Blaeuer. He passed away in 2018 from cancer. His passing was devastating to me because I wasn't aware of his fateful condition and expected we'd pick up our conversation at some point after his condition had improved.

Around the time of his funeral service I wrote, "I despise clichés and death is the worst one. But some Joseph Campbell comes to mind: 'We're not on our journey to save the world but to save ourselves. But in doing that you save the world. The influence of a vital person vitalizes.'"

That's who these professors are to me: saviors of the world; vital persons who vitalize.

83. Proud (November 2017)

It was the night of the 16th Annual Miami Short Film Festival and I would be attending the event to represent my 16th and final short film *The Promotion*. It was my third time having an official selection at the festival; previously with *Semester of Madness* in 2012 and *Leo's Love Letter* in 2016.

Arriving at the Cinépolis multiplex in Coconut Grove for my screening, I soon encountered my close friend Kieron Williams. He was dressed a touch more formally than usual and looked a bit on edge as this evening had much in its mouth for him as well. Kieron would be premiering his debut short film *It's Ya Boy* on the same night and screen as my short film. His piece would be playing in the first of two blocks of short films and mine would follow as part of the second block.

After a tight embrace in the lobby, we filed into the crowded auditorium. I took my seat next to Kieron and shared in his excitement and nervousness as we waited for the first program to begin.

It's Ya Boy is a two-minute, sketch-like comedy which unravels over the course of a single, unbroken take. It's about a young man who confronts a radio DJ with a surprising revelation that the DJ is his estranged father. Brief and comedic, it is a deft combination of writing, performance and hilarious sound design. Upon learning it had been accepted at Miami Short Film Festival, I was thrilled but I was even more thrilled when I learned our short films would be scheduled so close together.

Kieron had kindly shared his newbie effort with me some time before the night of this festival screening and I absolutely loved its riotous but heartfelt sense of humor! But how would the gathered audience of mostly strangers receive *It's Ya Boy*? We would find out in moments...

* * *

I first met Kieron under similar festive circumstances: at the closing night social event of the 2nd Annual FIU Student Film Festival at Florida International University in the spring of 2014. My 13th short film *Semester of Madness* had played earlier in the week to a full house in the largest auditorium at FIU and the response to it had been electric. Save for a slight award-disqualifying technicality, it had been poised to win the festival's best film award.

In any case, at the closing night festivities, I spoke with various young people who expressed great admiration for my film and were curious about me and my work. Among this group was Kieron Williams, an FIU student at the time and an aspiring writer. Kieron and I spent a fair amount of time discussing my short film and our individual creative processes. We clicked in a way I'd scarcely ever known. At one point, I offered up that my intent with my filmmaking was to offer an experience "better than reality." He seemed particularly smitten by that.

Kieron and I would later pick up where we left off at that closing night event when we saw each other again at a Fall 2014 convocation for new Communication Arts students at FIU. As chance would have it, we would be pursuing the same major as I resumed my undergraduate career at FIU.

As I continued my studies, Kieron and I found countless opportunities to deepen our friendship. We would wax on all manner of topics related to our respective crafts (i.e., writing and filmmaking). We'd also preview our latest work for one another and exchange ideas and experiences related to our shared pursuit of the sublime.

Kieron was an accomplished short story writer whose boundless imagination and fastidious orientation toward his craft were unlike anything I'd ever encountered in a young person. He shared many of his short stories with me, sometimes to simply share older works and other times to exact a critical response to a recently completed piece. He regarded my opinion of his writing as the result of someone with "more scrutinous eyes." Always a rewarding delight and never a taxing obligation, I constantly looked forward to reading Kieron's writings and relaying my thoughts.

With his friend and fellow FIU classmate Evan Burr as president, Kieron also helped run FIU's film club, Film Inititative: Underground. I attended their meetings as often as I was able, regularly participating in their many and varied workshops and discussions; offering my personal insight as a filmmaker wherever I could. Kieron was almost always in attendance.

Kieron also ran a separate club on-campus, called Creative Collective. This brainchild of his was intended for FIU students in the arts. Kieron presided over the meetings which offered any FIU student a quiet space to work on their creative projects and the opportunity to share their work with fellow creatives for feedback, support and positive habit formation.

In the spring of 2015, Kieron graduated while I was still halfway through the Communication Arts program. However, Kieron was hired by FIU's HR department not too long after his graduation and was able to maintain a regular presence on FIU's campus. As a result, we were able to continue our always lull-free conversational habit - albeit in hour-long, lunchtime intervals. We made the most of it and also met up for occasional film screenings.

Now sitting next to Kieron on the night of his momentous short film premiere, I couldn't help but think about the deep, abiding friendship we'd developed over the past three-and-a-half years.

Unsurprisingly, the strong comedic performances and deft writing landed exceptionally well with the night's gathered audience. Kieron's talent for storytelling and tickling an audience's funny bone was never more evident. *It's Ya Boy* elicited laughs in all the right places and when the short film concluded the audience paid their respects with vigorous applause and murmurs of satisfaction. Turning to Kieron with the widest grin on my face, he seemed overwhelmed by the unanimously positive reaction.

After the first block of short films wrapped up, I walked out of the auditorium with Kieron as he was met with a barrage of back-pats, embraces and enthusiastic remarks from his other friends and family. He was then asked to participate in an on-camera, red carpet interview with the festival's video crew.

After Kieron confidently fielded every question with his characteristic intelligence and charm, I approached him.

"Congratulations, man!" I offered him emphatically.

"Thanks, Gabe!" he responded with matched energy.

Kieron then apologized for not being able to attend my short film's upcoming screening due to a pressing family dinner invitation.

"No worries at all! Go celebrate! You've earned it!" I told him.

"Let's get together soon?" he floated.

"Sure thing!" I assured him.

Kieron then left with his family and I made my way back into the auditorium for the resumption of the night's screenings. However, as I retook my seat in the theater I wasn't thinking about the imminent screening of my own short film but reeling from the intense pride and respect I felt for my friend.

My amazing friend.

84. Radical (October 2007)

Earlier in the year, I had traveled from University of Central Florida in Orlando to Washington, D.C. to participate in a march against the Iraq War with my fellow sds (Students for a Democratic Society) members.

Now in the fall, a new series of demonstrations was expected to take place at the U.S. capital. This time, however, the target was the globalization movement; namely, the actions of the World Bank and the IMF (International Monetary Fund). The two organizations were set to meet in D.C. over the weekend where hundreds of activists would be there to greet them.

This October Rebellion, organized by the October Coalition, demanded wiping out the debt of developing countries, ending structural adjustment policies which prioritize profit over people and ceasing oil production, gas production, mining and other kinds of socially and environmentally devastating infrastructural development.

Intrigued by another opportunity to express my dissent over the status quo at no less a pressure point than the very seat of U.S. power, I readied to make the trip!

Unlike last time, though, I would be more visually in-line with my cohorts. The night before our departure, I visited a shopping center where I acquired a black hoodie, black bandana and a sinister-looking skull-mask. I planned on documenting the protests but I knew, if the time came, I would be participating in some degree of civil disobedience with my fellow student activists.

The drive was long and I mostly kept to myself. My creeping psychosis, several weeks from its full unraveling may have had something to do with my slightly greater-than-usual asocial disposition over the course of the trip. In any case, I preoccupied myself with trying to anticipate what form the documentary I was planning to make about the experience would ultimately take.

As the road trip neared conclusion, a familiar sight soon appeared in the far distance: the blinking red light atop the Washington monument; again, like the ever-watchful Eye of Sauron in *The Lord of the Rings*.

The group of sds'ers I was with had, with the aid of the event's organizing coalition, arranged to stay at a local community center for the brief duration of our activities in D.C. As soon as we arrived at the location in the early morning hours, we determined our sleeping quarters and turned in for the rest of the night.

The first order of business on our itinerary was to attend a rally at the headquarters of U.S. Immigration and Customs Enforcement. Only a few hundred demonstrators partook in the event, assailing problematic overseas economic policies believed responsible for excessive immigration, but I was sure to have my video camera out and documenting. I was surprised by the make-up of the crowd which was fairly heterogenous: young, old, male, female, white and persons of color.

Later that day, my fellow sds'ers and I visited a home that on the outside appeared like any other suburban edifice. But on the inside, it resembled a cluttered way station of some sort. Purely utilitarian. There was all manner of anti-globalization and anarchist literature on tables and specially demarcated areas for LGBTQ+ individuals. It was a safe house for all of the visiting student activists. The adults who ran it felt like everyone's caring and supportive parents. We half-expected peanut butter and jelly sandwiches to be passed around at some point.

At this location, my group and I took part in some tactical training with other young activists to prepare us for the approaching evening. No doubt of anarchist authorship, these exercises were intended to prepare us for encounters with police... and police on horseback.

Later that night, the October Rebellion would be in full force! The plan was to march in black bloc formation through an area of D.C. known as Georgetown; a quiet residential area considered a kind of playground of the capital's elite. Many of the World Bank and IMF officials were believed to be staying there for the planned meetings.

While my valiant comrades and I dined at a local restaurant not too far from Georgetown, we received word about the substantial police presence that was amassing nearby. We also learned that shop owners in the area were being asked to board up their windows and evacuate.

As part of a black bloc march, there was an expectation that an order might be passed on to suddenly disperse and participate in wanton property destruction and violence against police. Although this wasn't a certainty, I was ready to keep my camera holstered if I found it necessary to take violent political action. For a time, I may have believed in the cause against a political status quo more than my own personal, artistic ambitions.

We soon approached the rallying point for the march on Georgetown. There were several hundred activists ready to go. Appropriately fully clad in black with my black bandana and skull mask, I locked arms with my fellow comrades as the march began.

Many storefront windows had been boarded up in anticipation of our presence. But their store owners had their allies in the countless police surrounding our daring but onward march. There were police on scooters, police on motorcycles and police on horseback. And they were all aggressive; taunting and inviting our ire toward them through their close proximity to our ranks.

Their operation was massive and I soon realized that despite our numbers and whatever tactical preparation we believe we possessed, the police would prove a highly formidable opponent.

Then, it started to rain. I almost didn't believe the source of so much water. I thought the police were using water cannons to soak us as some form of crowd control. But I was wrong. It was heavy rain compounded with spirited gusts of wind. Within minutes, my allies and I were soaked straight through from top to toe. But we marched on, against the tide of rain and so much police chaperoning.

After some time, the police finally showed a stronger hand in rerouting us and attempting to quell the march.

At one point, I found myself and a few of my fellow compatriots cornered by several police on horseback. The police used the considerable size, strength and intimidation of their mounts to surround us and compress us tightly before allowing each of us to squeeze out from this tactical boxing-in and refrain from any more black bloc formationing.

I soon regrouped with my familiar group of UCF sds'ers as we were all forced to vacate the area by threat of arrest. The march through Georgetown was over.

My group and I returned to our hosting community center and, despite all of us still sopping wet, found enough sleepy repose until the next morning.

But there was still one last item left on our weekend itinerary!

Later the following day, there was yet another demonstration planned. This time, at the World Bank headquarters, the site where the meeting between these major global financial entities would be taking place.

So, hundreds of activists, including myself, showed up to express our rancor. Near the entrance of the building, some of my fellow activists were able to engage with some of the financial ministers as they exited their luxury vehicle caravan and approached the building. "It's not our fault" was one particular refrain I happened to hear from one of the ministers as they scurried into the building.

And yes, there was yet another sizable police presence. At one point, a line of officers rushed us with their batons lifted. I narrowly avoided their sudden onslaught but some of my fellow comrades were not so lucky and even reported having been struck by the ruthless law enforcers.

The showdown soon subsided and our merry band of activists eventually disbanded not too long after all of the arriving financial ministers were all gathered behind closed doors.

Following this final event in D.C., the group of sds'ers I had traveled here with and I set out on our return journey to Orlando.

Ultimately, I ended up not making a documentary out of the footage I'd captured of the October Rebellion. I had become too engrossed in my own active involvement and neglected to film enough to warrant a proper cinematic treatment of the experience - even a perfunctory one.

Although I remained quiet and contemplative on the ride back to UCF, I returned with a feeling of having further fortified my political identity. I'd never given myself to a cause as much as I had to the October Rebellion. It almost frightened me to consider to what length and degree I was willing to fight and suffer for such a cause.

At the site of the third and final protest, I happened to find a black anarchist flag that had been left dropped by another activist. I still have it and I'll always keep it to remind myself of a certain spirit integral to my life.

A spirit of justice.

A spirit of the People.

A spirit of resistance.

85. Recruitment (May 2003)

After several months of production on my first short film *Mass Education*, it was finally time to orchestrate the most elaborate scene in the script. The scene in question involved the protagonist of the short film, played by stalwart friend Sam Williams (a non-actor), encountering a group of students exiting their high school library with boxes of books in tow. Numerous extras and cardboard boxes would be required for the ambitious staging of the scene. It would be shot in the hallway just outside the actual library at Miami Killian Senior High.

When I shared the particular demands of this challenging scene with my parents, my mother immediately suggested that she could easily provide a number of flat, pre-folded cardboard boxes for near-effortless assembly at the site of filming. At the time, my mom worked as a merchandiser for American Greetings and had easy access to such a supply.

So, boxes?

Check!

All I needed now was the group of student extras. But how difficult could it be to gather about 15-20 students at a high school populated by nearly two-thousand of them?

Cake, I thought. Surely I could count on my friends and classmates to fill the needed ranks.

And, of course, my mom volunteered to bake a large plate of brownie cupcakes as catering detail for all of the student extras. Mothers will be mothers!

With determination to spare, I soon set about inviting my friends and fellow classmates to stay at Killian after school hours on a chosen weekday. I may have asked about 15 or so young people if they would show up. I even mentioned the waiting plate of brownies for their time and effort.

In the end, I received many verbal commitments but, in my naiveté, I didn't realize how conditional and flimsy they actually were.

In any case, during the lunch hour on that chosen weekday I set out to map out on paper how I'd shoot the scene. The diagram I produced survives to this day and resembles a storyboard with added drawings indicating a top-down view of the relationship between the camera and the action throughout every stage of the scene. I applied the most pure and calculated logic.

With my plan for shooting the scene worked out to a tee, I spent the rest of my day anticipating a successful shoot after school hours.

However, after school let out I was surprised that almost none of those I'd courted to help me out had shown up in the hallway just outside the library for filming. When the moment of truth presented itself, only my lead actor Sam, my friend Braian and a friend of his Veronica Torres had come through.

I then excused myself to check if my mom had arrived with the pre-made boxes and brownie cupcakes.

She was parked just outside the school entrance.

I told her to stand by as my concern and disappointment mounted.

Returning to the indoor hallway and finding no one but Sam, Braian and Veronica waiting calmly, I was devastated. So much for counting on what I believed was a healthy camaraderie among young people at my school, especially as matters of independent creative endeavor were concerned. But from that point forward, I knew I would have to be far more persuasive in my future solicitations or simply not write in scenes whose essential elements I wasn't absolutely sure I could gather.

There in the hallway I stood with Sam, Braian and Veronica as my despair gradually replaced what had been my pent up excitement about getting this major scene filmed. I prepared to make my decisive next move: calling off the scheduled filming and to try another day.

But just as I was about to fold, I caught a glimpse inside the nearby library and saw the Killian basketball team stationed inside.

A bold but chancy idea grew in my mind.

"Are we still filming or what?" Braian asked.

"Wait a second," I replied before I innocently strolled into the library.

Inside the library, I approached the coach of the school's sports team and jumped into persuasion mode.

"Hi, my name is Gabriel Rhenals and I'm making a short film here at Killian. I was wondering if you would allow your team to help me film a short scene just outside the library here. It won't take longer than 15 minutes," I stated, overtaken with an unusual rush of confidence and fearlessness.

The coach was surprised but sensing either my pathetic desperation or mad earnesty, addressed his group of young athletes accordingly.

"Alright, listen up! You're all going to help out this young man here who needs to film a scene for a short film," the coach commanded.

He then stepped aside and allowed me the floor.

"Hi, everyone! Please follow me outside to pick up some boxes needed for the scene! There's a big plate of brownie cupcakes waiting for everyone who helps out!"

The coach abided, "Let's go, guys! You heard him!"

Immediately, the basketball players rose and assembled in orderly fashion as I led them out of the library to my mom's car parked not too far from the expected site of filming.

The entire group, including Braian and Veronica, each grabbed a single flat piece of cardboard from the trunk of the car and were instructed to fold them into box form. They did so as I led them back to the hallway outside the library.

With Braian, Veronica and each basketball player now holding a fully-formed box, I gave them instructions to line-up just behind the library doorway. I told them that they would be exiting the library in a line on my mark and proceeding down the length of the hallway close to the right-hand wall.

I next gave some simple instructions to Sam as I prepared my video camera and makeshift Steadicam for filming. For Sam's part, he only needed to approach the library and observe the box-carrying line of students in surprise.

The process took a number of takes and I noticed that the number of basketball players decreased with each subsequent take. It seemed my charisma had its limits. In any case, I was ultimately able to acquire enough footage to make the sequence work in the editing.

After the team's work was done, I presented the large plate of brownie cupcakes to them and the offered baked goods disappeared in a flash!

I then thanked the student athletes, their coach as well as Braian and Veronica for all of their help but no words could do justice to the intense gratitude and satisfaction I felt.

After Sam and I flattened the used boxes and put them in the trunk of my mom's car waiting outside, my mom and I gave Sam a ride home.

The experience of directing this sequence had been challenging but exhilarating! And with the most difficult stage of production on my first short film now squarely in my rear view, I proceeded with the rest of filming on *Mass Education* with more confidence and surety than I'd ever known!

86. Refused (September 2003)

It was the start of my senior year at Miami Killian Senior High and I'd completed a short film script, titled *Body Master*, over the summer. It was my sole preoccupation during those warm, out-of-school months. I'd actually begun writing it months before I'd completed my first short film *Mass Education* at the end of my previous year at Killian.

Body Master was envisioned as an allegorical story about racism; a far more mature, ambitious project than *Mass Education*. It involved the relationship between an athletic trainer and his trainee which grows increasingly personal and fraught with animosity. At the end of the story, there is an eruption of outrageous violence and only one of our two main characters is left living. This climactic fight to the death would have involved filming underwater using special housing equipment for my submerged video camera.

I was particularly excited about filming *Body Master* at certain locations in the suburban area of Kendall where I lived. The underwater sequence mentioned would have been shot at an Olympic-sized swimming pool at nearby Miami Dade College. Also, I would have shot some introductory and concluding scenes in the backyard of my home (I even performed some early lighting tests). The film would have also featured the trainer character resting under a massive oak tree in a spot on a local golf course that I'd wanted to film at for years.

With a script in a more-or-less finished state, I decided to ask two of my fellow classmates who I'd been eyeing for the two principal roles since the start of the school year. As far as I knew, they were non-actors so I felt I had to be particularly persuasive.

One morning before class began, I popped the question to the first of the two candidates. However, midway into my humble presentation, the student turned me down politely. Citing a general disinterest in acting, the classmate I was soliciting seemed unalterably decided. Nevertheless, I approached the same student the following day with an added promise of compensation for his time and effort. He politely turned me down yet again.

Still hopeful I could recruit the other Killian student I had in mind, I went ahead and made my best effort to ask for his help. I was summarily turned down here as well. The student cited a lack of time and no amount of money I had to offer could sway him either.

Devastated by the refusals to participate from the two propositioned students, my plans were thrown into a whirl. I had banked fully on the cooperation of these two students and didn't have any alternative options for casting. So, I consequently abandoned plans for the production.

I was deeply hurt and needed time to lick my wounds.

Upon recovery, my new plan was to write something far less ambitious involving a single actor and a single location. I soon set about writing a brand new script.

Some months later, I came up with a detailed outline but not a complete script for my latest effort. The new project, titled *All Super Summer Long*, was a simple home invasion story. One actor and one location, as previously determined.

Thankfully, I was able to enlist a classmate of mine in the lead role of a gun-toting man gripped in fear of having his home besieged and infiltrated. We shot some scenes despite the lack of a complete script and I was confident I would see this latest project through to its completion. However, the irregular shooting schedule caused the lead actor's interest to wane and I was soon compelled to abandon production on yet another project.

Graduating from Killian and entering the summer break before my freshman year at Florida International University, I was resolved to come up with yet another short film project. This new untitled effort involved the Florida legend of Sasquatch and I eyed filming at a school where I'd taken my SATs. I would spend numerous months writing this untitled project and it would end up evolving into several different ideas. Unfortunately, all of these resulting offshoots would meet the same fate as *Body Master* and *All Super Summer Long*.

Although it would take some time to realize the follow-up to my first short film *Mass Education*, I owe my continual resolve to never allowing any setbacks or failure to dislodge my ultimate goals and ambitions.

That and my patience.

Much patience.

87. Rejection (July 2003)

When I was an overweening sophomore visual art student at New World School of the Arts in 2001, I spent some time looming over a group of senior visual art students working on a short film they were making. They were reviewing an edit of the short film's opening sequence in the school's iMac-filled computer lab. One of the students, presumably the director of this amateur filmmaking team, uttered something which I, despite all my infinite filmmaking inexperience at the time, immediately took offense with.

"We have to keep in mind what the audience will think," the young director stated.

I immediately balked at this suggestion and lost all interest in further shadowing this misguided band of newbies!

What nerve! What gall!

Later, I would elucidate my view on the matter to my mom during a subsequent car ride. I did not believe in making films for an audience. I felt prioritizing the consideration and taste of an audience was a cardinal sin and that the satisfaction of the artist him or herself should be the principal motivation and goal behind a work of art - especially a film!

After I completed my first short film *Mass Education* in 2003, I still nursed this idea and relished any opportunity to playback my short film on my desktop PC in the darkness of my bedroom for the explicit joy and appreciation of one person and one person alone - myself. This steely disposition of mine precluded any involvement with film festivals and other forms of public exhibition of my work for nearly a decade.

Despite this staunchly held view, I did envy to some degree the attention garnered by filmmakers on the film festival circuit. Even in the early 2000s, I was aware that an independent film movement was taking off thanks to the advent of the internet and DVD. I thought submitting my debut short film to a major film festival was a sure-fire way to establish myself as a professional filmmaker; by that time, a role I was fully envisioning for myself. But I knew I wanted to reach those heights without compromising my integrity by deferring to some need and regard for audience approval. Was it possible?

So, I did a bit of research and decided to submit *Mass Education* to an offshoot of an offshoot of Sundance Film Festival: Slamdance Film Festival's Anarchy Online film competition. The event sounded grungy, underground and too-cool-for-school. In other words, I felt it was a suitable complement to my view of myself and my renegade filmmaking mentality. Mainstream audiences be damned!

If I'm not mistaken, no film festivals had the means of accepting DVD copies of film submissions at the time so I had to prepare a VHS copy of my short film and thus did so. I actually thought the conversion of my short film to an analog medium helped disguise my film's digital origins; as I still harbored a digital inferiority complex which was common at the time.

With my self-authored VHS in the mail and on its way to Anarchy Online, I waited.

And waited.

A few months passed.

Finally, I received a response from the festival.

Mass Education had been politely rejected by Anarchy Online's programming committee.

I was disappointed, to be sure, but it was the first film festival I'd ever submitted to and it was my first short film. It was also a fairly major festival and my entry may have been competing with thousands of other submissions. The likelihood of rejection was to be expected and, despite my woeful inexperience, a part of me fully understood this. Still, I suffered from the burning rub of defeat.

That's why I didn't send *Mass Education* to any other film festivals after this experience. In fact, my engagement with festivals in the years following that somewhat stinging rejection was extremely limited. I was still operating on the basis of my own personal satisfaction with my work as the principal focus. I desired to be above the fray... above approval...

above rejection.

It wasn't until some years after completing my 2008 short film *The Nap* that I made a far more concerted effort to court the film festival world - with that particular short film.

Perhaps I felt I was now mature enough to face more disapproval and rejection without it affecting my self-esteem too greatly?

In any case, my renewed attempt would land me my first major film festival experience at Gasparilla International Film Festival in 2011 - and a glowingly positive one it would be! That's why from 2011 forward, film festival submissions became a regular consideration with every completed short film thereafter. Of course, there were plenty more festival rejections to follow but I was certainly no longer challenged or cowed by such outcomes.

As my experience attending film festivals and seeing my work screened publicly grew, so did my awareness of the immense social good of a generous and magnanimous artist; one who seeks to satisfy an audience as much as himself. In time, I would develop a greater appreciation of the symbiotic relationship between filmmaker and audience.

Despite the occasional "We regret to inform you…" emails, there was rich and fertile ground in this newfound relationship.

I no longer balked at the notion.

I no longer feared rejection.

I'd come a long way.

88. Relapse (June 2009)

A pair of EMTs lift me off of my bedroom mattress and onto a stretcher. Strapped in, I am carried onto an ambulance parked in front of my home.

"Deep breaths," one of the EMTs commands repeatedly. However, I mishear his words as "deep breasts" and assume the EMT is assessing the consumable meat content of my upper body.

The ambulance then departs.

A swirl of medical jargon from the busy emergency personnel fills my ears as their vehicle takes off. The transport's sirens clear the way.

When the ambulance arrives at an undisclosed location several miles away, my upward-locked view prevents me from seeing it but I hear the sonorous propeller-engine of a waiting helicopter.

Mounted onto the helicopter, an EMT applies a breathing apparatus to the lower half of my face. With my nose and mouth covered, I inhale an anaesthetic and lose consciousness moments later.

Nothingness.

When I regain consciousness, I can feel myself being lifted off of the helicopter and wheeled off a helipad and through a set of double-doors into the quiet retreat of a hallway. I am relieved that a violent mob with potentially cannibalistic intent are not waiting to intercept me. Perhaps staved off by the building's security? I'm not certain and the anaesthetic soon kicks in again.

Nothingness.

In a bright, fluorescently lit room, more medical personnel surround me. I lift and look at both of my forearms. I see jagged, three-inch-long incisions across both wrists. A surprisingly clear network of tendon, muscle and bone reveals itself from both openings in the flesh.

"Oh, god!" I cry. The anaesthetic takes effect once more.

Nothingness.

Upon recovering from another bout of chemically-induced sleep, I hear a soothing female voice.

"What is today's date?" the voice asks.

"March 17th," I reply. My birthday.

"What year?" she follows.

"1986," the year of my birth.

"Do you know where you are?" I am then asked.

"In heaven," I reply assuredly and soon capitulate to the sleeping gas yet again.

Nothingness.

When I return to wakefulness, I am now bound to my stretcher and parked near a nurse's station on a hospital floor. Both of my wrists have been bandaged.

My mom, dad and older brother Juan soon appear before me. They inform me that the surgery on my injuries was successful but express some confusion about why I chose to harm myself.

I opt not to reveal the secret reason I did so. My family profess their love and support but I can't bring myself to tell them that I believe a nuclear war is imminent and I, the Antichrist, am solely responsible for it.

An hour or so later, I am strolled into the reception area of a nearby mental health hospital. I will be interned there for two weeks.

At the start of the Spring 2009 semester, I was back at University of Central Florida after being required to enroll at a local college in Miami for a semester to prove that I was fit to continue at UCF following my mental health crisis in the fall of 2007.

Returning to the familiar surroundings of UCF's film school building fresh from winter break, I encountered the professor of my first class that day, Film History II (one of two courses I had with this particular professor that semester). I struck up a brief, friendly conversation with her before class time. Though charmed by her kindness and pleasantries, after some time in her classes, I developed a far less superficial fondness for her upon learning of her background as a graduate of a doctoral cinema studies program at University of Chicago.

I participated avidly in her classes because I found the class content, particularly of her more theoretical course The Film Audience, eminently fascinating.

As the weeks wore on, I attended all of my classes, worked diligently, made many new friends and generally made my best effort to fulfill the promise of a prosperous return to UCF following my past mental health challenges. However, believing that my Fall 2007 bout of mental illness had been an acute episode, to occur once and never again, would prove a calamitous and near-fatal mistake.

Some time later in the professor's other, theory-based class, my gradually deteriorating mental health condition reared its terrible head.

After a screening of Rainer Werner Fassbinder's 1978 German film *The Marriage of Maria Braun*, I overheard at least one student make a racially insensitive comment about this rather provocative film which centered on a fated interracial relationship. Unusually distressed by the remark, I remained in my seat brooding after the class had let out and only the professor remained.

Feeling offended and unsettled, I confronted the professor in the empty auditorium classroom about her choice of film. In a greatly agitated state, I sharply accused her of having ulterior motives in choosing her course content. However, I quickly relented and calmed down at both her urging and my realizing how frightening my initial burst of anger may have appeared. I quickly apologized to the professor and left the room.

My thoughts and emotions were clearly off.

A few days later, the professor was ready to discuss a film we'd seen in a previous class session, Tomás Gutiérrez Alea's 1968 Cuban film *Memories of Underdevelopment*. The film dealt with a bourgeois intellectual's account of a post-revolutionary Cuba.

I couldn't sit still. This time, I wasn't triggered by some errant, ignorant remark from an anonymous student. Instead, I felt completely isolated from my fellow classmates due to my strong affinity for revolutionary politics, particularly in Latin America. I felt that everyone around me, including and especially the professor, were brainwashed infidels that were sympathetic to the enemies of the Cuban Revolution and shared the same ambivalence toward social justice as the main character in the film.

As soon as the professor began her presentation, I fidgeted in my seat and agitatedly shuffled through the papers in my notebook. I felt like I was drowning! In the throes of intense social anxiety and paranoia, I messily grabbed all of my belongings and bolted out of the classroom.

I exited the film school building and found a bench in a nearby breezeway. I lay down on the outdoor furniture, perspiring and breathing heavily. Had I suffered another, yet milder, panic attack? Apparently so.

Several days later, I received notification that UCF's Office of Student Rights and Responsibilities was interested in having me participate in an OSRR committee meeting. I had been deemed a "student of concern."

At the meeting I was asked dozens of questions about the incident in which I angrily confronted the professor after class but responded to everything in the spirit of contrition. I knew how I'd behaved was inappropriate and concerning. But seeing how level-headed and rational I was, the committee members felt I no longer posed any threat to the safety and well-being of anyone in the UCF community. The meeting was adjourned and my status as a "student of concern" was stricken.

I met with the professor some time after the OSRR meeting and I apologized for my recent actions. We were back on regular terms and I would be free to continue attending both of her classes.

Following the incident and OSRR meeting, I had arranged to see a local Orlando psychiatrist in order to treat what I feared was a return of what had been diagnosed as a delusional disorder in 2007. I was prescribed a dosage of antipsychotic medication. Unfortunately, it wouldn't be enough.

Some time later, I asked the professor if I could meet with her in her office about one of the assignments in her film theory class. I was given an appointment and showed up promptly.

During the meeting I was still suspicious of the professor but felt compelled to share with her my views on a variety of film-related topics to prove my distinguished character. However, at one point in describing my attitude toward my classmates and UCF's population of students at large, I began to tremble and break down in tears, uttering "All I see are flesh and clothes." The professor hid her shock at my latest emotional disturbance well because moments later, having recovered from my unusual spell of strong emotion, I was able to engage in a normal, closing conversation with her as I accompanied her out of her office and to her upcoming class.

Owing to the mounting grandiose delusions I had about myself, my behavior in class became characterized by wholly uncharacteristic arrogance and boisterous participation. I felt I alone was the proper key master to all paths of enlightenment. My comments and questions became products of an unusual degree of uninhibitedness not unlike alcoholic intoxication. According to the professor, many students were offended and generally made uncomfortable by my in-class behavior.

But my in-person behavior wasn't the only concerning facet of my hastening re-descent into madness. My email communication with the professor took on an unusual and concerning character as well. In one email, some suspicious, semi-paranoid ideas about other students showed up: "During our conversation yesterday, I cited a showing of the 1995 film, *Showgirls*, as an example of how I became alienated from film criticism and how that experience caused me to consider the prevalence of group-think or a herd mentality in the practice, particularly among film students (ugh, can we consider [a new on-campus film student organization] the result of an inbred dynasty?)"

On another occasion, I overstepped my bounds by inquiring about the professor's personal political viewpoint: "I was somewhat surprised at your response to my query regarding how you saw yourself and the objectives of your course in relation to the goals of the university or traditional Enlightenment ideas like freedom, democracy and equality; and additionally, what your own personal political convictions were." Ironically, I would ask that I be exempt from disclosing my personal ideas in an autobiographical assignment; requesting to be allowed to interview someone else instead.

But no clearer was my unraveling than when I suggested the following in another email to the professor: "However, I was somewhat put-off by your reference to yourself as being 'a student of [Gunning, a renowned professor at University of Chicago].' Adds to my growing sense that there exists a subterranean world of worship and fanaticism that subverts your advanced notion that it's about the ideas, not people..."

To make matters worse, my frequency of contact and entanglement with the professor gradually produced in me strong feelings of affection and, to some degree, infatuation. I also suspected that my feelings were reciprocated despite any proof. These budding erotomanic delusions couldn't have been more misplaced.

On the night of the first meeting of the aforementioned "new on-campus film student organization," I arrived at the newly formed club's inaugural meetup and saw that the professor was also in attendance. We interacted briefly at the start of the meeting but I soon left as a scheduled film screening was about to take place.

After leaving, I went to the Student Union at the center of campus to have dinner and write. I was planning on returning to the film club meeting as it was finishing up in order to seize an opportunity to speak with the professor in private and admit my feelings toward her. I believed such an admission would purge the pain of harboring such misplaced sentiment.

When I returned to the meetup, the professor was on her way out of the film school building where the meeting had taken place. I trailed her down a hallway as I attempted to gather enough courage to call out to her. Before reaching one of the building's exits, the professor entered a nearby restroom. I paced in the lobby. When she re-emerged from the women's lavatory, we saw each other but I couldn't muster the will to do anything except wave to her as we passed each other. My confession would have to wait.

The next day, my paranoia intensified when I suspected the teacher was involved in some sort of tryst with one of the student founders of the film club of the previous night's occasion. I believed a secret, potentially sexual rendezvous was underway in the professor's office between her and the student. Her office door was closed on this occasion whereas during my meetings with her, it was always ajar.

Without fully considering the consequences, I pounded my fist against the outside wall of her office and her office door as I walked by them. Immediately embarrassed by what I'd done, I raced out of the area and visited the film school office to speak to the chair of the program about what had just happened. Unfortunately, the chair was not available. So, I left the building greatly flustered and ashamed over my rash action without being able to be held to account.

During the professor's class the following day, my outlandish behavior in-class, motivated by familiar feelings of persecution, persisted. However, this time I was determined to be upfront with the professor. So during an early break in the class period, I asked to speak with the professor in private. She was reluctant to do so but obliged.

We both exited the classroom and made our way some distance away from any other students. I was finally ready to say my long-waiting piece.

"Do you know who it was who banged on your office door yesterday?" I started.

"No, who?" the professor replied.

"It was me," I admitted.

The professor's eyes grew wide in shock.

"I have to get something off my chest," I prefaced.

"I'm obsessed with you," I said with a touch of melodramatic intent. "I know it's wrong but I need you to tell me it's wrong," I added.

The professor responded that she was open to talking about the situation further but my burden felt so entirely lifted that I quickly concluded the interaction by thanking her and swiftly left the film school building. I felt utterly relieved! I even called my oldest brother Alonso and expressed as much immediately following the interaction.

However, a day later, I was contacted by Detective Powers of the UCF Police Department. She wanted to interview me at the on-campus police station about my recent interactions with the professor.

In this interview, I was asked about what I'd admitted to the professor and again confessed my feelings. The detective cited the inappropriateness of a student-professor relationship and warned me not to contact the professor again in any way, shape or form; otherwise, a criminal investigation would be opened. I was also informed that I could no longer attend the professor's classes. I agreed and the meeting was soon over.

As I made my way out of the police station, I couldn't believe the professor would ally herself with the police in this manner; without further dialogue or involvement in some mediation process. She'd suggested as much at the end of our last encounter.

I soon learned that the professor had consequently accessed the Orlando court system in order to petition for a temporary injunction against me (lasting 15 days). This temporary injunction prohibited me from contacting the professor in any manner.

Unfortunately, I was incapable of contesting the grounds for either the temporary or a later final injunction due to a bungled informative effort by the court (they sent the relevant documents to an out-of-date address). Therefore, my chance to address the professor and the court in-person was dashed as well as an opportunity to more fully appreciate the harm I was causing and how sincere the professor's actions against me actually were (if that was even possible in my precarious state). In my absence, the professor's petition for a temporary and then final injunction was summarily approved.

In response to these alarming events, my parents drove up from Miami to help me find a lawyer to deal with the matter. The hired lawyer was competent and helpful but my interactions with her were vaguely flippant and disrespectful. It all felt woefully unnecessary.

Despite the new legal help and the detective's earlier warning, after the temporary injunction's 15-day time span, I sent the following social media message to the professor: "'Discipline and Fun: Psycho and Postmodern Cinema?' I would have never shut up! Or maybe I'd just stay quiet... :) (By the way, everyone's telling me to consider you persona non grata [I beat my lawyer to the term] and I'm perfectly willing to comply with the mandate, but I had to relate to you how insightful I found this article. There, bye."

The message's playful tone suggested that I was clearly oblivious to the severity of the whole situation.

A more severe final injunction would later be granted to the professor and, in effect, prevent me from being able to step foot on campus - even to attend my other classes. If I violated this court order, I would be subject to criminal prosecution. But even in the face of such unremitting harshness, I still didn't believe that the professor's actions against me were product of her own accord. Her hand was being forced, I thought. She wouldn't do this to me.

Moreover, the final injunction, while also prohibiting any contact with the professor, additionally restricted me from visiting campus for any reason without approved consent from UCF administrators for an entire year. However, this final injunction was never served on me by a court-appointed member of law enforcement.

Realizing that the professor's final injunction would bar me from attending the end-of-year showcase of the film program, I was livid! I had been eagerly anticipating seeing the work of a number of friends I'd made upon returning to the film school that semester as well as my former classmates from my earlier time in the program who would soon be graduating. Still, I clung to the belief that the professor was still sympathetic to my plight and open to some form of diplomatic dialogue. In fact, shortly before I was restricted from visiting campus I believed that the professor was communicating to me through cryptic drawings left on a drawing pad in the film program's main office.

Confined to my off-campus apartment, my desperation over being unable to attend the end-of-year film school showcase provoked the following message to the head of the OSRR office: "Please do not deprive me of this opportunity to be with most of the only friends I have. We have learned, worked, joked, and in some cases, lived together, and some them I may never see again."

In a follow-up email, I made reference to the professor not being included among the recipients of the OSRR's response - my bizarre ideations on full display: "Did you ever consider the possibility that [the professor is] the only person in this insulting, sordid situation whose opinion may actually matter? It is my most sincere contention that the UCF administrative and legal authorities (i.e., *my* greedy lawyer) have transformed this simple conflict - completely overlooking its peculiar but nevertheless significant idiosyncracies - into a situation filled with all the false dichotomies of what I'm certain are their own private sexual fantasies regarding swarthy, aggressive males and fearful, chaste females. To all involved, **GROW UP** and realize that some people are in fact genuinely interested in being thoughtful, productive, creative individuals in absolute fear of being driven by sexual appetite or other such base, selfish pursuits. But of course, who would understand that in a time and place like this..."

And then, in a fateful, self-inflicted blow, I copied the professor on an email to UCF administrators re-asserting my request to be allowed to attend the year-end screening event: "Allow me to repeat my *deepest sentiment*: No consequence could be worse than robbing me of, to a very unfair and damning degree, the only thing that matters to me, past all flesh and logic, my agendaless love for the art of motion pictures. A threat to that is a threat to me and I'm perfectly willing to go to the gallows for it."

I was warned by the OSRR officials to refrain from emailing the professor again due to the terms of the final injunction but I remained defiant and sent another email to the professor, foolishly requesting amnesty: "You have the power to end this comedy! Please allow me to attend the screenings."

That was the last straw.

The following day, I was contacted by Detective Powers and informed that I was promptly going to be taken into custody. I was completely surprised by the consequence of my actions and within an hour the UCF police arrived at my apartment complex. I was arrested and charged with a single count of stalking, a first-degree misdemeanor. Two additional charges relating to a violation of the final injunction were dropped because, again, the final injunction was never served on me.

I was alarmed and perplexed that the term "stalking" had entered the picture.

Jailed for the first time in my life, it was generally a regrettable experience despite my tolerance of its more degrading aspects. But given my history of mental health issues, I was relegated to the mental health ward of the Orange County prison which seemed like a slightly more hospitable environment for first-timers.

After a night in the pen, my parents made another trip up from Miami to pick me up upon release.

My arraignment was scheduled soon after. The legal help I'd enlisted to assist with my earlier conflict with UCF was no longer able to help me with my criminal case as I'd breached our contract with my illicit actions. So, at my arraignment, I was referred to Orlando's public defenders office.

My family was not in the position to afford a private lawyer.

With a trial looming in the coming months, I also had to contend with a conduct hearing by UCF's Office of Student Conduct. The hearing's purpose was to assess an alleged violation of university policy, specifically cited as "Disruptive Conduct and Harmful Behavior," in order to determine my status as a student and apply any necessary sanctions.

Before the conduct hearing took place, I was made aware of and provided with an extensive account of my behavior the professor had produced and shared with UCF police. I was stunned beyond all measure by the professor's rendition of events; an inverse reality to my own which sadly also included some complete fabrications.

Knowing the conduct hearing committee would be privy to this elaborate document (no doubt owing to the professor's scholarly background), my principal strategy for the hearing would be to contest the professor's account point-by-point. Suffice to say, I prepared thoroughly.

However, at the hearing, my most earnest preparation was undone by a thinly veiled irreverence toward the committee and the whole occasion. My manner was brash, arrogant and somewhat theatrical. While my behavior may not have appeared clearly pathological, a familiar elevated and even messianic view of myself was taking hold - yet again.

After the conduct hearing committee convened in private to discuss their recommendations, I was informed that I was found in violation. I was to be suspended for an entire school year, placed on conduct probation for the remainder of my studentship, assigned a reflective essay assignment and required to meet with a local victim's advocate about the effects of stalking. After four years, my time at UCF was now over.

I returned home to Miami not too long after the conduct hearing. Being back with my family was a welcome reprieve from the constant embattlement of the past few months in Orlando. But the tranquility and calm of my present circumstances would not last for very long.

Despite the comforting trappings of home, the stress and concern over my seemingly ruined college career and remaining legal predicament loomed heavily. In time, I would need to return to Orlando to meet with my state-provided lawyer and prepare for the bevy of legal consequences resulting from my actions. The immense pressure and anxiety about my future coupled with my under-medicated mental health condition was a recipe for certain disaster.

About a month after returning home, my unusual thoughts and behaviors finally reached a fever peak and I suffered another psychotic break from reality. Like the crisis that had befallen me in the fall of 2007, my mind was flooded with grandiose delusions, paranoid fantasies and constant ideas of reference. But unlike the fall of 2007, my psychotic episode would result in a suicide attempt.

One morning in the depth of my madness, I believed that a savage, right-wing mob would visit cruel designs on me and my family for reasons more bizarre than my sane mind could ever imagine. Convinced that torture, death and a possibly far worse fate was at hand, I grabbed the nearest sharp object I could find - a small pair of scissors - and retreated into my bedroom.

I proceeded to slit my wrists open in an effort to bleed out till death. To hasten my trip to the afterworld, I also stabbed my chest twice in an attempt to critically puncture my heart muscle. In what I believed were my final moments, I dipped one of my fingers in a copious pool of blood and scrawled my initials on my bedroom wall: G.R.

Not long after I'd commenced my bloody work did my dad open the door to my room and see me in my pathetic state. He was shocked but in characteristic control of his emotions.

"I'm the Antichrist," I uttered softly.

911 was immediately dialed.

After two weeks of receiving in-patient treatment at a local mental health hospital, I was assigned a new regimen of psychotropic medication which I now understood and accepted that I would have to take indefinitely. Although some side effects persisted, I trusted my doctors and would remain in close contact with them as I eased out of my latest and quite traumatic emergency.

I soon returned home but I was still contending with the somewhat debilitating side effects of my medication (e.g., lethargy and akathisia) and certain lingering but subsiding psychotic beliefs. To make matters worse, I was now faced with the unwelcome expectation of needing to prepare for my trial which was to take place in two months. Out of the frying pan... into the fire.

Loathing all of the legal business which now lay before me and dreading its possible injurious outcomes, I had to travel back to Orlando with my parents to meet with my appointed public defenders. My demeanor was vacant and distracted during my first meeting with the legal help. But despite my checked-out and irritable affect, my parents and I decided we would reject an offered plea deal and move forward with a jury trial. The professor had rejected a pretrial diversion program (i.e., a more rehabilitative legal sanction intended for young people). She wanted blood.

One of the most absurd turns of the screw in my legal plight was that I would not be able to invoke an insanity defense or mention any issue with my mental health during my trial. My lawyers strongly advised against it and informed me that the penalty for claiming insanity or mental illness as a factor in my defense would involve an indefinite stay at a state mental health hospital; a far worse fate than not doing so, even if found guilty. So, this absolutely critical dimension to my actions would be completely suppressed and not referenced in any way during the trial. I had to answer for actions that were carried out while I was not in my right mind.

About a month later, the day of the trial arrived. However, on the first day of the proceedings the state triggered a mistrial by identifying my lawyers as public defenders. It was an immediate foul but I'm convinced the move was intentional to forestall a perceived advantage on my defense's part. However, I'll never know for sure. A new trial date was soon set for the following month.

Making matters worse, the lawyer I was initially working with had to take leave due to her pregnancy and she was replaced by another not as well versed in the minutiae of my case. I was moving forward severely compromised.

The day of the second attempt at the trial was soon upon me. As with the earlier trial, I had to endure the professor's account of great fear and alarm over my behavior as part of the prosecution's case. It felt like listening to the victim of an imposter who bore my name. It was also difficult to hear what the professor had to say as my high regard toward her never wavered; even in these circumstances.

Still affected by the side effects of the medication, I was expected to take the stand myself and provide testimony for my case. Responding to questions from my lawyer, our back-and-forth felt awkward and uncoordinated. I'm sure many of the jurors minds were easily made up at that point. And when it was the state's turn to cross-examine me, my responses were also adversely affected by my condition. I had difficulty immediately comprehending the questions and my speech was somewhat slurred. Falling for some blatant rhetorical traps, I was far from demonstrating the accomplished speaking ability I'd acquire years later as a member of Toastmasters International.

The state had to prove that I was guilty of stalking beyond a reasonable doubt. The definition of stalking involved repeated, malicious and willful following or harassment (i.e., behavior that causes substantial emotional distress and serves no legitimate purpose). The state faced some difficulty in assessing malicious intent because the content of the online communication entered into evidence and nearly all of the in-person interactions I had with the professor described were school-related. The weight of the state's argument rested primarily on the idea that my perception of the professor's emotional state and let alone the entire situation were askew and contrary to reality. Well, they couldn't have been more right. I was psychotic!

After closing arguments, the jury deliberated for just under an hour. Upon return, they issued a verdict of...

Guilty.

"Sorry," my lawyer consoled as she gently placed her hand on my shoulder.

My sentencing took place shortly after the verdict was read. The state wanted me to receive the maximum sentence for my offense: one year in jail. However, upon hearing the professor's victim impact statement in which she stated, among other hard-to-hear sentiments, that she believed I was "mentally unwell" (she was partly aware of my 2007 mental health crisis), the judge passed down a far more lenient sentence of one month's jail time. The judge also handed down several rehabilitative penalties:

probation, community service and mental health counseling.

My mother sobbed as I was remanded into prison custody moments later. I would be out on bond the following day as the result of my lawyer's motion to appeal the judgment.

Returning home to nurse my wounds, my recovery grew more difficult. Beyond coping with the side effects of my medication, I had to add a bottomless depression to my troubles.

Following my trial and conviction, I began to openly fret over my criminal record, dashed film school career and, not so openly, a strong remnant of feeling toward a professor who no longer existed. My mood was so shot that I began a regular habit of making insincere suicidal threats to my parents. In turn, they had me Baker Acted multiples times in the ensuing months over fear that I would take my own life.

These frequent stays at various local mental health hospitals were a hell I'd never known. I felt so lost during this time period that on one occasion I managed, out of whim and boredom, to successfully escape the mental health hospital downtown, make it home for a few hours before the police came knocking and then be forced to return to the hospital. This elopement (of which the mechanics are rather faithfully reproduced in a scene in my 1st feature film *For My Sister*) took place before a resulting two-week stay which would thankfully mark the end of this period of constant sanitarium internments.

A gradual return to normalcy and creative activity took place in the months after my final hospital stay. Although I'd been seeing a therapist regularly in the aftermath of my relapse, I began to more earnestly participate in sessions and enhance the therapeutic relationship.

And my art, always open-armed and welcoming, was a life-preserver after the desperate weathering of such stormy seas. After such a tempest, I began to write more regularly, plan productions and reintegrate with broader society through my interacting with film students from University of Miami's film school, helping out on a variety of their student productions. All of these positive developments set me on a trajectory that has continued, quite profitably in terms of creative output, to the present. As John Milton wrote, "Long is the way and hard, that out of Hell leads up to light."

Will I ever apologize to the professor for those actions of mine which incurred her unsparing wrath as well as that of the university's student conduct office and the Orlando legal system?

Probably not.

Renowned author William S. Burroughs once wrote, "This is a war universe. War all the time. There may be other universes, but ours seems to be based on war and games." I actually agree with Burroughs' sentiment but with a nod to the exception that there exists a small red wedge tirelessly besetting our universe's foundational bellicosity. This small red wedge is art in all its attendant spirit of creativity, cooperation and non-destructive competition.

As a practitioner of art from the youngest age, I believe in the premium art places on sensitivity, expression, magnanimity and cognitive reverie. This ageless, mystical and deeply human endeavor has defined nearly all of the most significant relationships and experiences of my adulthood. The proof is in the pudding.

When my guilty verdict was read to the court, my parents and I heard an audible sigh of pleasure from the professor. The expression of delight seemed instantly abhorrent to me for such a solemn occasion, no matter for whom the trial resulted in favor of. The professor treated her outcome as a victory to relish rather than the result of a legal process necessarily predicated on dispassionate and objective remove. In my admittedly venerative regard for the professor from our first interaction up until that revealing sigh, I was far too trusting and naive. But this late realization served to reinforce my core values and reveal those of others.

I believe in art.

The professor?

In "war and games," it seems.

89. Rescue (May 2007)

"This may work," I thought.

I'd have to rely on several intertitles as crucial connective tissue to tie the three distinct sections of the piece together and clarify the overall direction of the documented event's narrative. But with the certitude of this approach, I could comfortably proceed with the assembly of my 3rd short documentary and 9th short film *March on the Pentagon*!

There was a surprising cohesion to the recorded footage that I couldn't appreciate in the immediate aftermath of its gathering and didn't appreciate when I had the opportunity to review the footage later on. My videography was more competent than I had initially comprehended; creating a strong, vivid impression of a rather epic protest and subsequent showdown on a gloomy, overcast day at the nation's capital back in March.

At one point in my editing process, I pulled off one of my proudest editing maneuvers: faking a camera whip-pan by creating an accelerating and then abruptly stopping crab movement between two separate, stationary shots. The result was highly encouraging!

Such clever and effective choices contributed to a growing sense that putting this short documentary together would be a wholly worthwhile effort - even if it had taken me months to fully realize it.

At the conclusion of the eponymous march in Washington, D.C. back in early spring, I had been overwhelmed by the size of the demonstration. There were so many different people, creative displays of resistance and more moments of human interest than could ever be recounted with proper justice. On top of this over-stimulation, I was also indecisive about what shape the eventual documentary would ultimately take. So, at some point while marching with ample company down a road that led to the Pentagon, I allowed these dual frustrations to cancel my plans to make a brief documentary from my footage.

Nevertheless, I continued to record footage of my surroundings despite having no grand scheme in mind for its use.

After the march concluded, I returned with my valiant comrades to our lodging site rather disappointed. However, this bitter taste in my mouth was a familiar one. Even at this early juncture in my filmmaking career, I had abandoned about as many productions as I had completed. So, I was used to it.

Days after the march my friend Chris Walker, a dedicated documentary filmmaker who'd also been filming the event, announced that he was going to screen his footage from D.C. to all interested sds (Students for a Democratic Society) members at his off-campus apartment. Of course, I planned on attending.

While Chris's work certainly captivated the gathering of our fellow comrades that one evening, I soon learned that Chris was not planning on editing together the footage into any form. I was surprised by Chris's declining to do so but this bit of news may have triggered a reconsideration on my part to do something with my own footage. After all, the march at the very center of U.S. imperialist power had meant so much to so many.

Busy with my 7th and 8th short films, both products of film school assignments at University of Central Florida, I became open to the idea of finally transferring my footage off of tape and importing it onto my computer for further consideration. But this activity would have to wait until I returned home to Miami after classes broke for summer.

Energized by the generally positive reception to short films number seven and eight at their respective end-of-year showcase screenings, I knew that I didn't want my momentum to stop in the summer stretch before school recommenced in the fall. I felt like I was on fire

So, I eagerly took up my earlier promise to give my Pentagon march footage a fair shake and upon reviewing all of the footage, I saw a potential I'd been blind to before.

"Would it work?" I wondered.

* * *

As day and night blended together in a manner characteristic of my occasional editing frenzies, I grew oddly mesmerized by the restrained color scheme of the footage I was manipulating on my desktop PC. I found the varying gray of capital roadways and the distant Pentagon building all under the whiteness of an oppressively cloudy sky appropriately grim. That drabness offset by the pale blues of lens flares and police vehicle emergency lights. Both students and police were almost exclusively outfitted in black, representing the tactical and the anarchistic, respectively. But the youth were dappled in red; indicative of a passion as thick and coursing as blood!

To complement these visuals, I made use of a some fife and drum recordings from the same source as certain selections used in my 2nd and also politically-themed short film *Does Free Speech Matter?* The music lent the proceedings a feeling of militant energy and implicit historical rhyme.

Upon completing the editing of the body of the piece, I spent a great deal of time refining the opening scroll text which had become an expected feature of these short vignettes. An obvious nod to the opening of the *Star Wars* films.

The resulting *March on the Pentagon* would be my 3rd and final short documentary of my pre-high-definition short film output. It was the final entry of a trilogy of short documentaries preceded by *May Day! or: Two Americas* in 2006 and *3,000 Too Many* in 2007. A fourth entry abiding in form and subject matter would be produced four years later.

In short, I'm glad I was able to save this 9th short film of mine from complete abandonment. I feel it preserves an important political event in recent history that would otherwise be swiftly overlooked. And I must admit that I've always seen these politically charged short films of mine as honoring the spirit of something New Hollywood filmmaker Brian De Palma (*Blow Out*, *Scarface*, *The Untouchables*) once said: "I'm amazed, when you can make movies for nothing, there are not people out there making these incredibly angry anti-war movies. How come?"

Yeah, how come?

90. Resuscitation (October 2012)

During the making of my 14th short film *Proteus* at my oldest brother Alonso's townhouse in Tampa, I was all set to film the opening scene of the uniquely silent short film. Involving my brother and his recent bride Paola, the scene involved the protagonist of the film Mr. Baldman (Alonso) arriving home and flirtatiously acknowledging a nearby jogger (Paola) who ignores his attempt to charm her as she jogs past him. Uncomplicated enough.

However, moments before we were set to film the scene, I experienced great difficulty in determining the editing of the scene in my head. And for someone who was growing increasingly used to shooting with a strong sense of the edit in mind, this was a significant lapse. Regardless of this perceived foible, I gathered my camera, tripod and willing acting participants. But as I led everyone outside I simply couldn't shake the vacancy in my mind about the fundamental construction of the scene. I was underprepared and proceeded without a firm plan.

Standing by my tripod-mounted camera for the first shot, I was immediately flustered and unsure of how to proceed as my actors waited for direction. But not only were my mental modeling instincts seemingly null and void at this moment but my compositional sense faltered as a response. I had no idea what I was doing and my actors pressed me to give direction I simply couldn't provide.

As the intense pressure and miserable stasis persisted, I stalled behind my camera for what seemed like an eternity. Sweat ran profusely down my forehead on this warm, late-summer afternoon.

Finally, I provided some direction. Alonso and Paola listened intently as I started. I surprised them by announcing an end to the day's filming. More than that, in fact, an end to the entire production! I was abandoning the project which felt like the worst creative enterprise I'd ever willed into existence. So was the depth of my feeling of incompetence at that point. This major decision was also prompted by the fact that I hadn't been able to review the roughly 1/2 of the short film I'd shot up to that point. As a result, my pessimism about the overall quality felt fully justified in the absence of any positive reinforcement which may have been present had I known what I'd shot.

With this decision, I felt a surge of relief instantly but it was coupled with some oddness because my brother so casually and complacently assented to my forfeiture.

With my tail firmly between my legs, a dark cloud loomed over me as I kept to myself during the long ride back to Miami. My choice to abandon *Proteus* gave rise to an acrid feeling despite my otherwise comfortable and stress-free circumstances.

But maybe I was asking too much of myself. After all, I'd completed the extremely well-received short film *Semester of Madness* earlier that same summer. Years ago, I'm sure I would've questioned my very identity as a filmmaker over a failure of this scale but, in the present, I saw this as a mere bump in the road - not a dead end. I needed to look ahead and move past this episode, however bumpy it was. In time, I'd be fine.

Still, I couldn't help myself.

On a lark, I gave into the allure of reviewing the footage I'd shot in Tampa during my prematurely aborted stay.

But reviewing the footage wasn't enough. I wanted to put it together in the form that it would've taken had I decided to finish it. With ample placeholder visuals and temporary intertitles, I was able to cobble together a fairly cohesive piece that was checking enough boxes to my 10-year filmmaker mind. Among the scenes included was the very climax of the short film's narrative whose shots had taken a great deal of effort to achieve. How could I have abandoned something so belabored and so clearly working, even if in a half-completed state?

I immediately uploaded this extremely rough but promising cut of the short film and sent the link to Alonso.

"I think it's tight and definitely works. I'd like to hear what you think. Call me back! :)" I wrote to him in an email with the link enclosed.

His response a few hours later?

"You're an idiot," he told me over the phone.

The production's completion was now back on the table. I would return to Tampa in short order to finish the job.

As eager as I was to finish *Proteus*, the challenge of production would be further compounded by the scarcity of a key resource - time. Alonso and Paola were planning on moving to a newly renovated home of theirs in about a week. This meant that I would have to complete all of the filming in their townhouse before the move. No time could be wasted or I would have to live with a promising but permanently incomplete short film. I would not let that happen and rallied my most sincere energies and sound calculations to avoid such a cruel fate.

Upon arriving to Tampa, I had every shot and edit squarely in mind. I was able to overcome whatever previous block existed. There would be no room for improvisation or shooting-from-the-hip. I would simply execute on a now fully realized mental model of scenes which remained.

I prioritized filming scenes involving the character of Proteus (played by Titan, Alonso's Staffordshire Terrier). It is a general rule of thumb that working with animals is notoriously difficult and there was no exception here. The trick to Titan's "acting" was simply producing a particular stimuli (e.g., clapping, calling, holding a treat, etc.) just off-camera to achieve any variety of simple responses from the animal. That said, luck was also a major factor as well as having enough patience for so many repeated attempts to exact the right reaction.

After the crucible of working with Titan, directing and filming the human-only scenes was a relative breeze, including the opening scene that had been my Achille's heel. I completed it on the final day of my stay in Tampa with absolutely no room for do-overs.

Returning to Miami once more, I felt a new and deeply satisfying relief knowing I had a fresh short film waiting to be completed.

I swiftly engaged with Adobe Premiere in yet another of my characteristic editing marathons. The digital fruit of my return to Tampa was soon quickly filed into acceptable form and combined with the earlier material I'd shot and already edited together. I was thrilled beyond belief with the result... and a kind of redemption!

I had visited the deepest pit of self-doubt but through faith in my abilities and the toil of their application I'd emerged victorious with a film I was unreserved in considering my finest yet.

But this essentially silent short film needed one final, crucial ingredient - an original score from end-to-end! Little did I know that the creation of this finishing touch would land me in the company of someone who would become my most valued creative collaborator...

91. Retail (June 2004)

My first summer job was as a customer service associate (i.e., cashier or stock boy) at an Eckerd, which later became CVS, located in Town & Country Mall in the Miami suburban community of Kendall. I entered my small corner of the workforce right out of high school, freshly and adequately conditioned to accept directives from unquestionable authority, uphold a strict standard of dress and conduct, memorize countless procedures and related details, keep my surroundings clean and, above all, stay productive.

I was able to commit to the store as a full-time employee and the dough gayly streamed in. And, for the longest time, I tolerated this drab, sterile, fluorescently lit, liminal space between high school and college.

Thoughts of filmmaking would find absolutely no purchase here but the experience seems to have molded me in ways that would benefit its practice.

Toward the end of my employment, which lasted all summer long and partly into the fall, I began to see this job in an odd but luminous way. In the brief moments between tending to customers at the cash register, I would look out at the expanse of the store and see not aisles, products, customers, co-workers or glossy floor tiles but the management of this little store in our massive consumerist continuum as a deeply abstract reflection and microcosm of an ideal existence.

The unassailable authority represented a inviolable will, the strict adherence to code was ascetic self-discipline, the memorization of countless details was razor-sharp cognition, the stress on organization was harmonization of reality itself and the emphasis on staying busy was the potent fuel of constant occupation.

My summer dalliance with CVS came to an end after six months but I'll never forget what my service to that store revealed to me.

18 years later, I shared a social media post about a visit to the mall (two years after the start of the coronavirus pandemic) which had been the home of that cherished retail job:

I didn't even get a chance to say goodbye... :(

On a trip to Town & Country mall earlier today, I was surprised to see that the CVS formerly occupying this spot in the mall had been replaced by a Five Below. In the summer of 2004, I was a customer service associate at that CVS. It was my first job. I ran the cash register, restocked shelves, swept the aisles, occasionally worked in the photo development lab, etc. I was a stalwart employee and have many fond memories of the experience and my long-gone co-workers.

I would occasionally revisit that CVS over the years and soak in the nostalgia I'd feel amid those familiar retail store trappings. It's too bad I won't be able to do that anymore.

92. Retooling (September 2012)

I had recently completed my 13th short film *Semester of Madness* and its immediate reception among friends and family was most encouraging. Many of the film festivals I initially submitted the film to responded in kind by selecting it for their respective line-ups. Energized by the momentum, I immediately began to think about my follow-up short film.

For some time, the idea of producing a video with viral potential had been percolating in my mind. I knew that if I wanted to produce something with broad, popular appeal I had to include my oldest brother Alonso's pet dog Titan. Centering on that particular element was a no-brainer because who isn't charmed by well-made pet videos?

Titan "SunBolt" Rhenals was an American Staffordshire Terrier who'd been my brother's furry, four-legged companion for about five years at the time. Titan was well-bred, well-trained and well-behaved. If I were to involve Titan, I knew it'd be a challenge but not impossible. So, I began to consider what a mini-video featuring my brother's dog might look like.

Unfortunately, I hit a snag.

My last three narrative short films had been between five and ten minutes in length and, quite frankly, I was constantly thinking about stories with such an abiding degree of narrative expanse. At the time, I'd never produced anything shorter than one minute, a critical trait of the kind of video I was now considering making.

So, I turned the issue over and over in my mind. Although I came up with a few extremely short-form story ideas, nothing was passing muster with me. I simply couldn't break from the storytelling paradigm I'd grown accustomed to. The most exciting ideas I had were too largely proportioned to fit into a 30-second or even 1-minute video.

With a somewhat heavy heart, I finally dropped the viral video ploy and opted to make a more formally conventional short film instead.

However, the idea of including my brother's dog Titan turned out to be a most welcome holdover from my viral video brainstorming.

Freshly unshackled by the limitations of viral content, I succeeded in writing a script in record time that would make effective use of Titan, Alonso, his wife Paola and their home in Tampa. It was titled *Proteus*, a reference to a common name for a dog in antiquity. Far from the brevity of a viral video, it would be a deliberately paced domestic drama about a man who receives a troubling letter in the mail.

Inspired by the same impulse to shake up my creative process a bit with a viral video, I made a choice to forgo spoken dialogue in the short film. Instead, all of the short film's dialogue would be presented through intertitles and the only sound heard would be that of an original musical score like silent films of old (with one crucial exception for the climax of the film). This choice also conveniently allowed me to mask the fact that I'd be employing non-actors, namely Alonso and Paola.

The short film would also contain some rather unique features as far as my oeuvre was concerned: Except for one shot at the film's climax, every shot would be captured on a fixed tripod; I'd be working extensively with an animal who had to look as though he was responding to and interacting with his human counterparts; the entire story would take place in a single location; and I'd be dealing with a theme ripped straight from the headlines - the country's economic crisis.

With script approval from Alonso and Paola, I soon made plans to travel to Tampa for the purpose of shooting the film. Although I'd face a serious calamity during my trip, *Proteus* would ultimately be completed and take its place as my 14th short film.

93. Return (August 2009)

Two months earlier, I had been discharged from Jackson Mental Health Hospital in downtown Miami after a two-week stay in one of their inpatient housing units. I had been interned due to a second serious mental health crisis: a psychotic break from reality which culminated in a bloody suicide attempt. I'd relapsed and I was not well.

Although the psychosis had been treated during my hospital stay, I returned home to a litany of challenges and frustrations:

- As a result of psychosis, my brain needed to time to recover from its trauma and I felt constantly overwhelmed by the complexity of most film, music, television or art in general. I was creatively incapacitated.
- The medication I had received in the hospital for my psychotic symptoms caused akathisia, or restlessness. It was like chemical torture and it would be several weeks before I was prescribed a different medication without that particular side effect.
- Knowing that I would now have to take medication indefinitely to prevent another relapse, I had to monitor the side effects of various psychotropic medication and keep up regularly with my doctors to find a tolerable combination. A long trial-and-error process would be involved.
- My home was in a state of some disorder as my parents were preparing to sell the property. I was expected to clear out much of the content of my bedroom and perform other related chores despite my devastated condition.
- My dad had axed our family's cable television subscription during my hospital stay leaving me without the comfort of a variety of entertainment choices in my desperate state.
- A temporary side effect of one of the initial medications I was put

on was a pervasive lethargy and dampened mood. Almost nothing interested or excited me. I felt like a zombie.

- My recent legal predicament involving a UCF film professor had plunged me into a deep and unsparing depression. I felt immensely frustrated over my inability to mollify the offended party. I was powerless in the face of looming and dire legal consequences.
- My film school career was hopelessly dashed. It looked increasingly unlikely that I would be able to safely return to UCF after the aforementioned legal predicament. My future looked gravely uncertain.
- Some of the nightmares I experienced at night during this period were the most terrifying and stifling I'd ever experienced. Insanity was a common theme but no words could do those night horrors justice.
- Over the past year or so, I'd gained a tremendous amount of weight. Being overweight sunk my self-esteem and offended my personal constitution which, for the longest time, prioritized health and fitness.
- Already strained from an earlier mental health crisis in 2007, my friendly relationships with the UCF film school classmates I was closest with grew increasingly estranged. I was too ashamed and besieged by difficulties to work on repairing those relationships.

Despite the staggering and unprecedented adversity I faced, about two months after my release from the mental health hospital, a small step in an abandoned but familiar direction was about to take place.

One quiet morning I decided to seize my writing portfolio from under a pile of medical and legal documents. I hadn't touched the leather-bound portfolio in months. Settling into my living room amid household silence and calm, I began to write again. And in this much-needed repose, my many troubles became secondary and I began to tango with my creative ideas once more.

The past two months had represented the longest period of creative inactivity since I first embarked on my titular filmmaking journey. Now, it was time to reassert my will and put an end to my costly creative deprivation.

I continued to write regularly from that day forward and I haven't stopped writing since.

94. Revision (May 2004)

"Art is never finished, only abandoned."

-Leonardo da Vinci

Toward the end of my senior year at Miami Killian Senior High, I visited the school's library and observed that the facility was undergoing an extensive renovation. The floor carpeting which spanned the full expanse of the space was being removed in favor of smooth tile. To accommodate the change, all of the books which had populated the many shelves were now stored in boxes at the feet of the those shelves.

Not too long after being witness to this curious sight, I figured I could use the situation to the advantage of my first short film *Mass Education* which I'd completed a year prior. The short film featured a narrative about a high school administration's sweeping directive to remove the institution's only library. I couldn't have asked for a better way to illustrate the turnout of a fictional order by a fictional administration at a fictional school than adding unmanipulated shots of so many boxed books and empty shelves. It would be the perfect cap to my short film!

Having forged a strong relationship with at least one of the librarians thanks to the experience of making *Mass Education* in my junior year, I was readily granted permission to film in the library in its upside-down but cinematically propitious state.

During a single lunch period, I quickly acquired a variety of carefully composed shots with my camera and tripod. The ecstasy I felt while securing these visuals that would markedly improve the visual character of my first short film effort was indescribable. I returned to class after that day's particularly fruitful lunch period feeling the most intense satisfaction!

While this new version of the film would be considered the latest and most definitive version upon addition of those prized shots, I'd actually produced several versions of the short film after its initial completion. These earlier versions featured differences in scene order, soundtrack and title cards.

Even from the start of my filmmaking career, I was a consummate tinkerer and partial to an iterative creative process.

Three years after incorporating the new shots of the library, I went ahead and added some establishing shots of Killian to the short film as well as a close-up of a document being signed. I also corrected a handful of amateur technical flaws.

Why did I do this? Simply because certain aspects of my debut piece had always bothered me and I saw no harm in improving upon an article of creation I know I'd have to live with for a very long time.

After years of experience as a filmmaker, I developed an increasingly nagging habit of revisiting my earlier short films to correct perceived flaws and whip up the work into what I considered a state of absolute perfection.

Here's an extremely abbreviated list of some of the changes I made over the years to each of my 16 short films:

- Adding establishing shots and a close-up to *Mass Education* (2003)
- Replacing television screen and a poster in *Does Free Speech Matter?* (2005)
- Adding a company logo to a beverage cup in *The Procrastinator* (2006)
- Adding factual intertitles to *May Day! or: Two Americas* (2006)
- Improving composited elements on a dinner table in *Meat on a Grill* (2006)
- Redoing the opening graphic of *3,000 Too Many* (2007)
- Adding foley sound effects to *Breakfast, Lunch and Dinner* (2007)
- Redoing all visual effects shots in *Jesus Christ Goes to Mars* (2007)
- Removing a number of shots in *March on the Pentagon* (2007)
- Re-compositing various elements in *Rough Cut* (2007)

- Revising end titles in *The Nap* (2008)
- Horizontally flipping a shot in *Occupy Miami!* (2011)
- Removing a revealing reflection in *Semester of Madness* (2012)
- Shortening a shot in *Proteus* (2013)
- Correcting end title spacing in *Leo's Love Letter* (2014)
- Adjusting the volume of sound effects in *The Promotion* (2016)

Because filmmaking in the digital realm is as chock-full of choices and possibilities as it is, any practitioner can easily be swayed by the lure of further improvement and modification far beyond an initial completion date. But a custom of revisiting work with such a mindset has an insidious underside.

My preoccupation with making changes retroactively grew to an almost pathological degree toward the latter part of my short filmmaking career. I found myself regularly overcome with anxiety and stress over the concern of not addressing what I often felt were glaring flaws (they were not). This uncomfortable pressure arose over considering additive choices as well as second-guessing already-made ones. And the immense irritation of needing to square all stored copies of the short film's video files, including uploaded versions on online video hosting services once the changes were made, only compounded the problem.

Thankfully, my condition was helped along by some keen advisement from one of my doctors. Upon explaining my harrying predicament, my doctor kindly countered by explaining to me a tradition among the quilt-makers of the Native American Navajo tribe. These quilt-makers would intentionally weave flaws into their quilts to reinforce and protect against a desire to produce a perfect quilt. In their eyes, nothing in nature was perfect and they wanted to imbue their craft with the same spirit - and perhaps stave off that potential anxiety and stress. Smart cookies those Navajo.

While I'd like to say that my doctor's advice did the trick and immediately put an end to this frustrating habit, I believe the actual anecdote was simply time and maturity. Over time, I may have managed to tickle the work as much as I possibly could. And with maturity, I've come to stiffly resist the urge to make further changes to newly finished pieces by establishing a personal policy of refraining from casually reviewing them post-completion.

But however the worst of this practice was quelled, I developed a strong compulsion to not allow the influence of perceived flaws to bog down my forward momentum as I moved forward with bigger and more elaborate projects.

I'd learned to accept imperfection.

Like the Navajo.

95. Satellite (November 2016)

The Addition Delay

July 1, 2000, 4:27pm

The Addition was scheduled to come out the day before the day it really came out. All Gabriel can do is apologize for this delay. He wishes to rekindle the light his viewers lost at this startling and unexpected delay. Nevertheless, Gabriel always comes up with a way to fascinate as well as educate his viewers. He promises that July will be more exciting and unpredictable than June and the months behind it. That means more updates and new sections as well as a more in-depth look at the workings of 'The Garnobian Chronicles'.

The Addition Is Now Fully Operational

July 1, 2000, 4:35pm

We are just moments away from releasing Gabriel's long-awaited sections of 'The Garnobian Outpost'. Hopes are really high right now. Gabriel wishes that he will win over all the viewers to coming back to the site and enjoying it as much as they used to. The tension is really building.

-Two updates from 'The Garnobian Outpost', my first website

After graduating from Florida International University as a Communication Arts major, I decided to begin looking for work in the corporate world. Since I was on-track to finish my final short film *The Promotion* and feature filmmaking seemed a distant proposition, finding a job in the corporate communication field felt like an appropriate interim step. So I applied to countless positions but, to be truthful, my efforts in this arena were half-hearted.

Over the few months I was actively pursuing work, I landed a few interviews but failed to adequately prepare and make a strong impression. My bliss, it would seem, was elsewhere.

Despite my lack of enthusiasm over those several months of job-seeking, I would visit FIU every few weeks to meet with my program's academic services coordinator Ms. Gabby Portela for assistance with my job search. Ms. Portela sent me some fitting job postings to which I readily applied. She also advised me on other practices to bolster my appeal as a job applicant.

However, one measure Ms. Portela recommended was creating a personal website to serve as a kind of online portfolio. Doing so would allow prospective employers to independently gauge my fitness for a particular position. The idea hadn't crossed my mind before and I gave it some sincere consideration.

I wasn't completely new to website creation. While I was a middle schooler in 2000, I used a custom website building service called Homestead to create *The Garnobian Outpost*. The site was a repository for my artwork, music MP3s, musings and other odd ephemera. It was active for a few years before I deleted it.

In college, I had also created several simple websites to make the short films I'd completed up to then easily accessible. They also allowed me to share a blog-like account of my filmmaking activity.

So taking up Ms. Portela's suggestion, I paid for a subscription to a custom website building service called Wix and registered the domain name www.gabrielrhenals.com. This new website would represent my media production work but initially serve chiefly to give potential employers a sense of my abilities as a communicator. So the earliest iteration of my website included a bio, complete resume, writing samples and the considerable attention my short film work had received from film festivals.

After launching the website, I couldn't get my hands off of it. I began to fill the template-based website with more content related to my work. I even began a blog on the site in anticipation of regularly sharing developments in my career as a communicator and filmmaker. However, the tremendous zeal with which I approached development and maintenance of my website fell far short of the quantity I nursed toward the actual job search.

As the year came to a close, I completed work on *The Promotion* and my desire to execute a feature film production soon entered as a higher priority than my job search. But my website remained up and running. And when I came upon a source of funds for a micro-budget feature film, the job search was the first casualty as I redirected my energies toward writing a feature script.

Over time, the website would drop its communication focus in favor of a dedicated filmmaking one. I would continue updating it accordingly, seeing it as a source of leverage for possible film-related opportunities.

In the years since its inception, my website has served as an oft-referenced supplement to my work as a filmmaker. Its blog is regularly updated with news, updates and insight about my creative activity. The site is also a comprehensive source for all key information related to my major creative projects. It also boasts an extensive collection of my press and media appearances. Indeed, my website has grown so full with content that it pushes at the bounds of the standard Wix template.

In sum, I am so grateful to Ms. Portela for her encouragement about carving out my own humble little corner on the internet. It has served me most well.

96. Scoring (November 2012)

After completing the edit of my 14th short film *Proteus*, I needed to find someone capable of producing an original score for this unconventionally silent film about a man and his dog. Although I waited until this penultimate stage to look for someone to provide such a crucial element for this formally risky project, I was confident in my ability to find a dependable talent for the job sooner than later.

The composing task for the short film would necessitate the writing of nearly nine minutes worth of unbroken music of varying mood and tone. I also figured that synthesized music would be the only practical way of satisfying the requirement on a budget. Indeed, it was a heavy assignment for what would be a first collaboration with a composer but I didn't think it was an unrealistic expectation of someone roughly my age to accomplish whose focus was instead in the realm of music composition. And to help grease the wheels, I'd provide temporary tracks sourced from some Hollywood movie soundtracks to help assist whoever I found to do the work.

"My name is Gabriel Rhenals and I recently completed a short film that I would like to have an original score composed for..." I posted to social media in an open call for a composer among my online social network. I continued, "It's a silent film, meaning that the dialogue is presented through title cards/intertitles. This also means that music is absolutely integral and must accompany the entirety of the short film... There are moments that are serious and dramatic as well as moments of levity. I have fitted the short film to temp tracks and have a fairly good idea of what I'd like. Now, I don't have professional training in music, but I'm a huge classical and film music aficionado."

Unfortunately, my social media posts resulted in zero leads. I would have to look beyond my immediate social network.

My first in-person effort to find a composer involved attending an event called "Scares and Scores" at University of Miami. At this event, small ensembles would live-perform the musical scores of several horror-themed short films from filmmakers with whom the composers had been paired with earlier on. As much as I enjoyed the novelty of the event, I immediately engaged with the organizers in order to gain access to a mailing list that would allow me to broadcast my search for a composer among the composing student population at UM.

Although I was unsuccessful in gaining access to such a mailing list that evening, the person who I'd ultimately collaborate with happened to be in attendance at the event. While our paths wouldn't cross this particular evening, they soon would.

My 2012 short film *Semester of Madness*, which I'd completed earlier in the year, was an official selection at the 11th Annual Miami Short Film Festival. At the festival's opening night festivities I found myself reunited with various UM film students whose acquaintances I'd made over the past year or so volunteering on their student film productions. Some of their films had been selected to screen at the festival.

One of the UM film students I spoke with on this occasion was Ryan Davenport, an amicable and talented enrollee at the university. He'd become aware of my search for a composer and kindly recommended the services of one Ben Morris, a UM music composition student who Ryan had some experience working with. Ryan spoke very highly of Ben and promised to forward my open call information to him.

Days later, Ben responded to me via email with acceptance of the job and great enthusiasm. We set up a date to meet on the UM campus for a spotting session (i.e., to determine the entire approach to the music of the short film).

My first impression of Ben was astonishment at his considerable height, towering at nearly seven feet tall! But more substantially I was impressed by his confidence and professionalism. He exuded these qualities right from the start of our earliest encounter.

As we engaged in casual introductory chit-chat on our way to a computer lab on the UM campus, I was also struck by Ben's gentle and generous spirit which masked but in no way diminished his fierce passion for music. We became fast friends.

Arriving to the computer lab, we swiftly set ourselves to the work and discussion at hand. I accessed a copy of my short film on the available PC and we went through the entire length of the video identifying the musical needs of the project in great detail. Ben's ideas and applied knowledge flowed like a river and we united in attitude and taste at nearly every juncture of our spotting session. If there were any disagreements, I usually deferred to what I was quickly becoming aware of was a preternatural musical talent. Concluding our spotting session, Ben had taken copious notes and I felt relieved that I had found a collaborator of sterling artistic deftness and sensitivity.

As we walked back to one of the campus parking lots where I was parked, I spent more time chatting casually with Ben. We both loved film and shared equally particular views toward certain films and film composers (e.g., John Williams, Michael Giacchino, James Horner and Alexandre Desplat). Ben was also pleasantly surprised to learn of my love of and familiarity with classical music. In all, there wasn't a single lull in our conversation. And leaving UM that afternoon, I not only knew I'd found a formidable collaborator but a very good friend. This meeting would be far from our last!

Ben turned in his completed score for *Proteus* shortly after his winter break, as we'd arranged, and I couldn't have been happier with the results! His music was nuanced throughout, varied where appropriate and in absolute union with the emotional currents of the short film's narrative. It was an impressive accomplishment for someone so early in their career.

Although it would be some time before I asked Ben to compose music for another short film, we maintained fairly regular, friendly contact in the years following our first collaboration; both online and in-person. We'd discuss the latest movies we'd seen, his latest concert pieces, my first attempt at a feature-length script and other topics related to music and storytelling.

While Ben was at UM, I also routinely attended performances of his latest jazz and contemporary chamber work as part of the university's Society of Composers, Inc. I also met up with Ben for some screenings at UM's Canes Film Festival. We always spent a significant amount of time conversing after each event.

After my time working on my aforementioned first feature-length script, I returned to short filmmaking with my 15th entry *Leo's Love Letter*, about a young man trying to repair a damaged personal relationship. For this short film, I once again collaborated with Ben on the score. We met at his apartment for another rigorous spotting session and he ultimately produced a relatively simple synth piano score (compared to *Proteus*) that matched the short film to a tee.

When it was time to score my 16th and final short film *The Promotion*, about a young woman who's all about her career. Ben and I collaborated remotely as he was in Texas pursuing his master's degree. Despite the geographical separation, the time we spent conducting our spotting session via video conferencing technology was just as blissful and productive. He turned in another synth score that elevated that short film far, far beyond what I could ever muster on my own.

Ben and I would continue our collaboration into my feature-length filmmaking phase. And although we would continue to perform our spotting sessions remotely in those instances, it never adversely affected the quality of Ben's work. In fact, I have dubbed every occasion of receiving finished music from Ben as Christmas morning, no matter the date.

To this day, Ben remains one of my closest friends and our work together represents my longest-running and most fruitful collaboration.

97. Search (February 2007)

With one semester of University of Central Florida's limited-access Film BFA program under my belt, I entered the Spring 2007 semester full of enthusiasm and, along with my fellow same-year classmates, ready to fan our feathers in our first major production-based course Directing I. Our competitive drives were unspoken but revving up.

Resided over by the passionate Professor Lori Ingle, a former Hollywood editor, our first Directing I class session was replete with so many of the familiar terms and concepts I had come to know since high school. Moreover, I arrived at the class having completed four narrative short films and one documentary short film on my own. With the two short film projects to be completed as part of Directing I, I expected to add two more short films to my oeuvre.

The first project on the docket was simply referred to as "P1". My class was to produce a dramatic, narrative short film that must take place off-campus, involve no college stories or moments, feature neither dialogue nor music, involve two people at maximum and have a runtime that could not exceed one minute. This assignment was generally familiar to me as I had made my 3rd short film *The Procrastinator* earlier at UCF in accordance with most of these guidelines.

I began brainstorming right away.

My first idea was set at a "U.S. Marine Recovery Facility" and focused on a conflict between two patients; one with life-like prosthetic limbs. It ended with an ironic display of patriotic fervor. However, I'd soon drop this idea for another.

This new idea took place at a local Orlando news station and revolved around a misfit employee's inability to communicate through written means. It addressed the limitations of language. But this idea too would be dropped in favor of another.

I briefly considered what would have been a VFX-heavy idea inspired by Darren Aronofsky's 2006 eras-spanning drama *The Fountain*. However, this idea didn't make it very far developmentally and it was also abandoned.

During this search for the right P1 idea, I was failing to meet script deadlines. Professor Ingle grew increasingly disappointed with me as the weeks passed and I'd failed to materialize at least a first draft.

I spent many nights taking long walks around campus with my notebook in hand. I'd find quiet, secluded areas to sit and try to tease out the best of what the right half of my brain had to offer. But alas, any progress I'd have with generating ideas would often be undone by subsequent examination and scrutiny.

As my fellow classmates discussed their finished scripts and production plans, I struggled with writing and grew increasingly reclusive. Sometimes skipping class.

In turn, my concerned friends attempted to reach out but I would often meet them behind the locked door of my on-campus dorm room. I couldn't come out to play.

As the weeks wore on and I remained scriptless, a sensation of free fall overcame me. Here I was, having uprooted myself from Miami to Orlando and qualifying for UCF's exclusive film program, and I was fundamentally failing in my role as a producing filmmaker. My response was to double-down and continue treading deep into the recesses of my mind until I struck something rock-solid.

And eventually I did.

My first reference to the germ of an idea that would ultimately become my P1 or 7th short film *Breakfast, Lunch and Dinner* was phrased in my notes in the following way: "A worker receives money from mother - spends on vending machines". The arrival of this fragment of thought was accompanied by a sudden jolt of supreme clarity I'd experienced in earlier successful writing efforts. As with these previous instances, I could clearly see the underlying skeleton that would with certainty provide the necessary basis for a completed film - or P1, for that matter.

In the resulting short film, the narrative involves a young corporate employee who spends a father's monetary gift over the course of one day only to return home with a surprise for the viewer.

I indicated the change from a mother figure to a father figure with an idea for an accompanying sound effect: "From Dad - Iron hitting, real solid". The sound effect of a miner striking metal with a pick axe would make it into the final cut.

This seed of an idea was further developed and consequently expanded into a short film with an expected shot count of 43 shots. The ending was determined two days after the idea was first wrought: "Fridge is chock full of the necessary ingredients [for meal preparation]".

With all of the writing and outlining involved clicking stiffly into place, my confidence returned in full measure. I re-assumed the expected duty, attendance and timeliness of a proper UCF film student as best I could and swiftly completed an assigned "director's book" for the short film which included a breakdown of the script, a narrative analysis, a shot list, overhead floor plan of shot setups and a storyboard. The professor was glad to see my fresh output even if she had to deduct several points from my grade due to the lateness of this deliverable.

With my elixir firmly in hand, I began production on my P1, *Breakfast, Lunch and Dinner* - as virtually all of my fellow classmates were starting production on their P2s.

Despite my lagging performance, I met with Professor Ingle in private toward the end of the semester to screen a near-finished cut of my hard-won P1 for her. She had many encouraging comments about the resulting piece but her overall response is best summarized by what she told me at the conclusion of our meeting: "Thanks for taking your work so seriously."

I would ultimately be permitted to screen my P1 at the end-of-year showcase (while everyone else screened their P2s) and Directing I was the last course I'd have with Professor Ingle during my time at UCF. Shedding the P1 designation, my resulting short film *Breakfast, Lunch and Dinner* would become the 7th in my canon.

Following that semester, I would occasionally see Professor Ingle in the hallways of the film school building and we'd often acknowledge each other warmly and occasionally with a brief comment about our continuing adherence to the directing principles explored in her class.

I regret that I failed her class that semester.
But I'm glad she recognized how serious I took my work.

98. Seniors (September 2005)

A few weeks into the Fall 2005 semester at University of Central Florida, the film school was buzzing with activity! Classes were in full swing, the film school colloquium was routinely packed, the well-attended UCF Film Club met twice-a-week and the film school hallways regularly alternated between vacancy and teeming with social activity.

I'd arrived at UCF knowing absolutely no one but I was already well on my way to building up a sizable social network. The first member of which was my off-campus apartment roommate Garrett. He was also a prospective film student waiting to apply to the film program later that year. Thankfully, his welcoming and generous demeanor was matched by virtually everyone I met in this new, exciting environment.

By virtue of the numerous connections I was making, I soon came into contact with students who were soliciting their fellow schoolmates for help on a variety of student film productions. Some of these students were delegates representing upperclassmen and their senior thesis short film projects, commonly referred to as capstones.

Bright-eyed, bushy-tailed and green as hell, I soon responded with bubbling interest to one such capstone crew call. It would be the closest experience I'd had to working on a professional film set and I looked forward to it with all due enthusiasm!

The first production meeting would take place at the off-campus apartment complex of one of the seniors. I would be attending with Garrett.

On the evening of the production meeting, Garrett and I arrived at the apartment complex. The meeting took place in a small screening room on the apartment complex premises.

The meeting was conducted by the producer of the film and addressed basic information related to schedule, locations, crew positions available, etc. During the meeting, I raised my hand at least once; more to demonstrate my eagerness to participate than ascertain any particular information.

After the meeting was concluded, Garrett and I signed up to be PAs (production assistants) on the project. Then, I managed to speak with the producer about the extent of their pre-visualization process. I was curious to know how prepared these filmmakers were. The producer replied that the short film had been storyboarded "to a tee." I was delighted to hear that! Receiving that response ostensibly confirmed my highest hopes that these were the kind of exemplary film students I'd hoped to be in a few years.

Later that night, I spoke with the director of photography on the production. I had heard he'd worked on a top-tier Hollywood production over the summer but I fought any feelings of intimidation and engaged in some conversation with him. I asked if he'd ever considered using 3D design software to experiment with lighting scenarios before orchestrating them for real. He didn't seem too interested in the possibility but I didn't mind. It was thrilling enough to know I'd be working with someone with experience on a major studio film.

The first day of production on the capstone soon arrived and it was a night shoot in a wide, recreational park. I arrived with Garrett and we quickly found and joined the crew on-site.

As one of several PAs, I was responsible for following the lead of the assistant directors. Their first task for us was unloading lighting equipment from the equipment supply truck. This included numerous massive lights, light stands, ballasts (power sources for the lights) and sandbags (to keep the tall light stands from toppling). I reasoned that the cinematographer's plans involved illuminating parts of the field for the background of the night's planned shots. So much equipment needed to be hand-carried across a large stretch of field that the work was immediately grueling and unpleasant.

The luster was fading.

When the work was done, I retreated to a corner of the field with some of the other PAs as we observed the night's shooting.

Among the PAs was a young man named David Pritchard. I got along with him almost immediately and learned that he was a pianist and composer. Later on in the evening, he would introduce me to the game of Sudoku with some handy print-outs he had brought along with him. We would become closer friends as time went by.

I also met a young man named Michael Schatz who was a most zealous film fanatic (it takes one to know one). I was particularly charmed by his quoting of behind-the-scenes content from *The Lord of the Rings* films. A few days later, I'd watch some of his recent short film work and express a favorable opinion of them. Michael would also be a regular fixture during my time at UCF.

And then there was a curious young man named Tim. He had an amicable if quiet presence and I'll never forget a rather bold admission he once offered up. "All I want is that statue," he'd said in a deeply determined tone. He was of course referring to an Academy Award or Oscar. However, months later he seems to have dropped out of UCF. My film school compatriots and I never heard from him again.

As the night wore on, I decided to pay closer attention to the filming occurring on a nearby basketball court. Apparently, the filmmakers were going over-schedule but were desperate to pull off an ambitious oner (a lengthy, continuous take free of any editing) of various young men engaged in a match concluding with the ball being thrown successfully through the hoop. However, the young men involved couldn't land the closing shot and were growing increasingly exhausted. Take after take, it just wasn't happening and the wearying effort also caused the Steadicam operator involved to warn of increasingly compromised performance due to physical strain.

After an obscene number of takes, the shot was finally achieved. However, I highly doubt the final, successful take looked nearly as good as the earliest takes despite the ball making it through the hoop.

In any case, the night's filming concluded and I soon left the park with Garrett. The closest experience I'd had to working on a professional film set had left me physically depleted but, more significantly, rather disillusioned.

I would ultimately see the completed short film some months later and nothing about the final product demanded the desperate one-take exigency that had closed the night. The filmmakers had let needless extravagance overtake practical considerations, not to mention their image in the eyes of impressionable underclassmen film students. From what I continued to observe, even a basic grasp of montage theory would have made their production far more efficient and the resulting film infinitely tighter.

My skepticism about the seniors in the UCF film program would only grow with my increasing exposure to their creative processes. Seeing so many examples of what wasn't working in production and in the final result provided me with a myriad of new knowledge and a bit of wisdom; and with that illumination came greater confidence in my own filmmaking which would be put to the test during my time at UCF.

99. Shrine (December 2013)

Three major creative events occurred in 2013: multiple film festival acceptances and screenings of my 13th short film *Semester of Madness*; completion of my 14th short film *Proteus*; and, most significantly, the start of writing my first feature-length screenplay *The Cult of Truth*.

Despite appearances, my creative activities are usually laced with a fair amount of uncertainty, doubt and even failure. But the fresh screenplay writing challenge I'd embarked on earlier in the year had turned the typical mix of production and writing challenges into those strictly of the latter variety.

So, at year's end with Christmas fast approaching, I decided to reward my hard-won screenwriting gains with a set of gifts to myself.

What gifts did I have in mind?

For the longest time, the walls of my bedroom sat mostly vacant apart from a few instances of framed generic art selected by my mom and a movie poster my parents had gifted me in 2001.

My bedroom had passed from my older brother Juan to my younger brother Daniel and then to me based on my older two siblings' moving out of our family home. Up to now, I'd been the room's inhabitant for roughly six years but only now did I feel it was time to give the space a more personal touch.

So, I ordered two new movie posters to accompany the one I already had hanging across the foot of my bed.

Which posters did I purchase?

Well, the one gifted to me by my parents over a decade prior had belonged to the 1968 sci-fi epic *2001: A Space Odyssey*. It captured a space scene of a domestic spacecraft jetting away from a massive space station with the earth in view. The two new posters would be 27" x 40" theatrical one-sheets of 2008's racing drama *Speed Racer* and 1962's WWI epic

Lawrence of Arabia. The *Speed Racer* poster captures the titular character holding a white helmet marked with a red "M" while standing in front of his race car with matching "M" and color scheme. The *Lawrence of Arabia* poster features a large, ominous face in shadow surrounded by illustrations of the main characters. These three posters represented my top three favorite films of all-time!

But not too long after I'd placed the order for those two posters did I realize that there was still enough empty wall space for an additional poster. So, I went ahead and ordered a third poster belonging to 1976's urban drama *Taxi Driver*. Its poster features Robert DeNiro's character brooding as he walks down a city sidewalk. Another top-favorite film of mine!

When the posters were delivered via cardboard tube, unfurling these big and beautiful pieces of vibrant promotional art was quite a thrill!

Anticipating their arrival, I had already purchased a set of appropriately-sized poster frames from a local crafts store. I had also quite logically and mathematically worked out the exact height and position they'd be hung in my bedroom. Their arrangement wasn't exactly feng shui but I put a great deal of care into figuring out the particulars.

When all the posters were frames and mounted on my room's walls, they gave my personal living space a unique flavor compared to all of the other rooms in my family home. The time, effort and expense that had gone into enlivening my room had definitely been worth it.

I'd describe the function of these posters in a personal essay write-up for an art appreciation class at Florida International University a year later. "The walls of my room or private living space are covered in framed movie posters and serve as a constant reminder of the identity I've avowed for myself," I wrote. "[The wall adornments] all serve to keep me focused and intensely attached to this sense of myself as a filmmaker."

Someone help me.

100. Solitude (June 2002)

The end of my sophomore year in high school marked the end of a school year that had seen me coldly booted from a prestigious arts high school in downtown Miami (New World School of the Arts) and dolefully completing 10th grade at a regular one (Miami Kilian Senior High). Released into the summer, I was determined to continue the new cinematic direction my life was moving in. I accordingly set my sights sharply on finally writing a script for my first official short film production. No more dilly-daddling.

Not too long after school had let out, my parents, aware of my growing interest in writing for film and reading about film, suggested Florida International University's Green Library as an ideal setting for both activities. They explained that my older brother Juan, an FIU student at the time, could drive me to FIU's campus and drop me off at the library while he attended his classes. Such an arrangement sounded appealing to me right away and before long I was on my way to FIU with Juan to visit its library for a few hours. It would become a regular habit that summer.

Following my brother onto FIU's campus for the first time was rather overwhelming. I was immediately intimidated by the size of the many buildings, the quantity of winding walkways and my rank unfamiliarity with the entire sprawl.

But I felt safe and comfortable amid my alien surroundings in the carrying of my trusty implements: a binder filled with lined paper and a supply of black, ball-point pens. Earlier on in high school, I had begun carrying a composition book for notes related to my earliest film-related musings. I had also become rather accustomed to lengthy and solitary writing sessions in school. This too would provide some measure of safety and comfort in this new environment.

Before I was left to my own devices, Juan recommended floors 6 and 7 in Green Library to write and read; the quiet floors.

Departing for his classes, I ascended to one of those floors and quickly chose a secluded cubicle to conduct my business. The floor was almost completely quiet and still. An occasional student walking by or the light patter of rain on the windows were the only intruding disturbances. This accommodation would be most conducive to my creativity, exploration and focus. My parents were absolutely right.

And so, I wrote and I read.

It is no coincidence that my first short film would resultantly revolve around a library-dwelling high school student. I couldn't help inserting my own predilections into my early filmic envisionings but such was the impact of this new and comfortable setting. This space so facilitated my creative process that I at once expected to have a final draft of my short film script ripe and ready before the end of the summer with the intent to begin production in the fall.

While attending New World, I had started to develop some ideas for a potential first short film and even produced a first draft based on one of those ideas. But in my domain of solitude at FIU, my most earnest and practical energies were mobilized like never before. Working out the broad strokes first, the details would follow after the thematic and structural foundation had been firmly established. And while my developing script would evolve substantially before the end of summer, most of the surviving aspects were wrought at FIU early on.

I read in great volume as well.

Upon breaks from my principal task of writing, I immediately sought out the film section of the library's vast collection. Some of the first books I seized were making-of books of Stanley Kubrick's 1968 sci-fi epic *2001: A Space Odyssey* and David Lean's 1962 WWI biopic *Lawrence of Arabia*. I also explored film theory books from Soviet filmmakers and theorists Sergei Eisenstein and Vsevolod Pudovkin. Beyond these selections, I also delved into books featuring interviews with two of my favorite filmmakers, Orson Welles and Martin Scorsese.

Suffice to say, I seldom grew weary of either writing or reading due to my habit of alternating between activities. And when my sessions at FIU's library would elapse, Juan would check out books for me, often more than one at a time, so I could continue my study or perusal at home.

In time, I would be introduced to the 5th floor of the FIU library which housed its equally vast media collection and an assortment of media consoles for playback of chosen content. I immediately seized the opportunity and compelled Juan to check out select VHS and DVD titles for home viewing (I quickly learned that watching films on the library consoles was prohibited). Among my selections were Ingmar Bergman's 1957 Swedish drama *Wild Strawberries*, Vittorio De Sica's 1948 Italian neo-realist drama *Bicycle Thieves* and Sergei Eisenstein's historical dramas *Battleship Potemkin* and *Alexander Nevsky* from 1925 and 1938, respectively. Arcane choices but they were films I had long desired to view and understand. A film school before film school.

My early writing experiences and certainly my visits to FIU this one particular summer were instrumental in establishing the heart of all of my ensuing filmmaking activity - solitude. It is this enduring capacity to work out scripts and plan productions quite single-handedly that has defined much of my work in the realm of filmmaking. This solitary tendency is quite contrary to the usual gateway into the practice for many young people; making irreverent videos with a group of friends. Rather, my early filmmaking activity was a touch more targeted, deliberate and discrete.

Leaving New World and starting Killian on my own, I had virtually no friends and I tended toward a rather asocial inclination. My principal preoccupation in those days was shifting my concentration from the nearly life-long involvement with visual art to the newer, greener pastures of filmmaking. No doubt it was a lonely endeavor but I was rarely if ever lonesome as I worked to find my footing in the latter area.

To write, produce, direct, shoot and edit all of my films was the ideal from the start. Since my introduction to the concept of the auteur theory, which posits that a film's director should be seen as the sole author of a film, this idea was immediately attractive both in thought and practice. This singularity of vision has always been a consistence facet of my work as well as sitting alone and thinking it all up, as I did so often at FIU's Green Library.

101. Speaking (April 2013)

"I'm in one of the films," shared a fellow film festival patron seated next to me in the lavish, expansive and gradually filling-in auditorium.

I was at Adrienne Arsht Center for the Performing Arts in downtown Miami at the 2011 edition of Borscht Film Festival; a one-night event showcasing an eclectic variety of short films from area filmmakers. My own work was not being shown.

"You're an actor?" I asked the outgoing patron.

"No, I'm an insurance agent but I heard that the Meza-Valdez brothers were looking for extras so I showed up," he clarified and added, "I'm also a Toastmaster."

"A Toastmaster?" I asked.

"Yeah, Toastmasters is a public speaking and leadership development organization," he revealed. "They train you how to speak without fillers. Like 'uh,' 'ya know,' 'so'," the patron explained. "It's an amazing organization. They have clubs all over the world," he stressed.

I let his curious words waft over me as I nodded slowly in comprehension.

Though I was attending the film festival to expose myself to the cinematic offerings of the participating local filmmakers, my most potent takeaway from that evening at Arsht would be the new knowledge I'd gained from the kindly patron. Toastmasters International, the organization referenced that night, was set to play a major role in my life and second wind as a university student.

Why was I so intrigued?

Because there were some specific moments earlier on in my adulthood where I became aware of the impressiveness and importance of exemplary public speaking skills.

The first was witnessing the refined verbal stylings of a legal advisor to at least one of the student political groups I was affiliated with during my time at University of Central Florida. John Barry, a practicing lawyer and a warm avuncular figure to us young whipper-snappers, was the first person I recognized as having the ability to address groups publicly without letting a single filler (e.g., uh, ya know, so, etc.) slip out of their mouth. During instances of his remarkable elocution ability, I would glance at my fellow radical comrades to see if anyone else was catching on to this marvel of expressive ability.

Inspired by this peculiar fascination, I later enrolled in a public speaking class in my Fall 2007 semester at UCF; also a convenient general education requirement. Here I was able to put my own rhetorical metal to the test in both classroom and auditorium settings before many of my peers. My appreciation for refinement in public address only grew in intensity during that class; how appropriate in a democracy where the People are expected to exercise their voice, I maintained and often expressed.

Yet another example of bearing witness to such extraordinary ability lay at the closing night of the Gasparilla International Film Festival in Tampa, Florida which took place weeks before the Borscht festival. Here, renowned Miami documentary filmmaker Billy Corben (*Cocaine Cowboys*, *The U*, *Screwball*) presented his 2011 documentary *Square Grouper: The Godfathers of Ganja*. After the screening, Corben and the central personality featured in the film took the stage to talk about the events presented and field questions from the audience. Both Corben and the other gentleman were impressive speakers and I most certainly took note.

But one experience above others, however, prompted me to answer the call of what had been laid out in reverent tones that one night at Borscht Film Festival. About two years after that interaction, I attended a special advance screening of Fede Alvarez's 2013 horror remake *Evil Dead*. Presenting the film was none other than storied legend of B-movies Bruce Campbell (*The Evil Dead* trilogy, *Bubba Ho-Tep*, *Sky High*). But it wasn't the mere presence of a Hollywood icon that awed me; rather, it was Campbell's utter prowess at extemporaneous and filler-free speaking that completely entranced me.

My life would soon turn a corner.

Immediately upon return from the *Evil Dead* screening that evening, I queried the internet for the closest Toastmasters club and earliest meeting date.

I elected to attend the West Kendall Toastmasters club which met twice-a-month about 10 minutes away from my home at a local sports grill and bar. The club organizers always reserved a separate room for their purposes.

Upon arrival, I was intimidated by the older crowd but was warmly received and soon acclimated as the meeting got underway.

The entire structure of the meeting was intended to give as many attendees as possible an opportunity to speak in front of their fellow members. There were functionary roles assigned for catching fillers, judging grammar and keeping time. There were opportunities for long-form, prepared speeches as well as shorter, impromptu ones. And everyone was most supportive and maximally concerned with the flow and effectiveness of each meeting. It was all new and extremely fascinating!

Midway through my first meeting, I knew I'd be returning for more.

But those plans were soon curtailed by the awareness of another Toastmasters club in the area. The FIU business school had their own club run exclusively by students. I was curious and intent on attending that club straightaway.

I had begun my college career at FIU in the fall of 2004 and attended until the summer of 2005 when I transferred to UCF in Orlando to pursue a major in film production. My experience returning to the FIU campus for the Toastmasters meeting after eight years was deeply nostalgic.

When I arrived, I experienced the same warmth and hospitality I had received at the West Kendall Toastmasters club; a great feeling.

Familiar with the format of the meetings, my transition into the FIU student version of a Toastmasters meeting was nothing short of seamless. I found myself engaging socially with many of the members and established a strong rapport with many of them early on despite their more left-brain dispositions. A bit more comfortable around fellow young adults, I was far more open to participating in the functionary roles and performed them with surprising aplomb.

Some time later, at the urging of the FIU club's coach, an older and fatherly gentleman who also attended the West Kendall meetings, I was encouraged to give my first prepared speech and did so not too long after the pep talk.

Over time and with much practice, I grew more confident and capable as a speaker. Indeed, my experience at Toastmasters was so positive and life-affirming that it even forced my hand in picking a major when I decided to return to FIU to complete my undergraduate studies (which had been tragically interrupted at UCF in 2009 due to a mental health crisis and legal quandary). The following year, I would resume my studies as a Communication Arts major at FIU. I would complete the program and receive my bachelor's degree two years later with a perfect GPA among all of my courses required for the major.

During my time as a student, my involvement with Toastmasters would continue and deepen. I attended every single summer meeting (taking place twice-a-week) and completed numerous prepared speeches. I also participated in more rigorous meeting roles and established a reputation among my fellow members as a highly competent speaker with an above-average vocabulary. Not too shabby!

Additionally, I took part in various contests and managed to win 1st place in the FIU club's impromptu speaking competition and achieve 2nd place later on at an area-level follow-up match.

To put it simply, my curious attraction toward finessed public speaking as a young adult irrevocably changed my life. My involvement with Toastmasters, aside from providing innumerable opportunities to cultivate my public speaking craft, substantially raised my confidence and self-esteem. It provided a much-needed shot in the arm following the fallout from an earlier mental health crisis and dire legal predicament. There's no doubt the skills and experiences engendered by my time at Toastmasters and my resurgent college career consequently paved the way for greater success in my filmmaking activity. For that, I am eternally grateful.

I still sing the praises of Toastmasters to this day.

102. Technology (September 2002)

"Every art form and every artist is struggling against the technology because art is technology... it's using technology to communicate emotion... whether you're telling stories, you're doing plays, you're doing music, you're writing books, you're painting pictures. It's all about the technology."
-George Lucas

Shortly after my junior year at Miami Killian Senior High began, I proposed to my dad that we build a $14 "Steadicam" using an online how-to guide by one Johnny Chung Lee. I was interested in using such a device for select scenes in my first fully-mounted short film production, *Mass Education*.

A Steadicam is, of course, a widely-used tool in the film industry which allows for the mechanical isolation of the camera from the operator's movement in order to produce smooth and steady traveling shots.

With parts gathered exclusively from Home Depot and following the online guide to the letter, the $14 incarnation I built with my dad's crucial handyman know-how operated on the same basic principle as the more impressive (and far more expensive) genuine article.

I had been inspired to add the device to my starting filmmaker arsenal by films that made spectacular use of the tool. These films included Stanley Kubrick's 1980 horror film *The Shining*, Paul Thomas Anderson's 1999 drama *Magnolia*, Martin Scorsese's 1990 crime drama *Goodfellas* and Alexander Sokurov's 2002 Russian experimental film *Russian Ark*.

Although my use of the home-made stabilization device was limited to two scenes in that first short film and discontinued beyond that, employing and embracing this technology suggested the alluring and intractable role of technology in art referred to by the George Lucas quote above.

Unfortunately, it's become rather prosaic to regard technology with suspicion and haughtiness these days but I firmly believe, when harnessed properly and astutely, technology can serve as a powerful extension of our best impulses, whether we're artists or not.

Thanks for your help, Dad!

103. Trust (January 2006)

One afternoon toward the end of high school, my mom picked me up from one of my frequent visits to the local library. I'd earn my driver's license shortly after graduation but for now I was reliant on parental car rides to get to where I needed to go. At the library, I'd read, write and often check out classical music CDs for listening (and to fashion MP3s from at home).

On this particular occasion, I had checked out a recording of music by Richard Wagner. I inserted the disc into the CD player of my parents' car.

The playback soon began as my mom exited the library parking lot.

"Short films are like calling cards," I bluntly stated to my mom as the Wagner piece was warming up.

We traveled down a main roadway toward our home.

"They communicate more than a story," I continued as Wagner's orchestrations continued to stir. "The work lets people know that I'm serious about filmmaking," I continued.

The music swelled into a greater fullness as my mom focused exclusively on the road.

"It proves my sincerity," I asserted firmly as the music climbed. "To help me attract actors and other people for future short films," I said, concluding my unusual moment of candor against the lush crescendo of orchestral music now filling the car!

"¡El volumen está muy alto! ¡Bájalo o lo apago!" my mom complained as she reached for the audio console's volume knob to lower the volume.

I huffed and spent the rest of the ride home looking out my passenger side window, listening to subdued Wagner and keeping my cognitive reverie to myself as my mom and I continued on our way home.

Some weeks into the Spring 2006 semester at University of Central

Florida, I was determined to produce a short film in the mold of a class assignment expected of freshman year film students (I hadn't yet been accepted into the Film BFA program). With an exciting, new and surprisingly brief short script in-hand, I had my eye on friend and fellow UCF student David Pritchard to participate as lead actor in the short film, titled *The Procrastinator*.

I met David Pritchard early on in my time at UCF. He arrived at UCF with a squad of students who'd completed a special college program elsewhere in Florida which had pre-qualified them for acceptance into the limited-access film program at UCF. Our first encounter took place on the set of an upperclassmen's senior thesis project early on in my first semester at the university. David was one of the most intelligent young people I'd ever met. We hit it off right away over our shared interest in cinema, classical music (he was also a competent pianist) and Sudoku.

Well aware of David's interest in acting, I decided I would entreat him in a rather strategic manner to all but assuredly secure his participation. I would keep my intent hush-hush and figure out a way to prove my ethos before I popped the question.

I soon landed on my approach. Having completed two short films, 2003's *Mass Education* and 2005's *Does Free Speech Matter?*, I decided that I would invite him to watch both and invite his participation on my 3rd short film production immediately after.

So, playing cool and cryptic, we arranged to meet up at his apartment. I had simply invited him to watch my two earliest short films, which he hadn't yet seen, without alluding to anything more.

When we were gathered, I took the USB flash drive, where I stored copies of my short films, from around my neck and inserted it into David's laptop.

Playback began.

David was captivated throughout our little private screening and reacted favorably to my amateur cinematic confections.

At the end of the second short film, he offered me his reaction in a capsule.

"These are very good," in his humorously frank way of speaking.

Following that, I popped the question.

"Would you be interested in being the lead in my latest short film?" I humbly inquired.

"Yeah, sure!" he replied with utmost casualness.

I was relieved and overjoyed!

With David committed, I immediately drew up more advanced and detailed plans for the production of *The Procrastinator*.

Production lasted well into the spring semester due to scheduling difficulties and my overly fastidious process. But David's unwavering alliance throughout production made the entire experience eminently enjoyable.

Most of the filming involved posing David a certain way for a variety of locked-down shots or shots involving precise camera movements. We were all over campus on the production and, at times, redirecting traffic and stifling certain campus activity in order to achieve certain shots.

Thankfully, David wasn't expected to do much in the way of conventional acting because there was virtually no dialogue or interaction with other actors - by design. Taking this approach allowed me to focus on cinematography and staging without worrying about the believability or nuance of an acting performance. This latter preoccupation would come later.

One particularly memorable experience working with David involved producing a shot in which he opens the door to his character's apartment bedroom and stands in silhouette against the lit wall behind him. For some inarticulable reason, I was dissatisfied with the overall movement of the action and David's resulting stance. We spent nearly an hour and more than 30 takes to achieve the final shot to some vague, undefined sense of acceptability. But David didn't mind the extreme mindlessness of the work because he trusted me and my process - even if I was still somewhat untested.

Overall, David and I fortified our friendship over the course of the production and he became more like a brother than a friend.

About a year later, I was devastated when David told me that he would be transferring to University of Chicago to pursue a more fervent interest of his - in economics. I expected that this change would upend my social life to a significant degree as David and I had established meeting routinely for meals at a particular on-campus restaurant from early on.

I was right and would deeply miss his distinctive intellect and humor; not to mention our remarkable compatibility.

But I'd never forget when David offered up one of the most flattering compliments I've ever received from anyone: During production of *The Procrastinator*, I rushed into one of David's classes during a short break to rapidly explain the logistics of an upcoming filming session on our short film. After I concluded my explanation, David was so impressed that he told his nearby classmates, "I would gladly rob a bank with this man."

Much love, David!

104. Twins (September 2005)

They were always willing to briefly talk craft in the hallways of University of Central Florida's film school building.

They regularly updated their website and kept it stocked with intriguing content related to their short films.

They were so prolific that I later learned I'd seen one of their *Star Wars* fan films years before I attended UCF.

They refuted a rumor that they dressed alike on purpose and asserted that their choice of clothing was based on frugality, not style.

They were kind enough to discuss their reading material during a chance encounter at the student apartment complex of their residence.

They were a focused, hard-working and two-man cinematography crew on the set of a mutual friend's Directing III short film production.

They were surprised by my awareness of an update to their website which they'd published in the early morning hours.

They shared their directorial and technical virtuosity at UCF's film club and at the end-of-year showcases to repeatedly enthusiastic reception.

They openly and candidly expressed their astute observations about the film school and other film students in the computer lab.

They were open to receiving links to YouTube videos about innovative imaging techniques and discussing them with underclassmen (me).

They enjoyed a proud and distinctive reputation among their peers and the film program's professors.

They conducted an audition with one of my closest friends with absolute authority and professionalism.

They inspired great praise, criticism and anticipation about their work among their peers and younger film students.

They allowed crew members to man an on-set video camera to capture their behind-the-scenes activity on one of their capstone short films.

They weren't too prideful to be impressed by my one instance of topping them on a *Star Wars* trivia question.

They alone ran the crowded set of one of their capstone short film productions with the might of a more conventionally-numbered production crew.

They were generous in time and attention to a question about their compositing techniques during breaks in filming.

They pulled off the most advanced visual effects seen at UCF on their far less than state-of-the-art computers.

They were some of the only film students at UCF to produce a feature-length film beyond the purview of the film program.

They are Robert and James Dastoli, identical twin brothers and two of the finest and most inspiring contemporary filmmakers I've had the privilege to know.

105. Undeterred (May 2006)

Amid troubled military campaigns abroad, unpopular presidential leadership and a creeping economic collapse, the UNITED STATES OF AMERICA faces yet another challenge - controlling immigration.

The Sensenbrenner bill, recently passed by the House of Representatives, threatens to criminalize and deport millions of hard-working immigrants.

As a divided Senate debates this highly contentious issue, immigration and labor rights groups, struggling for liberty and justice, unite in protest around the country....

After several months attending University of Central Florida, I had found myself in the company of sds (Students for a Democratic Society), a radical and well-populated student political organization. On occasion, they participated in actions organized by other leftist political groups in the greater Orlando area. One of the first events I took part in with them was a protest march and rally taking place in downtown Orlando on the first day of May (in 2006), otherwise known as May Day or International Workers' Day.

The event, prompted by general anti-immigrant sentiment among Republicans and resulting draconian legislation, such as the odious Sensenbrenner bill, was one of many events taking place across the country in solidarity with immigrants, particularly those of Central and Latin American origin.

I originally wasn't planning on attending but when I learned that a fellow UCF film school classmate was planning on driving downtown on an unrelated errand that morning, I asked if he could drop me off at the site of the protest after I'd visited my apartment to pick up my video camera.

He obliged and I was soon on my way downtown with a plan to document the event and perhaps cobble together some sort of documentary video.

When I arrived, I was overwhelmed by the sight of about 25,000 thousand protesters. Nearly every age was represented. This event meant a great deal to very many, young and old.

I soon found and joined my fellow sds'ers and was greeted warmly despite my fairly recent membership.

As the march began, I entered documentary filmmaker mode and wandered away from my compatriots as I captured various subject matter from numerous angles. This was a spectacle unlike any I'd ever seen!

Overcome by my zeal in capturing the alluring sights and sounds of the protest, I may have called a bit too much attention to myself by hopping the crowd control barricades positioned in front of various government buildings in order to get some better angles. As a result, the law enforcement monitoring the event soon intervened.

I was stopped by several officers and a fearsome K-9 unit. They then guided me toward the side of the street, away from the tide of protesters.

"What are you doing here today?" one of the officers asked.

"I'm filming a documentary. I'm a UCF student," I replied earnestly.

"Can we see some ID?" another requested.

"Sure," I replied as I retrieved my driver's license. "Why am I being stopped, officers?"

I handed over my driver's license.

"You look suspicious," an officer of color replied.

The officers examined my ID and relayed my information via walkie-talkie as the K-9 unit stood not more than a foot away from my fleshy limbs. I only looked calm.

"I'm doing nothing wrong," I insisted. "Who do I call about this?"

"Homeland Security," an officer informed me.

I froze.

The officers finished their walkie-talkie relay and, having apparently deemed me not a security concern, released me from their custody but not before prohibiting me from continuing to film the event.

I immediately contacted my fellow sds'ers via cellphone and described what had happened to me. They assured me of my rights and urged me to rejoin them.

As I made my way through the crowd of protesters to catch up with my schoolmates, I defiantly continued filming despite what the officers had said.

Among the sds'ers, I caught up with John Barry, an older gentleman who was a lawyer by trade and sympathetic to the cause of sds and other political groups on-campus. He had been informed of what had happened to me and was not surprised. Observing my unnerved state, he floated the term "chilling effect" to describe what had happened to me. The term refers to the deterrence of free speech and alike rights due to a threat of legal action by the state.

I remained with my fellow sds'ers till the end of the march. Afterward, I carpooled with the group back to the UCF area and my student housing complex.

When I re-entered the familiar tranquility of my apartment, I felt as though I'd been fundamentally changed by my encounter with the supposed Homeland Security officers. I felt alien among these familiar and mundane trappings.

After a while, I settled down in front of my bedroom computer and got started capturing and logging the day's recorded footage. In the days to follow, I'd succeed in putting together my first documentary vignette of the event, titled *May Day! or: Two Americas*. I added a rousing piece of music by Richard Wagner to suitably compliment the impressive fact that the event was the largest protest ever held in the city of Orlando!

During my time at UCF and beyond, I would continue recording video at other political protests and producing more short, rather intense documentaries about them.

My encounter with law enforcement on this memorable day in May hadn't deterred me at all, however; on the contrary, it seems to have emboldened me.

106. Uniform (August 2003)

A white dress shirt.

Slim blue jeans.

Brown boat shoes.

This was my wardrobe of choice for the first day of my senior year at Miami Killian Senior High. And the second, the third, the fourth, the fifth, etc. It was a uniform I had determined to wear every single day of my final year in high school.

I had a closet full of those white dress shirts - like Superman and his red and blue superhero outfit. They were regularly washed and I personally assumed the responsibility of steam-ironing all of them after every cleaning.

This unusual choice had precedent. The previous year, I wore the same corduroy jacket and slim blue jeans nearly every day. The only non-uniform element was my regularly rotating t-shirts. It was a less extreme practice but it still drew some attention for its peculiarity.

Some of my family members, except for my mom who had facilitated the purchase of the articles of clothing in question, were the first to call attention to it as they found it quite odd. But I ignored their puzzlement.

At school, I was already something of a loner so I wasn't too clued in on how my approach to dress was generally received by my fellow class and schoolmates. But it must have been more positively than negatively regarded because several students in my International Relations class once encouraged everyone in the class to pay homage to my uniform practice by asking everyone to dress in a white button-up, blue jeans and brown shoes on a particular day during the school year. When that day came, many did, including the teacher of the class. It was quite a humorous and memorable occasion!

Also, one morning toward the end of the school year before my first class began that day, one of my friends expressed his admiration over my uniform habit with a warm, sustained smile. I appreciated the support for my late-adolescent idiosyncracies.

This habit would persist into my first year of college at FIU. However, I would swap out the blue jeans for earthy-colored cargo pants. Ever the loner, I never noticed any kind of response to my wayward tendency but once a sociology professor, the late Dr. Barry Levine, favorably acknowledged my discreteness as a sign of self-actualization.

When I moved to Orlando to attend UCF, I substituted cargo pants with cargo shorts and wore sandals instead of the boat shoes. However, I permitted more variation as my time at UCF wore on. A few of my friends remarked in curiosity about my preference and one time a particularly loathsome, bullying student attacked me over it, likening me to "a cartoon character."

Despite my mental health crisis in 2007, I still maintained the custom as I recovered at home. Gray t-shirts and basketball shorts were the new duds over the following years but I would eventually become far more amenable to variation.

While I am still occasionally given to stretches of uniforming, I am far from following the austerity of my former clothing regimen.

Why did I get into the habit of donning a uniform?

First, the idea of reducing unnecessary mental activity greatly appealed to me. When you wear a uniform, you don't have to worry about clothing preference at all. And if you like what you wear (which I certainly did), the start of every day unfurls at a faster, smoother pace. I valued freeing up even such a meager quantity of mental capacity, enabling greater attention to what really mattered to me - my intellectual and creative processes.

Second, I wanted to project an image of order, consistency and conscious design. And I didn't at all mind if I hurt my social perception among my peers. Frankly, I was more interested in intelligence than likability. On top of that, I also happened to admire an image of Amish-like plainness and its reinforcing of said inner strengths and qualities. To me, the image I wanted to project was antithetical to capitalist and consumerist excess. I kinda liked that.

Lastly, physics tells us that everything in the universe is in a constant state of motion and change. So, in response to this most ancient of truths, I desired to daringly oppose this almighty, cosmic status quo. I wanted to assert my will against this unfathomably grand scheme of all things (a preoccupation that also informs some of my filmmaking). By adopting a uniform, I was resisting an enemy of the greatest scale imaginable!

So yeah, I was rather proud of my distinctive uniform habit.

107. Unprepared (November 2005)

Several months into my first semester at University of Central Florida, I was struggling with a short film idea, titled *The School Janitor*. I'd conceived of its premise shortly after getting fully situated at the Orlando university but I had made little substantive progress in the ensuing months.

The story idea tossed back and forth in my mind revolved around a school janitor and his last day of work before a major hurricane was expected to make landfall. The story involved visions of destruction, strange rituals among co-workers and a general atmosphere of existential dread. I suppose some of its parts had great cinematic potential but I toiled over developing a strong narrative backbone.

Despite being caught up in development hell, replete with all its characteristic indecisiveness and nebulousness, I decided to move forward with what little I had worked out and scheduled an evening of filming about a week later.

I reasoned that by establishing a definite start date and scheduling some actors, it would serve as a catalyst for me to figure out the rest of the script by the time I started filming. More foolhardy than clever.

In any case, I recruited my fellow off-campus housing roommate Dieri as the lead actor; a non-actor, in keeping with my well-established tradition. For the two remaining supporting roles, I cast a fellow film club member Sam and a film school classmate Lortir. Again, all non-actors but all plenty capable for the relatively simple requirements of what I had in terms of a script.

We would all convene after I was through with the final exam of one of my film classes. Locations would include UCF's math and physics building, library and two administrative buildings; without express permission and accessibility hinged upon the luck of the draw.

Suffice to say, I did not have anything resembling a complete script by the time that particular evening rolled around. In fact, even the material closest to finalization was far, far from polished. Despite my gross unpreparedness, I would be winging most of the nights' shooting and simply hope for the best.

What followed that evening was akin to the running around of a headless chicken. Plenty of activity and hustle but absolutely mindless. I arranged for the shooting of scenes vaguely reminiscent of what little I had on paper; moments with no clear relationship to any grander narrative scheme. Most of the scenes were silent and what little dialogue there was would be improvised.

Thankfully, our merry party of four was able to access most of the buildings that evening. We even managed to lug a garbage tank into the library and other buildings for several shots. My yet trusting band of allies worked throughout the night, however capriciously.

One of the last legs of our nighttime business involved filming some shots in one of the administrative buildings, Millican Hall. We were able to enter through an unsecured door but we may have tripped a silent alarm of some sort. While we set up and executed some shots, we soon heard another building occupant nearing our position. It was a police K-9 unit!

As the tethered canine and its uniformed master approached us, we froze in some fear.

"Is there a problem, officer?" I inquired.

"Are you students here?" he responded.

"Yes," I confirmed. "We're filming some scenes for a student film."

The officer's four-legged companion sniffed my pants leg.

"This building is off-limits to anyone without permission," he informed us.

"I understand. But can you give us a few minutes to finish up before we leave? We're almost done," I implored.

The officer considered my request and responded in kind.

"Okay, but hurry up," he said.

Relieved as we were, the officer and his furry friend soon left the immediate area. Then, my cast and I wrapped up a final shot and we made our way out of the building on the double.

The night had gone on long enough. Just outside of Millican Hall, I called time and announced that filming for the night was wrapped. Dieri, Sam and Lortir had all been most gracious allies throughout the course of the night but I felt like I didn't deserve their trust and confidence. In my mind, my project was in shambles. Half-formed ideas and half-baked execution.

I'd learned an important lesson about the dangers of inadequate preparation and a faulty writing process. I wasn't honoring the responsibility of a filmmaker and the goodwill of my collaborators with this shortage of proper planning and empty leadership. Still, it was better that I learned this earlier on the cheap rather than later with significant money on the line.

I would ultimately abandon this incarnation of *The School Janitor*.

108. Vagrancy (March 2008)

Amid an enrollment snafu during my time at University of Central Florida in the spring of 2008, I decided to abandon my off-campus housing and subject myself to several weeks of homelessness, returning to my apartment only for an occasional shower.

What exactly prompted this unusual decision?

I had received word from UCF administrators that my appeal to have a medical hold lifted had been denied. In the previous semester of Fall 2007, I suffered a dramatic psychotic episode and was hospitalized at an area behavioral clinic. As is custom in such situations, I was medically withdrawn from my classes that semester and a medical hold was placed on my account.

I returned to UCF in Spring 2008 believing that I'd be readmitted without issue but I was unaware that the medical hold was still in place. When I learned that it still was, I had immediately appealed for its lifting.

Apparently the medical hold hadn't affected my ability to enroll and attend classes two months into the semester but its application meant I couldn't officially register. I was a student in all but name.

In order to be released from the medical hold, I'd have to attend a local college at home in Miami in order to prove to UCF that I was fit enough to re-enroll as a student at the Orlando university.

So, I was unable to effectively exist as a UCF student and I had to wait for my parents to be able to travel up from Miami to pick me up. In the face of this liminal quandary, I became a person without a place.

During my vagrancy in-and-around campus, I wrote, thought, read, wandered, explored, observed, sang, soliloquized, dined and slept exclusively in public spaces.

Luckily enough, I somehow managed not to attract any perceptible amount of suspicion from either students or campus authorities. I also purposely refrained from interaction or contact with anyone in order to intensify what I began to treat as a self-imposed test of austerity and solitude.

One late night in my aimless meandering, I found myself alone in the film school building sitting across from the entrance to the production hallway.

Then a familiar figure soon appeared heading toward the key card-locked door. It was a former film theory instructor of mine, Professor Christopher Harris! I greeted him and asked him what he was up to. He told me he was going to the editing lab to review some footage he'd be presenting at a talk during an upcoming out-of-state trip. I asked if he wouldn't mind my joining him. He consented.

So, we both stood at a tall console capable of playing back nearly any type of media thrown at it. Professor Harris was reviewing footage of an interview with a female re-enactor of colonial New England times, if I recall correctly. However, Professor Harris pointed out that the women of this time were severely oppressed and subjugated. He felt that this woman's performance belied the truth of the historical circumstances.

During our late night coupling, Professor Harris also reviewed some footage of the sky, a parking lot and room service. It was interesting to watch the personal, creative work of a professor I held in so high esteem and to hear his self-reflective comments about it. A rare opportunity.

When Professor Harris was done doing what he'd come to the editing lab to do, I detected the chance for a different kind of special opportunity. I invited the professor to watch two of my latest short films *House Divided* and *Rough Cut*. Both experimental. He was sensitive about his time but I assured them that both were no more than a minute-long. He agreed and we exited the editing lab and accessed a nearby computer lab where I quickly cued up my short films.

He didn't seem to care too much for *House Divided*, an elaborate illustration of the uncanny dichotomy between various objects in my family home. It is no longer a part of my short film canon.

However, he was quite taken with *Rough Cut*, a simple visual tone poem about a man who mows the lawn. Professor Harris reacted quite audibly to some its most daring shots.

At the end of my little impromptu screening, Professor Harris and I parted ways. He probably had no idea how much what he'd shared with me and his positive reactions to my film meant to me. We wouldn't see each other again until after the mental illness-fueled drama which would ensue in the following year. Unfortunately, one of the most painful casualties I'd suffer was losing his and other professors' friendly regard toward me.

In any case, I was soon back to my ostensible homelessness for a few more days. Overall, the experience taught me, more than anything else, how to stave off vast stretches of tedium and become far more self-reliant. For these reasons, it was one of the most fortifying and valuable experiences I've ever had.

Not too long after, my parents were able to pick me up from Orlando and I returned home to Miami where I'd remain for the rest of the year.

109. Variety (June 2012)

"The film and entertainment industry brings millions of dollars into our economy each year, creates thousands of jobs, and supports local businesses. Public recognition is a great way to show our appreciation and support for Michael Bay who has contributed so much to the growth and success of the film industry here in Miami-Dade County," Miami-Dade County Commissioner Sally Heyman said in a press release about the issuing of a proclamation officially recognizing June 5th as "Michael Bay Day."

That's right. One of the most commercially successfully film directors in history and Miami Beach resident Michael Bay was honored with his very own day in Miami on June 5th, 2012. At the time, Bay was in-production on his relatively low-budget crime drama *Pain & Gain*, based on true events.

And on that Tuesday, I was actually in downtown Miami for a different, loosely-related special occasion: filming two shots I needed to complete my 13th short film *Semester of Madness*. I needed a daytime exterior shot of Ryder Trauma Center and a nighttime exterior shot of Jackson Mental Health Hospital to top off my story of a college student who loses his grip on reality.

Before night completely fell on the Magic City, I succeeded in obtaining the two simple hand-held shots and, with that done, production on my most personal film was officially wrapped! Filming *Semester of Madness*, perhaps my most complex short film, had been a long process but its production tested the rigor and integrity of my oft-touted one-man band ethos through the myriad of creative and practical problems I had to solve.

Here is an overview of the many challenges I encountered throughout the roughly five months of production and several weeks of ensuing post-production on *Semester of Madness*:

- As I wouldn't be requesting permission to film on the Miami Dade College campus grounds, I needed to know precisely where I'd be filming each scene. So, I borrowed my parents' digital still camera and spent hours roaming the nearby campus looking for spots and quickly evaluating their suitability for each particular scene.

- Also owing to a lack of acquired permission to shoot at Miami Dade College, I had to adopt a guerrilla-style, run-and-gun approach to filming and kept my footprint minimal at all times. I never worked with more than three actors at a time.

- Interested in using my neighbor's house as the exterior and interior of the main character's home, I prepared a presentation for the neighbor which outlined the areas I'd be filming and for what length of time. Despite some initial hesitation, my complete transparency about what I wanted to do allayed the homeowner's concerns.

- Mid-production, my lead actor Julian Malagon asked me to help out on a student film production he was participating in. During a lunch break on that particular film shoot, Julian expressed his concern about the scheduling on our film and urged to find a way to hasten the pace of filming. Later that day, I took a long, hard look at the schedule and found ways to speed it up.

- The climax of the film involved a messy and potentially surface-staining use of fake blood. To ensure that the furnishings in the room the scene would take place in remained unaffected, I appointed my mom as a set technician to ensure the filming process didn't leave a permanent trace.

- The final scene of the film called for some special effects makeup but I'd never worked with anyone who could provide them. Querying my parents about the issue, I was soon informed that a family friend's wife had some experience and likely wouldn't charge an arm and a leg for her services. So, I reached out to her and, while compromising a bit on the quality, the arrangement worked out.

- At one point in the film, Julian had to be shown exiting a series of storefronts to imply his character's failure at finding employment. In order to obtain the shots for this montage-like sequence, Julian and I stopped at every suitable storefront along US-1 for a stretch of a mile or two until I had enough shots to work with. We worked quickly and seldomly had to ask for permission; though when asked, it was granted.

- One of the proudest moments in making the film involved arranging for the appearance of a parked ambulance in front of the main character's home. Recalling the use of an emergency vehicle in a short film I'd seen recently, I was able to reach out to that short film's producer and acquire the information needed to hire an ambulance to appear in my film for a brief amount of time. I was proud of this occurrence because it illustrated the irony of putting so much effort, time and money into an element which only appears for a matter of seconds. That's filmmaking!

- Several shots required filming the exteriors of some residential buildings. In order to acquire the shots, I drove around my neighborhood with my younger brother Daniel and quickly gathered a variety of shots in front of various houses. However, a suspicious neighbor soon confronted us and I was prompted to de-escalate the rising tension between Daniel and the neighbor with an honest explanation of what we were up to and the presentation of my contact information for any necessary follow-up.

* * *

- For one surreal moment in the film, Julian's character peers into a classroom auditorium and sees a mass in session. To get a shot of a church service in progress, I actually attended a Sunday ceremony at the church up the street from my home. About ten minutes into the holy proceedings, I backed away to a mostly out-of-view area and surreptitiously acquired the needed footage before making a quick exit!

- Similarly, in need of some shots of a classroom full of students, I was initially concerned about a dead-end in the production because of how difficult I assumed getting such shots would be. However, I decided to take my chances and drop-in on random classes without permission. It took a few attempts but I was able to acquire the shots, including one with a professor who'd granted me permission to film him and his students, and I was thrilled with the results!

- Feeling I didn't own audio equipment of adequate quality to record two actors interacting in my home's outdoor terrace, I decided to dub all of the dialogue of that final scene in post-production. I performed the recording in my room with the aid of a pair of speakers purchased for the occasion and did my best to have Julian and Max Terlecki, who plays an interviewer in the scene, replicate their earlier vocal performances. The recording process went smoothly but the results were a bit less than seamless.

- Desiring to do something interesting with the opening and closing credits, I opted to take the creative approach of writing out the credits on paper. I thought it would pair well with the main character's passion for writing. The most difficult part of executing this idea, however, was flawlessly turning the pages one-by-one without having any of the pages stick together in a clumsy way that would necessitate starting over. It took many, many takes!

***

- I knew that I wanted my short film to have an unsettling aural ambience. So, it took me a while to decide what I'd do but I ultimately ended up browsing Freesound.org, a collaborative sound database I'd relied upon on nearly every project since the start of my filmmaking career. Scouring the site for hours, I ultimately found a selection of highly appropriate sound and music-like samples that would lend my film the perfect degree of dread and foreboding. I courteously credited their inclusion at the end of my film.

And so concludes my list of the diverse array of up-hill climbs I faced in the production and post-production of my 13th short film *Semester of Madness*. While these challenges pale in comparison to the stunt and pyrotechnic work on a Michael Bay film, I'm certain the intrepid spirit of practical and creative problem solving remains the same.

And in case I don't see you on June 5th, Happy Michael Bay Day!

110. Walking (September 2014)

Although production had only demanded a few intense days of filming and one major paper-crumpling task, editing together my 15th and penultimate short film *Leo's Love Letter* required several weeks. Perhaps in compensation for the short film's brief production, simple narrative and restrained visual approach, I felt compelled to lend greater sensitivity to the combination and timing of the audio and visual elements.

Editing the majority of the film was a rather uncomplicated process. Every shot of the short film had been determined by a highly detailed shot list and some of the film had been carefully storyboarded. Putting together the majority of the film in my editing program was a mostly swift follow-through.

However, the climactic scene of the film beckoned greater effort and consideration. It featured some visuals that were rather expensive to produce and time-consuming to pull off. They were the short film's nuclear payload and I had to serve them justly in the edit.

Unfortunately, I ran into a snag.

Before the reveal of a surreal mass of paper balls, illustrating the protagonist's superhuman effort to save his troubled romantic relationship, I initially wanted the camera to pan down to show some of the crumpled paper but stop dead at a certain point. However, most of the takes included a pan past the desired point.

I attempted to artificially slow down the shot to a complete stop in order to achieve the desired effect but that didn't sit well. It was far from seamless and such imperfection would fly in the face of the surrounding film which was characterized by delicate care from a technical point of view. I was also exasperated by the fact that re-shooting anything was completely out of the question as most of the paper balls used in the shots had already been disposed of.

Suffering from frustration over the issue, I attempted to evade the stress and uncertainty of my creative hurdle for a while.

So, what did I do?

I went walking!

And would you believe it? After about fifteen minutes of leisurely strolling away from my house, I landed on a solution!

While walking it occurred to me that a few of the alternate takes I'd filmed of the challenging shot in question involved an indefinite downward pan. Luckily, I had executed some of those downward pans with delicate smoothness as they captured the sheer glut of paperballs at the protagonist's feet. After concluding my walk, I returned to my desktop PC and accessed those relevant takes to see if they worked in the edit.

Seizing and applying the take with the smoothest and most uniform downward pan to the scene, my solution worked! It was definitely the better idea and I didn't once second-guess it.

The effectiveness of this touch would be constantly affirmed by the unfailing ability of this particular moment to elicit laughter and audible wonderment at virtually every public screening of *Leo's Love Letter* which would follow.

All I'd needed was some time to consider my problem with some degree of detachment in a less cooped-up environment. But my saving walk was more than a spur of the moment activity. It was, up to then, a serious habit roughly one year in age.

What began as aimless ambling around the neighborhood of my family home about a year prior gradually led to the discovery of a route which took me through a series of looped paths in my area and back to my home in almost one hour exactly; a total distance of about three miles.

Traveling the route became the basis for a daily or near-daily walking routine that served as a weight loss/maintenance and psychological relief mechanism; the same route always.

As a result of my rapt dedication to this habit, I've no doubt improved various facets of my physical health and enjoyed relief from so much unwelcome anxiety, pressure and stress. And, of course, it has allowed me to attack harrying creative problems from a different perspective on more than a few occasions with success more often than not.

I like to think of the practice as keeping my entire organism flushed, clean and in optimal condition. An appealing and potent image in my mind.

During my walks, I've also encountered countless neighbors and other witnesses of my routine exercise who've offered their appreciation and praise over my sustained devotion.

In fact, many years later, former Miami-Dade County Police Director Juan J. Perez, who happens to live along my route, was so impressed by my weight loss and consistency of habit that one day he stopped me to offer me a coin with his name, title and police force insignia emblazoned upon it. It's a traditional honoring practice known as coining that stretches all the way back to Roman times. He encouraged me to use my example "to inspire others."

My top priority will always be my filmmaking but if I can inspire anyone along the way with my walking habit, I'll certainly try to.

Thank you, Mr. Perez!

111. Zealous (March 2007)

Ever since I'd heard of a particular pair of Editing I assignments from the whispers of upperclassmen, I would salivate over the prospect of completing it myself until I was finally able to do so in my Spring 2007 semester. The assignments basically involved editing a sequence from Ridley Scott's 2001 war drama *Black Hawk Down* using raw footage of an aerial and ground troop invasion (our professor opted for the euphemism, "insertion," in his explanation) sequence procured somehow and made available by Professor Mark Gerstein. But the kicker was that students were required to apply any music of their choosing to play throughout the edit of the sequence; no other audio was allowed.

This assignment was personally significant to me because the practice of syncing movement and edits to music is a seminal reason I fell in love with filmmaking. My fascination with this facet of filmmaking was borne in my tween years as I re-watched and grew increasingly appreciative of films with tailor-made musical scores; chiefly, films featuring John Williams' music.

While I hadn't seen *Black Hawk Down* at the time, I avoided being unduly influenced by the official version of the sequence and so I refrained from seeking out the film to view it.

The amount of footage at our disposal was far from exhaustive but I saw great possibility in the bevy of open-ended takes. I was thrilled by the prospect of editing together such expensive footage involving elaborate aerial vehicle coordination, massive crowds, violent shootouts between opposing forces, stunt work, etc.

My first attempt at the sequence's editing would be juxtaposed with the energetic and counter-culture ravings of punk rock band Anti-Flag; specifically, their 2003 song *Sold as Freedom*. With lyrics such as "Pull on the trigger with your heart and soul, Cause war is peace now you know,"

"Fight for the wealth of the few! Wrapped in a flag and sold to you," "It's up to you to see through lies by those you've led us to endless world strife," I found its union with the visuals of modern warfare deliciously (and blatantly) subversive.

But aside from such subtextual interests, my general approach was to satisfy the goal of the assignment by telling a clear, linear story; accommodating the music with some matching cuts; and editing down some of the music to keep the entire edit lean and efficient. Some proud touches included opening with a propulsive electric guitar solo, milking the satirical bent by matching certain lyrics to certain visuals and adding a closing title card that expressed that the invasion was made possible by several participating oil companies.

When I met with Professor Gerstein at one of the editing stations in the film school's editing lab, he was amused by my song choice but had some critical but sensible notes about the logic of my work. He wanted me to "Dilate the opening," "Introduce HQ officials earlier," "Build up to RPG incident," resist making a plummeting soldier "look like a dummy" and "Add peril" and a "sense of opposition."

For my second attempt at the assignment, I would address every single one of his notes.

The second edit would incorporate several fused tracks from Basil Poledouris' rousing musical score for the 1997 sci-fi action film *Starship Troopers*. The effusively militaristic music would be implemented to match the visuals and my cuts exactly. Totally jingoistic! It was the exact opposite of the youthful irreverence of my first edit.

Some proud touches included some rather subtle visual cues appropriately paired with certain orchestral flourishes in the music, an added splash screen at the end with an ironic slogan ("Always strong, never wrong") and not following the basic beats of the first edit too closely in the interest of freshness despite using the same basic footage.

I was also rather proud of the fact that I'd put together this latest edit over the course of an all-night editing bender in the editing lab; an excess I was prone to from time to time.

When I sat down with Professor Gerstein to review my second and final edit of the *Black Hawk Down* sequence, he responded encouragingly as it played. I was most proud of this far more earnestly approached follow-up attempt and after the video had played, Professor Gerstein didn't offer a single note. Instead, he offered a simple verbal response I'll always remember.

"You mined it!" he exclaimed.

Part III: Feature Films (2014-2022)

112. Adaptation (April 2020)

While working on a screenplay poised to become the basis for the follow-up to my debut feature *For My Sister*, the coronavirus pandemic befell the U.S.

Soon, terms like "social distancing," "masking," "lockdown" and "quarantine" became a part of the popular lexicon. Within days of the outbreak, all of society seemed to come to a complete stop as we all braced ourselves for this mostly unprecedented threat to our way of life.

But as fear and uncertainty gripped the population, I was steadfast in my determination to finish my 4th feature-length script, titled *Zenith*, even though its fate as the blueprint for a 2nd feature film production was now cast in serious doubt. Yet a month after the pandemic hit and amid my personal lockdown circumstances, I completed the 93-page script. Described as following "a defiant, young neuroscientist who abandons home in pursuit of his grandest ambition - a journey that will lead him to the edge of his own humanity and beyond. It's a mixed bag of drama, humor, romance, horror and sci-fi insanity!" I was proud of my script.

However, the anticipated extent of the pandemic's hold on society would put the kibosh on my immediate plans. In contact with the prospective lead actor J.C. Gutierrez, I soon broke the news to him that we would not be proceeding with the script's production in the foreseeable future for obvious reasons. It was with a heavy heart that I would be shelving *Zenith*.

I soon determined that I'd need to adapt to my dramatically altered living conditions. Perhaps it would be possible to conceive of another feature idea that could be produced in these more narrowed straits?

Although I expected that forging a fresh concept would take some time, I figured I'd encounter greater ease by the fact that the concurrent societal lockdown prompted by the coronavirus kept me safely cloistered in my bedroom/home office, my usual writing space. Without a single excuse to be productive and a desire to see if I could write a script that could be made given present confines as well as be produced with less expense and greater speed than *For My Sister*, I set myself to think up and develop a new idea.

Far easier said than done.

Committing multiple hours each day to my writing process, I would spend just under a year in infernal pursuit of an idea that satisfied those desired requisites. Over the course of eleven months, I generated about ten ideas which each seemed initially promising enough to make for well-formed outlines. However, they were all ultimately abandoned one-by-one after their foundations crumbled in the face of my applied scrutiny. Welcome to my notorious writing process!

Even actress Stephanie Maltez, who'd worked with me on my two final short films and my first feature, characterized my process as involving my "disappearing for a year before returning with the goods." Indeed, my writing sojourns were always fraught with pain and frustration but there always seemed to be an elusive pot of treasure at the ever-beckoning, far end of the rainbow.

Accordingly and rather inevitably, I finally reached a familiar state of ecstasy when an eleventh idea occurred to me out of the ashes of its many fallen brethren. It seemed to check all the boxes: pandemic-proof, low-cost and with potential for a quick turnaround. It also embodied that rarest of aspirations in filmmaking - innovation! As I continued to revolve the idea in my mind and work out a series of increasingly refined outlines, the idea began to glitter as gold.

Having arrived at a well-developed outline, a sudden and powerful wave of activity followed as I began to tighten all the screws of the concept's narrative framework and produce many detailed notes; all in preparation to write a first draft of the screenplay.

My idea presented an account of the rise and fall of an aspiring, young civil engineer with a mysterious past in the fictional city of Verity Falls. My dad, a Massachusetts Institute of Technology-trained civil engineer himself, was an influence on some elements of the narrative. He also served as a technical advisor on the project during the scriptwriting process.

After approximately five months, I completed a 95-page script for what would ultimately become my 2nd feature film *State v. Unknown*. I accompanied my social media announcement of the completion of the first draft with the following playful use of language which hinted at the unique perspective of the film and its criminal subject matter: "I am immensely pleased to announce the completion of the first draft of my second feature-length film, *State v. Unknown*! At 95 pages, the scrINCOMING MESSAGE FROM CAPTAIN LEEROY DOWD, VERITY FALLS POLICE DEPARTMENT: OUR CRIMINAL INVESTIGATION UNIT IS IN THE PROCESS OF COMPILING A SIGNIFICANT BODY OF VIDEO EVIDENCE FOR THE PURPOSE OF PROVIDING THE STATE WITH A COMPREHENSIVE NARRATIVE ACCOUNT TO SUPPORT THEIR CASE AGAINST WHAT MAY PROVE TO BE ONE OF THE MOST SHOCKING ABUSES OF CIVIL SOCIETY IN OUR CITY'S HISTORY. PLEASE STAND BY FOR ADDITIONAL NEWS AND INFORMATION RELATED TO THIS ONGOING EFFORT AND ITS EVENTUAL PUBLIC DISSEMINATION. THANK YOU."

The script and determined production plans for *State v. Unknown* fulfilled all of the necessary conditions I'd set out to satisfy at the outset. It was pandemic-proof as the production could be achieved by remote means alone; using webcams exclusively to record all of the participating talent. And an early estimate of the production cost was roughly half the amount it took to produce *For My Sister*. And the production's completely remote approach suggested the potential for a speedier production process than on the earlier feature film.

The path to *State v. Unknown* had been long, winding and rife with many blind alleys. While the writing process was maddening at times, the feeling of near-absolute surety it ultimately offered up was a crucial form of insurance as I moved forward on this latest filmmaking effort - my most ambitious, collaborative and riskiest yet!

113. Collaboration (March 2018)

Prior to writing the actual script for what would ultimately become my first feature-length film *For My Sister*, I was interested in sharing an early synopsis of the film's narrative with two particular individuals. Their opinion would mean a great deal to me as I readied to begin the hard work of writing the script itself.

Having forwarded the synopsis to the two in advance of a meeting at a local Starbucks, they soon arrived to the coffee shop and enjoyable conversation soon followed. Their response to the synopsis was highly encouraging and I received a pair of spirited endorsements.

These two persons were none other than Matthew Racher and Carlos Larrauri. Both local mental health professionals and advocates, I had made their acquaintance through my affiliation with NAMI (National Alliance on Mental Illness) Miami-Dade to which they were both heavily involved in (Matthew's mother, Susan Racher, is president of the organization). They had attended the NAMI film festival a year earlier and had both been impressed by my 2012 short film *Semester of Madness*. We all got along instantly.

But Matthew and Carlos were more than community mental health workers, they were both exceptionally talented members of their two-man band FogDog. I had seen them perform their soulful blend of folk blues and acoustic rock music at the previously mentioned NAMI film festival as well as other NAMI events.

During that meeting at Starbucks, I had floated the idea of perhaps applying a song or two from the FogDog repertoire to my debut feature. The possibility thrilled both Matthew and Carlos. And as I continued to write and figure out the details of my film, the idea of needle-dropping (using pre-existing music) on my first feature made perfect sense.

Out of their catalog of songs, which they generously made available, their "You Are Not Alone" struck a particularly strong chord with me for its lyrics' thematic proximity to my film and, of course, its stirring emotional power. I would end up using "You're Not Alone" for the end credits of the film and another song of theirs "Hold On" as source music in the film.

After production was concluded on the film, Matthew invited Carlos and me to his apartment to record a new version of "You Are Not Alone". It was a spur-of-the-moment meetup and involved Matthew and Carlos constructing a makeshift audio recording booth in one of Matthew's closets using a variety of household items in clever ways. When they felt they'd succeeded at producing the conditions for a quality recording in their apartment using what was available, I watched in fascination as they got to work recording their new rendition of "You Are Not Alone".

Despite a most valiant effort to make a walk-in closet-based recording work, the resulting audio quality was far too compromised. In light of this, Matthew and Carlos made an effort to arrange a professional studio recording of the song with the help of a recording specialist who would later assist FogDog with their debut album. Consequently, the new studio recording of "You Are Not Alone" was incredible!

I couldn't have asked for a more suitable ending cue than the one "You Are Not Alone" provided, powerfully punctuating the entirety of my 88-minute film. The introduction of opening guitar notes and Matthew's soothing vocals is richly satisfying. While the lyrics, "graced by this love we did witness" and "I am here, I am here and, Lord knows, I will try," evoke the depicted bond between the two sisters in the film and the desperate attempts on the part of the elder sibling to help the younger.

After seeing the film, both Matthew and Carlos were all smiles and offered up their most sincere expressions of satisfaction. I was glad to have gained their support on the project early on and then honor their musical talent by accommodating such an enjoyable and rewarding partnership. I would look forward to involving them again on future films.

114. Compromise (March 2014)

On the evening of Monday, March 10th, 2014, I was sitting at the desktop PC in my bedroom typing in a final remaining paragraph of voice-over dialogue. With this finishing touch, I had successfully completed the first draft of my first feature-length screenplay! Weighing in at a lean 104 pages, it was the hard-fought end-result of an eight-month-long writing process that had tested me like nothing before ever had.

The screenplay, titled *The Cult of Truth*, is a drama/comedy centered around the daring exploits of Frank Bone, an intrepid young journalist in the city of Rockview. Beginning with a thrilling introduction that operates like the conclusion of a previous adventure, we follow Frank Bone as he's befriended by the leader of a mysterious organization and must step up to protect his city when he discovers that the organization and its leader are more nefarious than they appear to be. The film culminates with an elaborate plot hatched by Frank and a newly formed, rag-tag team of independent media personalities to incriminate the duplicitous leader.

The primary impetus for writing the screenplay, aside from my desire to finally tackle a feature-length writing project, was the possibility of having the script sold to Amazon Studios, a media production/distribution subsidiary of the major online retail company. At the time, Amazon was accepting unsolicited script submissions from the general public and willing to pay handsomely for selected scripts ($10,000 if the script was chosen for development; $200,000 if the script was selected for distribution as a full-budget movie). Amazon's open submission program (now-defunct) launched in 2010.

While the opportunity to submit a feature script for studio consideration was compelling enough to get started, I was averse to the notion of potentially having to hand off my brainchild to someone else to produce and direct it. Despite this apprehension, I began to develop some ideas.

However, my brainstorming process posed some unprecedented hurdles right away. I had immense difficulty pulling ideas out of the ether that I felt could justify the runtime of a feature. It was frighteningly unfamiliar terrain as I'd never made an earnest attempt to write anything as extensive in length. But some time into the process, a flash of inspiration struck!

I knew the entire prospect of actually completing a script and then having my rookie effort catch the eye of Amazon of all places was a shot in the dark. But I was still unsettled by the uncomfortable scenario, however unlikely, of having to surrender producing and directing duty on my dear script to others. However, an alluring idea would soon occur to me that would allow greater success in my early brainstorming and resolve the tension I felt in relation to the ultimate fate of my creation to-be.

That alluring idea in one word?

Compromise.

That was my difficulty. I didn't want to compromise. I wanted all the glory of not only the development of the idea but the execution of its form as well. But this wasn't a surprise as I'd always jealously defended my interest in being the singular voice behind any work of art that bore my name. It was true of me as a visual artist and it remained true of me as an aspiring filmmaker.

But it was now time to relinquish some control.

When I decided to make compromise and my personal relationship to compromise the basis for the theme of this anticipated feature script, my mind was flooded with many new and appealing ideas. This fresh angle would yield ample story concepts and, just as importantly, the necessary personal motivation to succeed at this massive undertaking.

In *The Cult of Truth*, Frank Bone takes great pride in doing everything himself. However, dire circumstances soon compel him to cede control over his work and sacrifice the glory of succeeding by his own talents alone. In doing so, Frank grows into a wiser, more capable person. The story almost wrote itself.

Feeling I'd arrived at a strong enough foundation from which a feature script could be built, it was still only a mere seed. I would need to provide the sun, soil, water and untold amount of a farmer's daily toil to arrive at the completed work.

After brainstorming, the next step was gathering all of my ideas into an several-page-long outline informed by a three-act story structure. Making constant reference to several screenwriting books (i.e., Robert McKee's *Story*, Syd Field's *Screenplay*, Christopher Vogler's *The Writer's Journey* and Linda Seger's *How to Make a Good Script Great*), I was able to work out the broad strokes of the entire story effectively before any finer detail was applied. This is the way I typically went about writing almost all of my earlier short films.

After the outline was sufficiently worked out, I next prepared a treatment to help clarify the multitude of story beats and to see how these decided-upon beats operated in a more palatable narrative formation. Written in prose, the treatment for *The Cult of Truth* was 24-pages-long and the last vital step before I moved onto writing the actual script in the traditional film script format.

I would be using the scriptwriting software Final Draft to write the first and any subsequent drafts of my screenplay. The key advantage of using this particular software is its automatic, user-friendly handling of all the industry-standard formatting related to scene headings, descriptions and dialogue. By now, I was intimately familiar with those functions and others having used the program to write almost all of my short films.

Although I'd produced a thorough treatment which gave me great confidence in my story as I approached work on the actual pages of the script, there were still tons of details related to names, dialogue, incidents and staging that were in need of spawning from seeming nothingness.

Over the better part of eight months, I would carry a small notepad wherever I went but otherwise lived practically chained to my bedroom computer with Final Draft almost perpetually active on my desktop. I'd never served a project with as much routine solitude and focus as I did on this project. Holy cow.

Weeks after finishing the first draft of *The Cult of Truth*, I presented a speech about my writing process to my fellow Toastmasters during one of our meetings (at Florida International University). I concluded my speech with a glowing appraisal of the experience of writing my first feature-length screenplay, saying, "I find writing to be an immensely enjoyable pursuit. I imagine it could keep me busy for the next thousands of years - if I live that long... And I'm ready to restart the process the next chance I get. There are so many story possibilities; so many combinations and permutations of character and genre and situations and settings and tone and visual ideas. It's just endless. So, the sky has nothing on the limitations of the medium... Thank you!"

I meant every word.

115. Disappointment (June 2019)

With my first feature-length film *For My Sister* freshly completed, I now looked forward to screening the 88-minute film for audiences! I expected to have the support of grassroots mental health organization NAMI (National Alliance on Mental Illness) Miami-Dade which I'd been affiliated with in the past and had inspired some of the content of the film. I also expected at least a few film festivals, in South Florida and beyond, to bestow my film with an official selection nod given its merit as an artful offering made by modest means. On top of that, surely there were many other local theater venues interested in screening the work of an area filmmaker on a topic of considerable social relevance.

All reasonable expectations, right?

Thankfully, I was able to arrange two nearly back-to-back screenings of the film, including its premiere, at a local arthouse theater Coral Gables Art Cinema. It was pricey at roughly $650 per screening but my savings and help from a family member made it possible. I must also add that my experience working with the expert staff at Coral Gables Art Cinema over the myriad of technical details for each screening was resoundingly positive.

But after those two well-attended screenings, I didn't want to lose my momentum.

Regarding the possibility of working with NAMI, the film had received exceptionally well by both the president and executive director of the organization. At the conclusion of the film's second screening in Coral Gables, the NAMI president had called the film "a masterpiece" and immediately lobbied for its submission to the largest film festival in the land, Sundance Film Festival. She also casually assented to the possibility of hosting a third screening at Coral Gables Art Cinema. Straightaway, the prospects looked bright for a collaboration with NAMI.

However, some time later, the executive director of NAMI would inform me of some unfortunate news. After a review of my film by a special committee, I was told that NAMI wasn't interested in supporting it. Their concerns were few but fair. The committee found my film too steeped in science-fiction for their taste. They were also concerned about the potential audience response to the depiction of familial deception (at one point in the film, the main character laces her sibling's food with an anti-depressant). And lastly I was told that even if the film was deemed acceptable, paying for the cost of a theater rental was outside the limits of their budget. Despite their reasons, I harbored absolutely zero resentment toward NAMI afterward. But it was a bummer.

While I anticipated that major theater chains would charge a fortune to reserve an auditorium in their multiplexes, I didn't expect the utter coldness and indifference they displayed toward a local feature filmmaker upon speaking to their management to see if any exception or discount was possible. So, moving on...

I also reached out to an impressive outdoor venue downtown which projected selected films onto a massive wall before a grassy field where guests were encouraged to bring beach towels to lay on for the presentation. However, the coordinating group seemed more interested in screening classic studio films with broad familiarity than the work of home-grown talent.

Luckily, I was able to secure two educational venues later in the year. The first screening took place at Florida International University in collaboration with the NAMI chapter at the university, ironically enough. The second took place at the Homestead campus of Miami Dade College where I was awarded a plaque for presenting the film and leading a conversation about the film.

What about film festivals?

Not too long after submissions had opened, I submitted *For My Sister* to the 37th Annual Miami Film Festival, the most prestigious film festival in South Florida. I enclosed a substantial cover letter which described the film as a consummately local, micro-budget production and as a pioneering effort by virtue of its mobile filmmaking approach. I was also sure to mention my film's social topicality by stating the fact that

"Miami-Dade County has the highest percentage of people living with severe mental illness than any other metropolitan area in the country."

Despite making my best case, I learned that my film was not selected for their lineup a few months later.

Upon learning my film's fate at the hands of Miami Film Festival, my dad suspected that they and upper-tier film festivals like them are generally fearful of micro-budget films and filmmakers because the touting and promotion of them would inspire others to adopt similar means which would lead to a surge of rather cheaply made films. My dad believed this would result in lost patronage and sponsorship. I mostly agreed with this view. Most institutions made reputable by a cultural elite fear populism like death.

So, what about other festivals?

Scottish Mental Health Arts Festival?

Not selected.

Vero Beach Film Festival?

Not selected.

The REEL Recovery Film Festival & Symposium

Not selected.

NYC Mental Health Film Festival?

Not selected.

SMart: The London International Smartphone Film Festival?

Not selected.

These festival submission outcomes were certainly disheartening but early on I realized I wouldn't be comfortable with any sort of extensive festival run if I was't able to kick it off in the city where I'd proudly produced the film.

In any case, I believed in my film and valued its local, modestly budgeted, DIY (Do It Yourself) identity. I also had a inviolable belief in my abilities. If I wasn't fortunate this time around, maybe I'd have better luck with my next feature...

Or the one after that...

Or the one after that...

Or the one after that...

Or the one after that...

116. Effective (September 2018)

Once I completed the first draft of the script for my debut feature *For My Sister*, I immediately phoned Stephanie Maltez and Cristina De Fatima, the two actresses whom I'd written the two most important parts in the film for. Upon describing what the new film entailed narratively, they were delighted and greatly looking forward to working together. For all of us, it would be our first time making a feature-length film!

As I refined my first draft into a second and final draft, I started a WhatsApp group for the three of us and I began a routine habit of providing highly informative updates to Stephanie and Cristina as pre-production got on a roll.

I would use the online production management application StudioBinder to help me organize this production of personally unprecedented size. Instrumental to my early organization of the production schedule was the use of StudioBinder's stripboard which allowed me to arrange scenes (each assigned a strip) and group them together by shared location and filming day. This process allowed me to see the shape of the production early on and, more frankly, make it possible to wrap my head around the otherwise daunting proportions of the production. The stripboard also helped me determine the approximate number of days the entire production would take - 34 days.

With my rather precise estimation of the filming schedule established, I could now generate a rough figure for the expected budget. After running all the numbers, I determined that I'd likely end up spending no more than $6,000 for the entire production. All cast would be paid. And so, with this sum and the comprising figures all deemed acceptable, I continued my pre-production activity with more than a little pride in my micro-budget thriftiness. My friend, an editor based in Los Angeles, California, would later remark that "a production out here spends $6,000 on a single day's worth of catering!"

An early consideration for the organization of the production was to schedule the scenes involving interaction between Stephanie and Cristina's characters first. The loving but tested relationship between this sister-pair had to work in order for the entire film to do so. I believed in both Stephanie and Cristina but I wanted to nail this facet of the drama before I moved onto anything else.

On account of Stephanie's work schedule, I also determined that filming would need to take place primarily on weekends. The production would row at her pace because she was in practically every scene of the film as the lead actress.

Another key consideration involved casting and locations. I would be acquiring new cast members and filming locations on a rolling basis. While a risky proposition that could result in extended production delays, I had great confidence in my abilities to quickly raise talent and fish out available filming spots as need dictated.

With the logistics of the first stage of production (the crucial apartment scenes) sufficiently worked out, I was ready to begin production on *For My Sister*!

As the first leg of production commenced, I couldn't have asked for circumstances more conducive to creativity and collaboration. I had managed to secure my aunt's apartment for lengthy stretches at a time, day or night. This access was a veritable blessing as it gave me the time, space and quiet to work closely with Stephanie and Cristina without any unwanted encroachments. For the duration of the time it took to complete the key apartment scenes, the general climate among the three of us was respectful, cooperative and allowing of considerable candor. Stephanie and Cristina met the demands of each scene with inexhaustible enthusiasm and utmost professionalism.

But there were occasional challenges.

For instance, on one evening, I was particularly intent on having a door slam with a particular timing, speed and impact. Stephanie and Cristina were patient with me but it took an embarrassingly long time for us to work out the right mechanics. And to add insult to injury, we had to reshoot the scene and replicate the effect again later on due to a continuity-related snafu.

On another occasion, Cristina had some difficulty with her memorization of a set of lines on a necessarily long take. Unable to split up Cristina's delivery into more manageable parts in order to remedy the situation through editing, Cristina had to deliver all of her lines correctly in this minute-long shot. It took some time but after she managed to pull it off, I simply encouraged her to be more prepared in the future.

Another tense situation arose involving Stephanie's limited but sensible tolerance for numerous takes of shots a touch more physically demanding. In one scene where her character needed to rush into her apartment, scramble to the kitchen sink and rinse out some liquid from her mouth while pretending to be affected by the acridity of its taste, she only allowed me two takes. While I imagine I would have begged on my knees for another take if necessary, we were able to succeed on the second try. Thank heavens!

I also encountered my own personal difficulties. Toward the end of filming the all-important apartment scenes, I suffered a crisis of confidence during the filming of the film's very climax. Having felt that the preparation of a shot list or storyboard was unnecessary for the critical scene, I found myself conflicted over the results of my attempt to improvise. Caught in frigid indecision as I struggled to visualize a solution, my two actresses stood by for further direction. Although Stephanie and Cristina were patient with me, as the minutes wore on, I hadn't the faintest clue of how to proceed. "As long as I'm getting paid for this," Stephanie quipped. Thankfully, I overshot the scene from a variety of angles and was able to solve my creative problem in the editing room. But for a moment I'd tasted the bitter bleakness of unpreparedness.

While proceeding with this first stage of filming, I began to edit together the resulting footage as soon as I could and continue to refine the edit throughout the week (again, filming mainly occurred on weekends). This would allow me to make any necessary alterations to the script for upcoming scenes in the filming schedule. Able to improve the writing as I saw the film begin to take shape, this practice of editing straightaway and altering the script accordingly would become a regular habit throughout the rest of the production.

When I finished filming the pivotal apartment scenes between Stephanie and Cristina's characters, I was able to readily assemble the scenes together into a kind of showreel to share with both actresses. Their response to what I'd put together was highly encouraging and I thought so as well. The heart of the film had been forged!

After these apartment scenes were in the can, I now faced the second phase of production which would involve filling about 30 supporting roles. As mentioned, I would be enlisting the additional cast members on a rolling basis. Thankfully, with the help of my social network and the casting call website Backstage, my casting efforts were reliably successful and I was able to fill every role with great ease. Among the talent I recruited were more than a few FIU Theatre students. I also cast some non-actors in more abbreviated roles.

I believe my casting process was as successful as it was because I offered monetary compensation (a basic hourly rate) for their involvement; both principal and supporting actors. Sadly, this is something many aspiring filmmakers don't do.

In addition to the bevy of actors required were a multitude of locations throughout the sprawl of Miami. These included an office building, a drug store, a university campus, a park, an alley, a medical building, a cemetery, a legal office, a cafe, a remote street, a hospital and another apartment. I filmed at most of these locations with consent from the relevant point-persons but, in many cases, I engaged in filmmaking at certain locations without permit or consent. Guerrilla-style!

Despite the fairly smooth acquisition of cast and locales, I faced a number of challenges throughout this latter phase of production.

Some weeks after the first leg of production had concluded, Stephanie needed some time to recuperate from the demands of filming and the simultaneous stress of her day job. After she persuasively argued for some respite, I granted her the needed time-off. But now, I was faced with having to re-order the filming schedule to accommodate her leave. Luckily, I was able to swap out some scenes and make substantial progress despite Stephanie's absence. It was a bump in the road, to be sure, but an acceptable one.

Another challenge presented itself in the form of working with a child non-actor in a short scene involving Cristina's character. On a warm winter's day at a local park, I met up with Cristina, her two friends (cast as Cristina's character's friends) and a young cousin named Chiara Michel who was joined by her parents (Alba Lucia and Jack Michel, who facilitated my filming at an area hospital they own). I had opted to hire Chiara at my mother's urging and out of a dearth of options. While she didn't have any experience acting, I was confident in my abilities to craft a serviceable performance through a mix of strategic direction and crafty editing. She had her lines memorized and all she was required to do was take a seat on a bench next to Cristina and deliver some simple lines while holding a teddy bear. My strategy was to shoot all of her lines in one take to ease her into the general requirements of the scene and then, afterward, take a more surgical approach to perfect her performance line-by-line. After an hour or so of intense work, I suspected I had what I needed and my suspicions would later be confirmed after some judicious editing. In spite of her inexperience, Chiara pulled it off and I was utterly relieved that this simple but thematically resonant scene jived with the rest of the film.

While filming one night at a local hospital I'd managed to secure permission to film at thanks to the Michels, I faced two colliding obstacles. Juan Iglesias, an actor I'd worked with on my final short film, had some difficulty with delivering his lines verbatim, as required. But on top of that, I was at a loss for how to proceed in terms of my camera (phone) placement and my mental editing together of the scene. As Juan gave me mostly spotty takes, his bull's eyes were compromised by my uncertainties. As Stephanie, who was also in the scene, grew impatient and urged me to get it together, I realized that I had to move on and that I would most likely be saved by some clever editing. And I was right. But this delay prompted me to cut corners on the subsequent scenes that night and doing so was incredibly unnerving. But thankfully, some skillful editing was all it took to save me from absolute despair.

On the final night of principal filming (i.e., filming involving principal cast), Stephanie and I met up at a Metrorail station at night. Our first order of business was filming a long take of Stephanie walking down a nearby sidewalk against incoming traffic near the station. After two takes, the security guard of the property we were filming on called out to us and prohibited us from continuing to film. This encounter with a restricting authority would be the production's first and only. Luckily, the second take I'd managed to get was good. Not perfect but good. Stephanie and I completed the remainder of our filming that night without further incident.

With that night's filming complete, principal filming on my film was finally wrapped after eight long months.

There was no extensive post-production process on *For My Sister* because virtually all of the scenes were edited shortly after they had been filmed.

However, there was some second-unit filming that needed to be completed. This involved filming the footage for the Reveu promotional videos which bookend the film as well as a brief interlude toward the end of the film. The promotional video footage involving actual drones was filmed using a cousin's drone (they were made three with some digital trickery) suspended in front of a white backdrop in my kitchen on, of all days, my birthday!

A special effort was also made on one of the shots of the opening promotional video: a dry erase board covered in physics equations. The equations featured are as close-to-real as equations for time travel are likely to get. They were provided by Michael Cohen, a highly intelligent physics major who earned a technical consultant credit for his contribution.

My go-to composer Ben Morris was also tapped to add his magic touch in the form of some key music throughout the film. He provided original music for the Reveu bookends and interlude as well as the plot-critical therapeutic music along with several other instances of source music.

The last stage of post-production on the film required some painstaking rotosplining (frame-by-frame animation) in order to remove some intrusive and undesired Florida International University signage which appeared in certain shots filmed on the FIU campus. This work took hours and I did it all myself.

With the film more-or-less completed (on-budget and relatively on-schedule), I watched it several times in order to tighten any slightly loose screws in the editing. But I was brimming with confidence in what I'd created; to such a degree that I offered no sneak preview viewings to anyone, not even family. Everyone would have to wait until the premiere.

But where that premiere would take place was a pressing question shortly after the film was screening-ready. I researched numerous local venues until landing on Coral Gables Art Cinema which offered a quality venue at a relatively reasonable price.

My experience preparing for the premiere screening was nothing short of excellent! With a date set and the venue prepped with a DCP copy of my film, it was only a matter of time before I would expose my creation to the open air. The premiere audience would consist of family, friends, former teachers, critics, filmmakers, acquaintances, strangers and one Florida state senator. It would count as one of the most memorable days of my entire life.

On the phone with Stephanie Maltez a day or two after she'd completely tied up her work on the film, we spoke for over an hour. At one point in our conversation, the topic turned to how much time and effort I'd committed to the film since its conception; how much love and care I'd given it; and how proud I was of it. I was suddenly overcome with the most intense surge of feeling and soon broke down in tears. I had to take a moment to regain my composure.

I'd never known such joy.

117. Familiarity (October 2016)

Well before I completed my 16th short film *The Promotion* in the fall of 2016, I deemed that it would be the end cap to my nearly 15-year career as a short filmmaker. My ambitions now lay with the standard currency of the greater film world - feature films!

But my experience making short films had yielded great gifts. Through my writing, producing, directing, shooting and editing of 16 short films, I had developed an acute sensitivity toward cinematic design that was far beyond that which I'd started out with. Those years had also graced me with an affinity and extensive track record of collaborating with many others, in creative capacities as well as strictly practical ones. And most importantly, my short film experience helped wrought the confidence and tenacity I would need to tackle film projects of nearly 10x the size of those shorter-styled projects.

So, following completion of *The Promotion*, I began the writing process on the first feature-length screenplay I'd intend to produce myself.

Right away, I learned that finding and developing an idea that not only satisfied my creative hunger but conformed to my practical and budgetary limitations was not going to be easy. I stumbled more often than not and often found myself scrapping weeks' worth of work.

However, several months into the process, I landed on an exciting, high-concept idea which seemed ostensibly produceable with my admittedly meager resources. I succeeded in crafting a fairly detailed outline and a brief synopsis for feedback purposes.

The conceptually ambitious idea was a fast-paced adventure story with plenty of drama and levity. It followed Luna, a lowly waitress (in a part written specifically for past-collaborator, actress Stephanie Maltez), who experiences an unusual disturbance in her diner and consequently embarks on an epic quest with the aid of a surprisingly powerful Swiss

Army knife and a single-minded athlete to save a vast and mysterious multiverse from total annihilation!

The various realms explored would turn out to be the settings of a variety of videos saved to a hard drive (e.g., a music video world, a school presentation video world, an athletic training vlog video world, a wedding video world, a corporate video world, a vacation video world, etc.). The fantastical universe of the story was generously reminiscent of the world-building in films like *The Wizard of Oz*, *Tron* and *The Matrix*.

After writing my first-ever feature-length screenplay *The Cult of Truth*, which I never intended to produce myself, this second time around the block was characterized by greater comfort and ease. I was now all the more accustomed to habits that facilitated my workflow and productivity on these longer-form breed of writing projects. My story design instincts were also more attuned.

In January 2018, I announced completion of a first draft of the script, titled *Omni*. Writing this initial draft had taken me roughly half the time it had taken me to write *The Cult of Truth* - four months. But this script was 87 pages long and contained 207 scenes; far denser than that earlier effort.

However, reception among some friends was not wildly affirming. A close friend found the script far too complicated, another friend expressed concern about the excessive number of video worlds in the story and a close confidant likened the story to the simplicity and trappings of a video game.

While my peers' views did little to dissuade me from my fundamental enthusiasm, my own practical concerns would soon eclipse theirs. Even with my masochistic tendencies at the ready, I was doubtful I'd be able to pull off such a massive coordination of location, talent, and camera on my own. Also, the project would likely cost a small fortune, forsaking my career-long and proudly micro-budget filmmaking ethos.

In light of these concerns and with a heavy heart, I decided to abandon *Omni* weeks after completing its first draft. A leaner, more practical idea was desired and even if I had to restart from ground zero, I knew I'd find it.

And I would. Months later, I posted an announcement on social media: "Feature update: I shelved my completed script, *Omni*, in January in favor of a more bomb-ass one I've been working on since then."

That "more bomb-ass" idea would end up becoming my first feature-length film *For My Sister*.

118. LLC (December 2018)

Before I began production on my first feature-length film *For My Sister*, I realized that I'd eventually need to set up a limited-liability corporation (LLC) to establish a clean chain of title for distribution purposes and to facilitate a variety of necessary legal protections. I also saw starting my own LLC as lending greater legitimacy to my fledgling feature filmmaking operation which was starting humbly enough but would likely expand over time with more projects of increasing complexity.

Accordingly, I would register my LLC just ahead of the start of the new year following commencement of production on *For My Sister*. I would name my LLC after the fictional video recording service in my debut picture - Reveu.

Assisting me with the process of getting Reveu LLC on its feet was my dad. He was far, far more experienced in these purely practical, business affairs and his entrenched left-brain orientation was the perfect counterbalance to my almost-exclusively right-brain one. It is safe to say that there was occasional turbulence between us but we were generally effective together.

After filling out the proper forms correctly and paying the necessary filing fee required by the State of Florida, Reveu LLC was soon officially registered. I received my Employer Identification Number from the IRS not too long after. 2019 would be the first year of operation for my brand new LLC.

The next order of business involved setting up a separate business account for Reveu LLC. This was accomplished with assistance from my dad as well. The LLC's bank account would be used exclusively for cast payroll and production expenses.

"Is it French?" asked my bank specialist about my LLC's peculiar name.

With my new LLC on a roll with official registration and its own financial account, I had a new responsibility on my shoulders. I would be solely responsible for keeping track of all business-related transactions and accounting - even when it came to tax filings later on. But I was more than ready to shoulder such an important responsibility.

Although my dad had ample trust in my character and ability to manage these new affairs, he took a moment to share something from his past with me. The extremely well-organized and well-preserved accounting books for Hexatek, Inc.

What was Hexatek, Inc.?

When my family moved from Boston, Massachusetts to Miami, Florida in the mid-'90s, my dad had a plan to start working for himself as part of a fresh direction he wanted to take in life. So, in 1995, he established Hexatek, Inc. - his very own corporation!

The company's mission was to provide computer consulting services and software development for the international freight-forwarding market. The company's flagship product was a database application called InCargo, designed from scratch by my dad. As he describes it with some pride, Hexatek, Inc. was "a one-man enterprise." For better or worse, my dad was responsible for virtually all of the activities of Hexatek, Inc. It was active until 2011 when he dissolved the corporation upon returning to the workforce.

When my dad showed me his pristine accounting books, I sensed an implicit passing of the torch. As he leafed through the contents of the various binders and ran his fingers over the neat rows and columns of data, it felt like he was sharing the secrets of the universe with me. After all, I would be the first of his four sons to start their own company. I'm sure the opportunity to share these byproducts of his individual industry with a son embarking on a similar path meant a great deal to him.

Clearly a chip off the old block, I looked forward to the job of managing Reveu LLC with considerable gusto. I also understood the importance of cultivating a more shrewd business and managerial sense to essentially complement my otherwise exclusively artistic endeavors.

As it has been said, "If you don't do the business, the business will do you."

119. Mobile (August 2018)

Throughout most of my time in University of Central Florida's film school, I was a man apart when it came to my filmmaking ethos, particularly as it related to video technology. While virtually all of my classmates opted for high-fidelity video made possible by cameras with a triple-CCD sensor and then high-definition capability later on, I was still using the same consumer-grade, single-CCD digital video camcorder I'd used for all of my projects since my start in filmmaking. But as my dad often says, the tennis racket doesn't make you the more formidable athlete; training and practice does.

Far from being a Luddite, I absolutely understood the allure of the latest in filmmaking technology. Its seductive power no doubt strengthened by the example set by the Hollywood film industry; a status quo many of my fellow film schoolers and filmmakers I'd come to know post-UCF gravitated toward rather unquestioningly. But high-fidelity imagery and other cosmetic concerns have always been a lower priority to me than attempting to master the fundamentals of cinematic storytelling (e.g., screenwriting, directing, cinematography and editing).

A key advantage to eschewing more sophisticated tools, like advanced cameras or specialized lighting equipment, is that it doesn't invite reliance on the expertise of a cinematographer or other additional crew member(s). Indeed, a filmmaker with the right motivation can operate faster and more effectively on their own - now more than ever before. As the relentless Anton Chigurh from the Coen Brothers' 2007 film *No Country for Old Men* keenly advised, "You pick the one right tool." Yourself.

Despite my anti-technocratic mindset, I'd eventually upgrade my video camera toward the end of my time at film school (for a miniDV camcorder, the Canon HV20) and then again a few years later (with a

DSLR, the Canon T5i). My new equipment always consumer-grade and budget-conscious.

In 2017, after I finished writing *Omni*, a feature-length screenplay I intended to be my first feature film production, I spent a great deal of time considering what I'd use to film it. For this elaborate adventure story on an epic scale with extensive set pieces, I considered using the Canon DSLR I'd used on my previous two short films. I was more than comfortable using that particular camera but it seemed a daunting prospect given the anticipated complexity of the production. And I didn't want to hire a cinematographer. In fact, I wanted to execute my first feature-length production in the same manner as virtually all of my short films - on my own!

When I finally but reluctantly accepted how impractical it would be to produce *Omni* in that desired manner, I shelved the script.

Before I commenced serious work on a new script for my first feature film production, I knew I needed to nail down the technical means by which it would be accomplished.

During this ruminative period between scripts, I found myself in contact with writer/filmmaker David Bush, a former UCF classmate. Based in Louisiana or "Hollywood South", David has worked on a wide variety of TV and film productions in his local film industry but maintains a peerless devotion to his own projects which include several books, countless screenplays and a handful of feature films.

Having recently written and directed the TV movie *A Deadly Affair* for the Lifetime TV network at the time of the aforementioned contact, I was able to engage with David over his experience making the riveting Lifetime whodunit and his plans moving forward. Among the prospective projects he talked about was an upcoming indie feature film production of his own. But what surprised me the most was how he was planning on filming it - using a phone!

In the days following my phone conversation with David, I thought about the idea of filming a feature film using a phone. I'd never seriously considered it before but the prospect was bold and daring. To the filmmaking ethos I wanted to embody and project, it was an enticing idea!

After deciding that my new script would be written with the

expectation of using a phone for filming, I messaged David to ask for his blessing. After all, it was his idea before it was mine.

"Absolutely, do it. And best of luck," he responded.

Several months later, I completed a new, 76-page screenplay for what would be my debut feature film *For My Sister*. To accommodate the use of a phone for filming, I imbued the film's narrative with a distinctive choice of perspective: The body of the film would be presented to the viewer as though it was recorded by time-traveling nanodrones. With the exception of the bookends and a brief interlude, the origin of all the imagery being presented to the viewer was definite and known. Dispensing with the assumption of an omniscient POV or God's eye view, characteristic of practically all visual media under the sun, was extremely invigorating!

Opting for phone-based filmmaking would not only allow me to continue honoring my minimalist practical approach to filmmaking but enable experimentation with cinematic form itself. So with my plans firmly set, I now needed to prepare my phone for this novel undertaking.

The first step was to take advantage of a sales promotion offered by my phone plan carrier. I was able to upgrade my phone at the time, the Samsung Galaxy S8+, to a Galaxy S9+. At the phone store, I shared with the employees assisting me that I was planning to film a feature film using this new phone. They appeared to share the same half-curious, half-incredulous response as most everyone I revealed my plans to. "Okay..." I'm sure they thought.

With a new phone in tow, I wanted to have a bit more manual control over my phone's video recordings, including the ability to achieve a conventional frame rate of 24fps. So, I paid for and downloaded the mobile filmmaking app, FiLMiC Pro. This app would prove an indispensable tool.

With the basic video recording capability of my phone figured out, I decided that I'd need a gimbal to hold and help stabilize the phone as it was recording. I found a popular and well-reviewed model for $140. I was also lucky enough to find an extension for the device that would allow me to easily attach an external microphone for audio. While much practice was required to get comfortable with the motorized movement of the gimbal's phone-holding arm, throughout production the gimbal was occasionally temperamental.

Considering battery life was another important consideration. I initially believed I'd need to augment the phone's battery power with an added, gimbal-mounted battery pack. However, that plan was soon nixed when I discovered that the gimbal could only deal with so much weight. For the entirety of production, I relied on a single phone battery charge per each day of production; about five hours of activity.

With the phone and microphone attached to the gimbal, the result was a one-handed apparatus which felt great in terms of weight and range of movement. I immediately conducted a battery of tests. With one hand, I could tilt, pan and roll to accommodate almost any angle while my other hand was free to adjust the FiLMiC Pro app controls on the phone screen. In light of these promising results, I was ecstatic over the prospect of filming my first feature-length film with this flexible and easy-to-operate device (which I dubbed "The Excuse Destroyer" as there were none anymore)!

Soon enough, the day I'd long anticipated had arrived - the first day of filming on *For My Sister*! The afternoon shoot, which lasted about four hours, took place at my aunt's lent-out apartment and involved myself and actresses Stephanie Maltez and Cristina De Fatima. Not a single additional crew member required!

Although I'd performed a long string of tests prior to actual filming, there were still some kinks to work out after using my phone rig at length on the first day of filming.

After returning home to review footage from day one, I heard some clicks, pops and other distortions on the audio track. I considered what might be the culprit and observed that the microphone cable that fed into the phone was loose and likely causing some intrusive rustling on the soundtrack. So, I taped down the cable with some tape (a practice I'd have to repeat every single day of production) which partly resolved the issue. After consulting some mobile filmmaking forums, I learned that clearing all inessential phone operations while recording video would help ensure issue-free audio. And doing so did the trick!

Just after a few weeks into the production, I was able to appreciate some of the most significant advantages to filmmaking on my phone.

Firstly, I was able to accomplish nearly three times as many setups (different camera and actor orientations) than with a DSLR, my previously used recording device. The speed and efficiency were unprecedented to me. I'd never known such swiftness as a filmmaker!

Secondly, there was absolutely no downtime for technical recalibration or resetting between takes. This kept the actors plenty satisfied because they could do more of what they were essentially tasked to do - act. The phone's ease of use also allowed me to get more takes and, if necessary, turn on a dime with regard to new ideas or circumstances.

Thirdly, the capacity of my phone to handle low-light or otherwise problematic lighting scenarios was quite impressive. There wasn't a single instance of stage lighting on my film. Everything was lit by natural light sources and my phone was more than up to the challenge. The sensitivity of the phone sensor and its sharp grain texture always came to the rescue to ensure that my images looked crisp even when shots were substantially under-lit.

Some other advantages of shooting a feature on my phone included the ability to remain mostly inconspicuous while filming in public spaces, the welcome relief of relatively short days due to limited phone battery life (exhaustion hurts quality) and a lack of preoccupation with technical details which allowed more interaction between myself and the actors.

Throughout the entire production of *For My Sister*, going the mobile route would allow my focus and that of the actors' to remain fixedly where it mattered most - on our creative choices. They were freed to concentrate on performance and I on staging and composition. Regularly quick and nimble, we encountered no significant operational impediments. By seizing the power of the phone, I was once again championing creativity and self-sufficiency over technocracy and dependency.

Some things never change...

120. Premiere (June 2019)

Two nights before the premiere of my first feature-length film *For My Sister* at Coral Gables Art Cinema, I posted a pair of screencaps from one of my favorite movies, Billy Wilder's 1957 biopic *The Spirit of St. Louis* on social media. The film is about Charles Lindbergh's historic solo-flight across the Atlantic. In that post, I quoted the accompanying lines from Lindbergh (played by Jimmy Stewart) in the film:

"Come on now, go to sleep. Cut your motor. Let it rest now. Maybe I should have spent the night in the hangar. Maybe that's what's keeping me awake. Maybe I should be with her out there on Roosevelt Field."

I couldn't easily surrender to sleep either! Even two nights away, I wanted to stay awake feeling the ever-rising peaks of anxiety and intense nervous excitement over my own flight - one which was finally due for landing! Writing, producing, directing, shooting and editing (and premiere-organizing) *For My Sister* was no easy feat. It was a year and two months of strenuous mental, physical and emotional labor. And beyond two close friends who'd offered feedback on a near-final cut of the film, no one beside myself had seen the film in anything near its premiere-ready form. Not cast. Not family. No one. And I'd been sitting on it for weeks!

But fearful of messing with my circadian rhythm too much, I eventually talked myself into getting a good night's sleep and so I did.

The following day, I couldn't help but play showman to my family and totally hype up the experience I wanted them to have without really spoiling anything. After 17 years as a filmmaker and shameless self-promoter, I've developed a talent for such theatrics. It was fun priming them even if I knew that it would make a lackluster reception in the theater sting all the more. But despite the occasionally descending fear of that happening, I actually had a complete, unwavering confidence and trust in what the supremely talented cast of this film and I had conjured before my trusty Samsung Galaxy S9+ (the phone I shot the near-entirety of the film on).

Throughout the remainder of the day, I busied myself refining the structure of my opening remarks as well as preparing as best I could for what I'd hoped would be a brief Q&A (which is no sweat to this decorated Toastmaster, I might add). I also checked in with Stephanie Maltez and the rest of the cast to gauge nerves/excitement and relish it with them. And I found it immensely helpful to visualize how I would want the event to go from start to finish. In retrospect, I made so many oversights on the day of the event that I should have spent far more time in this personal virtual reality space. A note for next time.

The venue for the premiere screening was Coral Gables Art Cinema. I was familiar with the elegant and roomy 141-seat auditorium as I'd visited it for four other film screenings in the past. They offer rental of the theater for a price but they stress an interest in providing it as a community service. That's admirable and certainly proven in that the theater coordinators and technicians I worked with throughout preparation for the event were all incredibly dedicated and hospitable to the event's every need. And it was a joy testing my film out on their equipment in the weeks prior to the event. Consequently, I can only give my highest recommendation to anyone interested in a theatrical exhibition beyond par!

As night fell, I got to bed early and managed to sleep through the night.

I summarily woke and readied for the big day with great ease. I could have easily fallen victim to a serious degree of debilitation due to all the nerves and pressures expected but that aforementioned confidence and trust was no passing fancy. At the risk of repeating this bit of biographical insight ad nauseum - after 17 years, I have a pretty damn good idea about what I'm doing. Spend a significant amount of time with any craft and you'll start to feel rock-solid cement beneath your feet.

And guess what! I had a friendly date to the premiere - Ms. Olivia Wills! Self-described as a "scientist, environmentalist and patriarchy-smashing feminist," we met when we were both FIU students in 2016. I had arranged to pick her up at her apartment and some light rain accompanied the arrangement but I certainly didn't invite such a wrathful monsoon to hammer down on all the fun! Seriously, it was the worst possible weather I could imagine for such a momentous day as I attempted to simultaneously make enjoyable conversation with Olivia and maintain vehicle traction on our way to Coral Gables. Nerve-wracking!

Luckily, we arrived in one piece and at the theater ten or so minutes before the doors were set to open for the attendees, allowing ample time for me to check in with the theater staff and receive any pertinent instructions. I hate being late to anything except maybe family gatherings.

Slowly, the attendees started to trickle in. So many familiar faces from both the past and more recent circumstances. In such inclement weather, I thought overall attendance would take a serious hit but that was so not the case. I tried to greet everyone and encourage them to find a seat as I wanted to start promptly at the expected showtime of noon. But it was very difficult to be so curt with some of the guests as they included the principal actresses and actor of the film, Florida State Senator Annette Taddeo, local film critics, local feature filmmakers, former high school teachers and so many more people very dear to me. It was the wildest intersection of familiar faces from such varied social contexts! Overwhelming!

The crowd in the lobby soon dissipated. Then, my older brother Juan interrupted me in conversation and described to me that the auditorium was at near-capacity. I didn't believe him so I casually approached the auditorium doorway, peered inside and...

Holy shit. He was right.

I entered the auditorium, surveyed the gathered audience, took a deep breath and then checked outside to see if there were any last-minute stragglers to corral inside. There weren't.

So? Showtime.

I re-entered the auditorium, retrieved the nearby microphone and commenced my opening remarks to hearty applause.

After addressing the presence of Senator Taddeo; making some dedications to my parents, the cast and the lead actress Stephanie Maltez;

acknowledging the graciousness of the theater venue and reminding the audience to practice proper phone etiquette, I signaled to the projectionist to roll the film presentation. Then, the lights dimmed, I took my seat next to Olivia and the show began...

I suppose it took some time for everyone to get acclimated to the unique form of the film but once that was done, the film's humor, drama and daring-do were all met with appropriate, consistent and substantial reactions from what I observed was a highly attentive and captivated audience. I couldn't have asked for more.

As much as I'd love to delve into a comprehensive account of my thoughts on how well certain moments played and the artful nuances of each of the performances from the cast, I risk spoiling the surprises laden throughout. And as filmmakers, what's behind those corners is our most potent implement. But I'll repeat something I wrote to Stephanie Maltez a few days before the screening: "The cruel fact of the matter is that filmmakers (including acting talent) never see the same movie as audiences do upon initial release. Magic only works on the unsuspecting, not those intimately familiar with the mechanics of illusion."

In a later conversation with Stephanie, I piled onto that notion that I could really only see the narrative and dramatic engineering behind my own film. I could certainly not feel the emotions of the characters and their situations in the same manner that an audience member coming to it all fresh would; not an iota of it. That's the unusual curse of a filmmaker completely enveloped by the totality of the creative process. So be it. I can always visit someone else's film at the local cineplex or arthouse cinema for that type of enjoyment.

As the ending credits concluded to a final round of applause and the house lights came back on, I proudly marched to the waiting microphone and then faced the audience. What followed is now an extended blur in my memory and perhaps it's better that way.

I immediately railed off some fun facts about the nature of the film's production: shot near-entirely on my phone, locally in Miami, employing 25+ local actresses and actors, for under $6,000, with no crew beyond myself and no equipment beyond a single-hand-held apparatus.

Then, I opened the floor to questions from the audience for what I expected would be a brief Q&A sensitive to the time period of the theater rental. But quite a few questions came forth and it went on far longer than I expected. The questions addressed the state of mental health care locally, the choice of shooting the film on my phone, the more fantastical elements of the film's events, the time-traveling nanodrones (of course), what was next for me project-wise, what challenges I faced in making the film, what inspired me to make the film and consideration of grants as well as other forms of funding for future projects. I don't want to recount my responses to all of these questions as something has to remain exclusive to such a special event but I think I handled all the questions satisfactorily even though I concluded the Q&A with an uncomfortable and uneasy feeling as is usually the case for me under such long-form, impromptu speaking situations.

As a crowd of relatives and close friends descended upon me after the close of my presentation, I was consequently stretched in a hundred different directions and struggled to extend my most sincere thank yous for attending to as many guests as I could. After the sea of attendees flowed back out into the lobby, there was a flurry of activity taking place which included numerous photo opportunities (many tragically dashed), initiated but unfortunately interrupted conversations, a Facebook Live broadcast (WTF?) and a countless number of smiling, seemingly satisfied faces. That last visual is one I'll probably remember for always.

The crowd soon dispersed back out into the city on a much cleared up Saturday afternoon and the event was concluded. A fine success, to be sure.

Two weeks later, removed from all the sound and fury that was the premiere screening of my first feature-length film, I sat reflecting on such an indelibly memorable experience amid promising progress on a second feature film project I hoped to have produced before the end of the year. I'd broken the money and technological barriers enough for some time and now I had my sights set on the time barrier! On top of my reflecting, I was monitoring ticket registrations and seeking promotional opportunities for a second screening of *For My Sister* at Coral Gables Art Cinema later in August which would be open to the general public.

At the time, I thought to myself: If I could think and work as I had for the past 17 years on projects of ever-increasing interest and collaboration with so many immensely talented individuals up until the very end of my life, I'd look forward to it with the same exhilaration as any aviator charting their course across the seemingly boundless and infinite stretches of land, sea and sky...

121. Preview (May 2022)

Good morning, everyone! Today's the day!

I just wanted to say that I'm extremely proud of all of you and the extraordinary work you all committed to this film. Thank you for lending me your time, talent and trust. I couldn't have asked for a more capable principal cast!

To those attending, take it easy this afternoon and savor the fruit of your labor! You've earned it and more! See ya in a few hours! :)

-My WhatsApp message to the principal cast of 'State v. Unknown' on the morning of Saturday, May 21st (the day of the film's sneak preview)

The evening before the day of a sneak preview of my 2nd feature film *State v. Unknown*, I was able to fall asleep fairly quickly and remain peacefully in slumberland for the duration of the night. Unlike the night before the premiere of my 1st feature film *For My Sister* three years ago, my nerves were firmly under control. In fact, after I was roused from sleep by the daylight spilling in through the gaps of my window blinds, I was soon brimming with great confidence and excitement! I was far more convinced that my 2nd feature film would be met with equal or greater enthusiasm than my freshman effort.

Before showering and getting dressed, I spent most of the morning reviewing what I was planning on saying to introduce the film, facilitate the Q&A and close-out the entire presentation. Over the past week, I'd managed to work my remarks into a finely ground verbal pâté. I'd let the film do most of the talking.

After I showered and dressed, I checked in with my parents. They were duly excited about the event but they of course grilled me about my expected number of guests, my time of departure, my plans to encourage some degree of social distancing, etc. While also informing me of a few last-minute cancellations by some family friends, my parents confirmed the attendance of a particular older couple who'd been friends of the family for decades and luckily happened to be visiting Florida this same month - the Másmelas!

Who are the Másmelas? Héctor Másmela had been a Massachusetts Institute of Technology (MIT) student at the same time as my dad in the mid-'70s; both studying civil engineering. They eventually struck up a friendship and soon Héctor, his wife Amparo and their two offspring, Jillian and Bernard, were regular guests at our home in Massachusetts (where my family lived for nearly two decades) for social functions and vice-versa. So close were the Másmelas with our family that Héctor and Amparo were named godparents to my younger brother Daniel upon his baptism. In all honesty, Héctor and Amparo were like another pair of parents to my siblings and me from very early on. They were ever-present and always caring. It is fair to say that they knew me even before I knew myself!

On the way to University of Miami's Cosford Cinema where the screening would be taking place, I accessed a particular soundtrack from a USB flash drive full of my personal music preferences. I opted for the energizing synth of Daniel Pemberton's score for the 2015 biographical film about a particularly thorny but brilliant technological innovator. The mood it contributed felt more than apt.

Arriving at Cosford Cinema primed for my event, I immediately found the theater manager Rene Rodriguez, greeted him and soon followed him up some stairs to the projection booth above.

In the projection booth, I followed through with a quick, last-minute test to assure that my film's video file would absolutely play without issue. I'd visited the theater a week prior to meet Rene for the first time and perform a basic test of the theater's projection equipment. Rene, formerly a film critic for the *Miami Herald*, had been hired as the theater manager at Cosford several months before and I found him a most dedicated steward of the facility and a most delightful personality. Rene's considerable knowledge and utter hospitality would be instrumental to the success of my event.

After Rene showed me how to operate the house lights, microphone and sound mixer, I checked the time and exited to the terrace outside the theater to receive the soon-arriving attendees. Outside the theater, I first spotted my family members, who'd planned to arrive early so they could place three bouquets of blue balloons (blue for a reason!) near the entrance of the theater to help guide everyone toward the rather nestled-in theater. Soon after, my event's attendees began to arrive in a fairly steady stream.

Many of the attendees were those who'd actually participated in the film and most of them came accompanied with a guest or two. My engagement with nearly everyone who showed up was voluble, spirited and bent on conveying my optimism about the expected reaction to the film. It meant a great deal to me that despite the event having been announced with such short notice (just over a week), many made and followed through with a commitment. I also relished the fact that it was my first time seeing many of the film's actors in-person for the first time. And of course, after each instance of brief chit-chat with my arriving guests, I was sure to remind everyone to socially distance inside the theater. The coronavirus pandemic still loomed somewhat over the event.

Just past 1pm, my younger brother Daniel joined me on the terrace as I kept vigil over the parking lot waiting for more guests to arrive. He suggested I not make the attendees already inside the auditorium wait too much longer. I knew it would soon be time to start but I was willing to wait a tad bit longer for any stragglers.

Soon sensing that no one else would be approaching from the parking lot, I entered the auditorium, snapped a few photos of the occupied audience gallery and then approached Rene and the waiting microphone. The event was now underway!

Ambling down the aisle toward the ample space between the frontmost row of seats and the screen, I immediately engaged the gathered audience with a confident greeting and stated that "the State [was] finally ready to present its case." Thanks to my past and extensive involvement with Toastmasters International, I experienced next-to-zero nerves.

I then acknowledged the lead actor (Andrew J. Garcia), the rest of the cast, my family, Rene and the audience. I announced that a Q&A would follow the screening, reminded everyone to observe proper movie theater etiquette and then encouraged everyone to "enjoy the show!" After some applause followed my opening remarks, I retreated to the back of the auditorium and dimmed the house lights to absolute darkness.

A few seconds of silence and pitch blackness elapsed before a special intro played. This intro was a little something I'd put together to commemorate my twenty years as a filmmaker (from 2002 to 2022) and showcased shots from all of my films, both short and feature-length. After that special intro concluded, *State v. Unknown* finally began...

In a blog post dedicated to the premiere of *For My Sister* which took place three years before, I noted that a filmmaker or anyone else intimately involved in the making of a film never has the same experience as the general audience does when watching it. This observation was as true in this case as any other. Throughout the entire film, I was watching the film presentation for issues related to editing, audio sync, perceived comprehensibility and the reactions of the audience (both verbal and nonverbal). It was a purely critical exercise but, as a result, I was able to gauge which moments were particularly effective. I noted that about 90% of the comedic beats landed and some of the dramatic turns in the film's latter events did elicit some gasps and other interesting, audible reactions. For all my cool detachment from my location at the back of the auditorium during the screening, I was thrilled that the audience seemed thoroughly captivated by what was happening on the screen. It felt like the last year-and-a-half of practical and creative labor had definitely paid off!

At the start of the film's end credits, the audience let fly vigorous applause. And when the credits concluded, the audience paid their respects with another round of hearty applause. After turning the house lights back on, I made my way back to the front of the auditorium and expressed my hope that the audience had enjoyed the film. Given another round of lively clapping, it certainly appeared so.

After rattling off some novel facts about the production, including the use of actual instruments for its musical score (a first in my 10-year collaboration with composer Ben Morris), I asked the attending principal cast members of the film (Andrew J. Garcia, Lorean Mapp and Florencia

Barletta) to join me at the head of the theater. With the available principal cast and *snickers* entire crew gathered, I began my moderation of the Q&A by asking the cast members to introduce themselves and then invited each of them to describe their experience making this film. They all remarked how unusual the process had been and how surprised they'd been by the quality of the final product. It was refreshing to hear, at the very least, that my dear and dedicated cast had been exceedingly pleased by the product of all our hard work.

The Q&A continued with a few more questions from the audience, coupled with some positive comments. My cast fielded the questions like the pros they are.

Following the Q&A, Rene surprised me by projecting the film's poster on the sizable screen behind us and asked all attending cast in the audience gallery to gather for a group photo op with the principals and myself. After plenty of photos taken by the other attendees, I announced the conclusion of the event and thanked everyone for coming. A fitting conclusion to a smoothly run event!

After thanking Rene personally for all of his crucial assistance before and during the event, I found myself in quick dialogue with various attendees who all unanimously expressed their appreciation and, dare I say, amazement with my sophomore feature film effort. In the terrace outside, I participated in more involved conversation but unfortunately I couldn't speak to everyone at length. Nevertheless, the feedback I received was extremely encouraging!

With nearly all of the attendees having vacated the Cosford Cinema terrace, I rejoined my family who were with the Másmelas. We would all be heading off to lunch. Daniel had suggested a restaurant called Havana Harry's in Coral Gables as the venue for our post-screening luncheon. So, we all convened there.

At the restaurant, I recounted every significant observation about the event to my parents. They were exceptionally proud of my accomplishment and echoed my view that the entire event had been a success and the general reception to the film itself undoubtedly positive.

I also spent a bit of time speaking with the Másmelas. Although their involvement with our family had been somewhat limited as a result of our move to Miami decades ago, their presence at the screening meant a great deal to me. They had known me since my earliest years as a rambunctious youth with a love of movies and a knack for drawing. But now, they were witness to a fully grown adult with more than a passing fancy for filmmaking. When I looked at Héctor and Amparo, I felt like I was back in Boston and at their house for movies and childish games under their familiar presence and care. Despite my maturation over the intervening years, they made me feel like I was still that same rambunctious kid madly in love with art. Because in many ways... I guess I still am.

Much love, Héctor and Amparo!

122. Remote (July 2021)

A year-and-a-half into the odious coronavirus pandemic, I was scarcely as resolute about starting a film production as I was now. With a script intentionally assimilated to present circumstances, I had conjured a bit of Jiu-Jitsu in harnessing the strength of an oppositional force to my distinct advantage. My script's fictional city of Verity Falls would be duly afflicted by a scourge similar to our own but with another name - the halovirus pandemic! And the selected law enforcement perspective of the entire film would justify using webcam recordings exclusively. It was a film idea begging to be realized during an actual pandemic. Like a mighty Arthurian sword, it was an opportunity too tempting not to wield.

So, despite the weariness of a society still dealing with troublesome waves of high disease transmission and all the accordant safety measures, I readied to produce my 2nd (and pandemic-proof) feature-length film *State v. Unknown*. The budget was set at approximately $3,000; half-the-cost of my debut feature *For My Sister*.

My principal cast was assembled fairly quickly. Andrew Garcia (Jim the janitor in *For My Sister*), Lorean Mapp (Dawn Hartwright in *For My Sister*) and Juan Iglesias (Dr. Castillo in *For My Sister* and Em's father in *The Promotion*) were all members of the same community theater group The Pelican Playhouse and I wrote each of their parts with them squarely in mind. Andrew and Lorean had impressed me with their talent and enthusiasm on my first feature and I knew I'd wanted to work with Juan for a third time. All of them eagerly accepted the offers to play their personally tailored characters.

The remaining two principal roles went to Mia Scornavacca and Florencia Barletta, who'd both also impressed me with their work and overflowing congeniality on *For My Sister*.

Casting was an extremely important consideration on this film.

Abandoning the traditional pictorial approach to filmmaking, my film would offer very little in terms of cinematography or visual panache. I was essentially throwing out my 20 years' worth of cinematic understanding; instead, relying on the spectacle of what legendary filmmaker John Ford once regarded as "the most interesting and exciting thing in the whole world: a human face."

This film would present a veritable sea of faces in the form of a cast numbering 53 individual performers in total. In my view, this would be the greatest spectacle offered by the film.

Before I began the filming process, however, I considered the possibility of recording each and every actor individually and then editing their parts together; a piecemeal approach which strongly appealed to me for its allowance of greater control and flexibility. While my first impulse was to orchestrate real-time interactions between two or more of the actors involved in a respective scene, closer evaluation deemed that method too logistically unwieldy and taxing in terms of time even if it lent itself to a more organic quality. So, favoring focus on one performance at a time, even if it required closer attention to how the performances melded with one another in the editing, I opted for the latter strategy.

I would be primarily relying on the go-to online meeting application Zoom (and the more mobile-friendly alternative Skype for actors only available via their phone). For every recording session with the actors, I would have the script of their scene on the left side of my screen (for rather intensive script supervising duty on my part) and their Zoom window on the right.

This general process of tackling each actor's half of a conversation by itself consistently allowed for a greater finessing of their performance. And I would always be on-hand to replicate the necessary emotional tenor of the absent performer's part with my line readings and facial expressions.

My production plan was to record all of Andrew's parts first. As he was virtually in every scene of the film (he had 119 scenes in total), this would allow me to gain an early read on whether the film was fundamentally working or not. And as all of the other actors' performances needed to meld with Andrew's, having this basic layer down first gave me critical reference when it came to knowing how to direct all the other actors subsequently.

For Andrew, I imagined the prospect of filming his part, which accounted for half of the entire film, in such an unconventional manner must have been a nerve-wracking proposition; especially as it was his first lead role in a feature film! But any apprehension I may have initially imagined he had was quickly assuaged by a remarkable memorization technique he employed. He was able to comfortably memorize up to 10 pages worth of dialogue for each day of filming, which numbered 12 in total over the span of a month.

After I finished recording Andrew's part, I invited him to share his highly effective memorization method with the other principal actors. He described it thusly: Read the lines to yourself quietly 10 times, read the lines out loud 10 times, audio-record the line readings and then read the lines 10 times again with the recording playing "so you immerse yourself completely." He said it "[worked] like a charm" for him. It certainly did!

Another potentially challenging part of production came with Andrew's Day 04 on the film which involved on-location filming at night in an empty lot downtown. This particular filming arrangement would be accomplished by having Andrew record his part using Skype on his phone. From my home office, or "the situation room" as I jokingly dubbed it, I could only see what Andrew was showing me. In order to direct him and what his camera needed to record, an exceptionally acute level of communication was demanded. Andrew needed to move the camera a specific way and maintain a specific orientation throughout. And he had to mind his performance all throughout the process. The experience was extremely difficult, repetitive and frustrating but never self-destructive or fundamentally compromising. It was a long night but neither Andrew nor I lost our calm or gave in to lower impulses. We trusted each other like brothers in arms and managed to accomplish what was head above tails the most challenging day of filming between us.

Yet another testing situation worthy of recounting involved filming Mia's part, which consisted of 25 scenes over the course of 6 days. At one point during our sessions, I offered an unsolicited line reading to give a clearer indication to Mia of the desired quality of a particular line; a habit of mine as a director. But being the professionally trained actress she is, Mia politely interrupted me and stressed her aversion to my practice of offering line readings. Her defense was reasoned, assertive and right. I admitted that I wasn't respecting her as an actress with agency and intelligence when I superseded suggestion and insisted on a particular line reading. So, at that moment, I committed myself as a director of actors to never again offer a line reading to an actor unless it was deliberately asked for. I became a better director that day and continued to work profitably with Mia for the remainder of our filming together.

Working with the rest of the principal cast (Lorean, Juan and Florencia) was not without its share of hurdles but all of them, like Andrew and Mia, demonstrated great confidence in this peculiar production with their routinely strong performances.

Having wrapped my principal cast after two months of filming, the film was now well over halfway complete. What remained now was hiring 48 actors (and non-actors in some instances) to fill 48 supporting roles. A supporting cast size nearly 50% larger than on *For My Sister*.

The plan was always to cast on a rolling basis because I was confident in my abilities to recruit and organize quickly. I relied on my online social network to reach out to potential actors as well as posting casting call announcements on several actor and filmmaker Facebook groups. Mobilizing my talent as a communicator, I would engage desired talent by social media or email first. If interest was expressed, I'd arrange to speak over the phone regarding all of the pertinent details. There were a few declinements but, in the end, I was more than satisfied with the considerable wealth of actors willing to collaborate with me. I was also able to work with some close friends and family members in a more abbreviated capacity.

My method of working with the supporting actors was identical to the principal cast. Script on the left, Zoom window on the right. However, I had to adjust to each actor's varying skill level and amount of experience. There were a few veteran actors that I couldn't be too fussy with. And working with several non-actors also prompted me to alter my basic approach.

The prospect of casting and working with 48 different actors was an intimidating challenge, to say the least. But I soon made plans to work bit-by-bit. I would engage, schedule and record all of the actors in six separate blocks with about eight actors per block. Manageable chunks. This staggered approach was far from the most expedient way to go but it leavened the filmmaking process a bit for me - an important stress-relieving measure for the singular driver of this project.

With my stage-by-stage approach and generally fastidious nature, managing a group of actors as large as eight at a time was mostly problem-free but I always dreaded the possibility of failing to inform the talent of a critical piece of information or forgetting to send a particular document with enough lead time. Thankfully, those fearsome predicaments never materialized beyond mere entertainment in my head.

Among the 48 actors (again, some non-actors included), there were a number of occasions in which a given actor simply wasn't delivering what I needed them to. But in getting them to where they needed to be, I was always supportive and encouraging; never letting anger or frustration take the reins. There isn't a single actor on the picture I wouldn't work with again. Everyone pulled through.

Similar to my process on my first feature film, I was editing together the footage as soon as it was available to work with. This included selecting Andrew's best takes when I had only his part of each scene earlier on. On account of this and as had been the case with *For My Sister*, there was no extensive post-production period. Some intertitle work, a few reshoots and a couple of pickups were the only outstanding tasks to accomplish on my end after principal filming had concluded.

However, I would turn over the film's musical scoring duty to my go-to composer Ben Morris, who would be composing a march and some other much shorter pieces of percussion music heard intermittently throughout the film. What Ben composed was then to be recorded by his go-to drummer Evan Hyde using Evan's live instrument set. This instance of using real instruments to record the musical score to one of my films was a monumental first after four previous collaborations with Ben.

After *State v. Unknown* was fully completed (coming in on-budget and more-or-less on-schedule), I also kept it tightly under wraps as I had with

For My Sister upon that film's completion; not allowing anyone to see it, including family. However, Ben was privy to a near-finished cut of the film for musical scoring purposes. His response to the film was rather encouraging.

Looking for a venue to host the film's sneak preview screening, I reached out to Coral Gables Art Cinema again. They'd been so gracious (at a fair price) three years before for the premiere of my debut feature. However, this time I wouldn't be able to organize the event with them on account of an air-conditioning issue.

Scrambling to find an alternative venue to sate my desperation about finally letting the cat out of the bag, I reached out to Rene Rodriguez, the manager of University of Miami's Cosford Cinema, to see if there was a chance the theater could be made available for my purposes. Several days later, Rene responded with great news: The theater, the largest single-screen venue in Miami, was available for use by local feature filmmakers. I was ecstatic!

I immediately scheduled the event and soon let everyone, both close and distant, know about it.

Unfortunately, among the many societal changes wrought by the pandemic was its effect on society's movie-going habit. I expected that many of my invitees would decline the invitation on account of their wariness about sitting in a theater close to so many others, especially as social distancing and masking measures were being largely relaxed.

Despite emphasizing that I was booking the theater at half-capacity in regard to those concerns, I had to come to grips with how much the world had changed since 2019. And there was nary a more clarion example than how I had to go about conceiving, executing and screening *State v. Unknown*.

123. Renewal (February 2018)

Finding my 2nd feature-length script *Omni* impractical as the basis for my first-ever feature film production, I decided to abandon it and restart my writing process on a new idea from scratch. This choice was disheartening but the prospect of a far more produceable script was motivation enough to keep me engaged through another months-long stretch of writing.

As stated, I was looking for an idea that was far leaner and simpler in terms of production logistics. After all, I was interested in being the film's sole crew member as had been the case with nearly all of my short film productions. This approach would allow for a swifter production as there was less reliance on needing to match up so many schedules in order to execute a production.

Re-entering brainstorming mode once more, I knew right off the bat that I'd want to involve both Stephanie Maltez and Cristina De Fatima, the two actresses with whom I'd worked with on my 16th and final short *The Promotion*. This choice lay in my interest of being resourceful but I was also interested in involving them once again in my work because I already had a sense of their strengths and abilities as actors. We had also developed a positive working relationship throughout the production of that earlier short film.

While I spent a month or so attempting to land on a fertile idea, I worked out countless variations of ideas involving two young women. Toward the later weeks of this initial writing stage, ideas related to mental illness became increasingly alluring. This was likely on account of my involvement with NAMI (National Alliance on Mental Illness) Miami-Dade at the time; a noble organization which provided mental health support and advocacy in the community. Mental illness was also a topic of great personal relevance as I'd suffered two several mental heath crises about a decade earlier.

Before long, a compelling narrative with an attractive blend of two female characters and a dire mental health challenge was birthed. But it needed a special ingredient to truly whet my filmmaking appetite.

This other ingredient would be a result of my unusual sensitivity toward the common assumption of omniscient perspective in film; versus a more finite, subjective one. Before arriving at my present idea, I had considered several others which toyed with the fundamental perspective by which a narrative or series of events are experienced through a film. I constantly thought about what film director and professor Alexander Mackendrick described as "the invisible imaginary ubiquitous winged witness," an idea introduced to my Directing I class by Professor Lori Ingle during my time in film school at University of Central Florida. This peculiar obsession about perspective would lend itself to one of the resulting script's most unique aspects - time-traveling nanodrones.

With a highly detailed outline struck and a profuse amount of notes gathered, it was time to commit to writing another full-fledged script. The process of writing a whole new feature script (my third at this point) would take approximately four months. But at the end of that time, I'd have the blueprint for a film I'd deem wholly worth giving myself over fully to.

After those four months elapsed, I announced on social media that I'd completed a 76-page script described as "[following] a young woman named Evie as she struggles to help her sister Tris with an ever-worsening case of depression - a condition that has already marked their family with tragic death." I added: "Out of time and patience but with renewed excitement and determination, I greatly look forward to realizing this feature..."

I would follow through with my promise.

And in what had become a tradition between my dad and me upon completion of each of my feature scripts, I allowed my dad to read the finished draft and offer his most frank and honest opinion. Thankfully, with *For My Sister* he gave me his most enthusiastic blessing, deeming the script "a serious work."

With that, I was off to the races!

124. Struggle (April 2019)

Weeks before the end of production on my first feature-length film *For My Sister*, I began my brainstorming process for a follow-up feature film. Confidence in my feature filmmaking abilities, which had now been squarely put to the test, was at an all-time high and, on top of that, I craved a head start on what I was all-too aware of was my notoriously drawn-out writing process. So, I settled into a renewed writing habit in an attempt to nip the problem in the bud. The process was initially fruitful as I was visited by many intriguing ideas for my next feature. But could I whip up a script faster than I'd managed to in the past?

Chief among my considerations for a second feature film was an anticipated collaboration with a former Florida International University Theatre student J.C. Gutierrez. I'd first met J.C. at an FIU Theatre film festival in which one of his short films was being presented (he's also an aspiring filmmaker). I was so charmed by his friendly spirit prior to the event and then impressed by his filmmaking metal during the showcase that I resolved to include him as an actor in my debut feature.

And upon working with J.C. on a one-scene part in *For My Sister* I was instantly reunited with his familiar kindness and sincerity. So, after the second screening of *For My Sister* at Coral Gables Art Cinema which he attended, I found J.C. and raised the idea of having him be the lead actor of my second, yet-unwritten feature film. He'd been greatly impressed by the film of mine he'd just seen and was at once honored and accepting of the prospect.

But I needed an idea worthy of his abilities!

I had kept up my writing habit all through the end of production on *For My Sister* and throughout the time of its few initial theatrical exhibitions. However, I soon experienced a peculiar emotional disturbance related to wrapping up work on my first feature. In what I'd liken to postpartum depression or a kind of separation anxiety, the sudden lack of a major, daily preoccupation left an uncomfortable void in my life. This void would appear after finishing my second feature as well but I was wholly unprepared for its first-time occurrence.

A deep and abiding depression soon followed and I found myself taking up some rather unhealthy and superficially comforting habits to cope. I kept nocturnal hours; sleeping in the day and staying awake at night. I also maintained a deplorable fast food binging habit. But as I grappled with a painful feeling of loss and impermanence, I did give some time to writing; continuing my search for a workable, new idea.

At the start of fall, I became unusually fixated by the image of a brain in a vat of sustaining liquid. I worked out a narrative to surround this peculiar visual and soon shared my idea with my good friend Kieron Williams. He was appropriately critical toward my potential script idea and asked all of the hard but essential questions about it. Although Kieron's feedback eroded some of my initial confidence, I persisted with my idea to the point of arriving at an outline which survived beyond my own personal scrutiny. That was far enough.

With the wick lit, I developed a more complete and final outline in rather quick time. A bevy of detailed notes then followed in short order. As my writing process entered a new, more promising stage with an outline and plenty of notes in tow, I was prompted to pick up healthier, more sustainable living habits. Before long, I was out of my funk and once again productive!

For this fourth instance of actual scriptwriting, I decided to mix up my usual approach a little. Rather than sweep through the entire first draft in one major push, I'd be implementing a two-pass process. This involved laying down action and temporary dialogue placeholders first, allowing me to see the consistency between action and dialogue early on; an important consideration toward my preference for more visually primed or cinematic filmmaking. After the broad strokes of the script had been worked out, I would start again from page one and fill in all the dialogue and more exact details in a second go-over. I'd employ this two-pass process on my next script as well.

Unfortunately, before I finished my first draft of the script, titled

Zenith, a certain global pandemic would obliterate my plans to produce it. Although J.C. was eagerly expecting to help me realize this new script, I would have to shelve the whole project for an indefinite period of time and put my collaboration with J.C. on hold for just as long. It saddened me to do so. However, I considered yet another feature writing experience as a benefit despite the early hardship. And as for my plans to work with J.C., thankfully we both understood the virtue of patience and waiting for the right circumstances.

In the mean time, I would see that many of the themes I found appealing in *Zenith* found their way into my following feature script and resulting 2nd feature film *State v. Unknown*.

125. Validation (October 2019)

After two well-attended and enthusiastically received screenings of my debut feature *For My Sister* at Coral Gables Art Cinema, I was interested in finding additional opportunities to screen the film at other local venues.

In the fall, my mentor and director of Florida International Univeristy's film studies program Dr. Andrew Strycharski helped spearhead a screening of the film at FIU with the university's NAMI (National Alliance on Mental Illness) chapter. At the modestly-attended event, I introduced the film and made note of the particular significance of screening my first feature in the same university I'd started writing my first short film 17 years ago!

Notable among the audience were Louise Farnsworth, a former Miami Killian Senior High teacher who'd been very fond of me when I was a student there, and psychologist Dr. Geysha Menendez from the hit Spanish-language TV show, *Caso Cerrado*. After the film played, I led a panel following the screening which addressed the topics of mental health and the stigma associated with mental illness.

Another screening at a different educational venue took place a week later. Invited to the Homestead campus of Miami Dade College by Professor Jessyca Perez, the event saw more seats filled by young college students. And after the film played there, I led another activity; a brief conversation also about mental health and mental illness stigma. At the end of the event, I was awarded a plaque for my filmmaking and advocacy efforts. A most kind gesture.

With the onset of the coronavirus pandemic early the following year, any plans I had for further theatrical exhibition of *For My Sister* were at once kaput. As the outlook turned grim for a return to normalcy in the foreseeable future, I examined my options for making the film available to as wide an audience as possible.

During May, considered Mental Health Awareness Month, I made my first move by deciding to make *For My Sister* available using the Vimeo video hosting service. For nearly three-week-long engagement, anyone could access the film without charge. I was more interested in sharing my film with as many willing viewers as possible. Profit has never been my foremost preoccupation as a filmmaker. The fewer barriers between my work and an audience, the better. Accordingly, I encouraged everyone to watch it on as an impressive display as they could manage.

The resulting view count for the special limited release numbered several hundred and I received numerous positive comments from many friends and acquaintances. However, I later realized most viewers could only access the film from their computers or phones and not through their televisions as I'd recommended. A major sticking point for me as I determined my next move.

Toward the end of the year, I discovered a reputable independent film distribution company called Indie Rights capable of securing placement of their films on major streaming services, including Amazon Prime Video. They regarded themselves as champions of independent filmmaking and they were led by a remarkable, hard-working woman named Linda Nelson. They also took a sensible percentage of commission from each quarterly payout. I immediately sent *For My Sister* to them for consideration.

Within weeks, I received a positive response from Linda herself and soon prepared my film deliverables to Indie Rights' exact, demanded specifications.

Weeks later, *For My Sister* was available on Amazon!

I was sure to make plenty of noise about it and spread word through the whole of my social media network. My actors were especially thrilled, particularly Cristina De Fatima, who remarked that making the film available on such a major streaming platform was "a breath of fresh air in the middle of this terrible pandemic."

The film would be available for free to Amazon Prime members some weeks later. It would also show up on other streaming platforms in the ensuing months.

With *For My Sister* freshly available on Amazon, my friends and acquaintances now had a chance to see the film on more ideally-sized screens and the film soon received a steady stream of positive worded reviews from many quarters:

- "I love the nanodrones for their surrealism... they add a whole other level of weirdness that works," wrote user DK.
- "[The film] was refreshing to see... excellent work," wrote user Jorge G.
- "Powerful story of two sisters... Hopefully after watching this film more people will not be afraid to get the help they desperately need... a touching film," wrote user DORIS MARCUS.
- "Definitely give this little gem a try!" wrote user BB.
- "Awesome work for a first-time director/writer," wrote user Raul E.
- "A very creative independent film that is very much worth watching," wrote user Mike D.
- "A gripping look at the trials and tribulations a loving, determined, young woman goes through to help her sister," wrote user Coppelia22.
- "The story, direction and performance of this independent film are both compelling and entertaining," wrote user Neelam Sheikh.
- "Powerful film about how destructive, if left alone, depression can be... very captivating," wrote user Nelson.
- "[The film] uses an innovative approach to storytelling to explore the very important topic of mental health," wrote user Justin.
- "Wonderful film. Really dismantles societal judgments on mental health," wrote user Karla.
- "I recommend this film for those looking for a story about bonds, sacrifice and prejudice," wrote user Peter S.
- "Great little independent film, with lots of heart," wrote user Alvaro Sanchez.
- "This film is powerful and gripping... it's a relatable, yet heart-wrenching story that I'm glad I had the opportunity to experience," wrote user Kaluohs.
- "A thoughtful and touching portrait of family devotion," wrote

user MDVIRTUAL.
- "Definitely one movie to watch many times," wrote user Kathy.
- "What a beautiful, poignant film. Thank you for such a touching piece," wrote user DK.
- "A wonderful independent film that explores mental illness through the lens of magical realism... A unique watch that stands out amidst the usual Hollywood fare," wrote an Amazon customer.
- "A beautiful film acted and directed masterfully," wrote user Christian Rivero.
- "The shining light in this film is the love between sisters and what we do for our family. I highly recommend it!" wrote user Paola Cruzat.
- "Watch this compelling human story and feel your soul moved a little bit. Thank you for this work of art," wrote user Marcile.
- "With impressive performances and genre blending filmmaking, it's definitely worth a watch," wrote user Evan Burr.
- "You will be thinking about this movie for a long time after you see it!" wrote user L. Weissman.
- "A well-done film that presents the reality of mental illness in an informative and empathic manner... A must-watch!" wrote user Elizabeth.
- "The lead, the incomparable Stephanie Maltez, is a treasure," wrote user Peter Alexander.
- "Beautiful story! A realistic presentation and excellent film. Strongly recommend," wrote user Ana Muller.
- "A well-made movie that makes you think," wrote user German R Hernandez.
- "Very powerful and needed message. Excellent!" wrote user jack michel.
- "Insightful and touching," wrote an Amazon Customer.
- "Simply amazing," wrote user Jonathan Ramirez.
- "I especially love how it's made on a shoestring budget, which is awesome!" wrote user JK.

* * *

After the approximately year-and-two-months it took me and the cast to make *For My Sister*, I greatly appreciated the outpouring of unanimously positive sentiment toward the film. It affirmed the worth of the entire effort and validated my passion for the art and craft of filmmaking.

Even since I was 16 years old and just beginning production on my first short film, I knew with great clarity and conviction that I wanted to do this work for the rest of my life...

About the Author

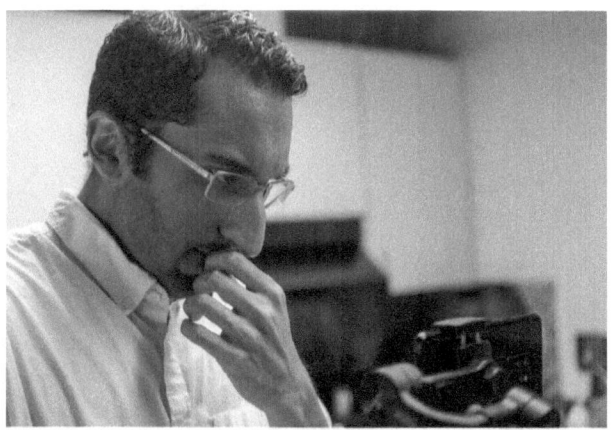

GABRIEL RHENALS was born in Boston, Massachusetts in 1986 and later moved to Miami, Florida with his family where he has lived for most of his life. From a very young age, he demonstrated a remarkable aptitude for the visual arts.

Throughout his K-12 education, Gabriel was enrolled in various visual art programs. In high school, he attended New World School of the Arts in downtown Miami. After high school, Gabriel attended the limited-access Film (BFA) program at University of Central Florida in Orlando and later received his bachelor's degree in Communication Arts from Florida International University in Miami, graduating cum laude.

Equipped with little more than his father's digital 8mm video camera, Gabriel began filmmaking when he was 16 and, between 2002 and 2016, wrote, produced, directed, shot and edited 16 short films. These short films have been accepted at numerous film festivals, both domestic and international, and distributed nationally on the National Endowment for the Arts-funded PBS television show *film-maker*.

ABOUT THE AUTHOR

In 2019, Gabriel completed his 1st feature film *For My Sister* as writer, producer, director, cinematographer and editor. He used his phone for filming and employed a cast of 30+ actors. It screened at local theatrical and educational venues.

In 2022, Gabriel completed his 2nd feature film *State v. Unknown* as writer, producer, director and editor. This pandemic-proof production was accomplished using webcams exclusively and employed a cast of 50+ actors.

20 Years a Filmmaker is Gabriel's 1st book. For more content by Gabriel Rhenals, please visit: www.gabrielrhenals.com.

www.ingramcontent.com/pod-product-compliance
Lightning Source LLC
Chambersburg PA
CBHW031603210526
45464CB00004B/1409